TOLEDO

GW00361980

Charles L. Johnson, Paul Harsh
Carlos Pascual

Senior Series Writer
Tom Burns

Edited by
Erica Witschey

Everything Under the Sun Travel Guide Series

First published in Great Britain 1987
by HARRAP COLUMBUS
19-23 Ludgate Hill, London EC4M 7PD

First published in the United States 1987
by NATIONAL TEXTBOOK COMPANY
4255 West Touhy Avenue, Lincolnwood, IL 60646

First published in Spain 1987
by NOVATEX EDICIONES S.A.
Explanada, 16, 28040 Madrid

Collaborator: Lettice Small
Cover Design: Jill Raphaeline
Cover Logo: Joan Miró
Drawings: Enrique Ortega
Maps: Javier Ruiz
Photographs: Photographic Archives of the Instituto Nacional de
  Promoción del Turismo, D. Cubillo, J. Dieuzaide, G. Moschioni, F.
  Ontañón
Senior Series Writer: Tom Burns
Series Editor: Erica Witschey

Colour Separation and Reproduction: Progreso Gráfico, S.A., Madrid
Electronic Editing: Isabel Balmaseda, software and interface by Protec
  S.A.
Printed by: Gráficas Estella, S.A., Navarre
Typeset at: Pérez Díaz, S.A. Madrid

ISBN 0-7471-0027-6
D.L.: NA-473-1987

Printed in Spain

Published with the co-operation of the Spanish Ministry of Culture

CONTENTS

TOLEDO: A LIVING MUSEUM OF HUMANITY

The first sight of Toledo, timeless atop its rock and girded by the Tagus river, is unforgettable. You know instinctively that **a mind-stretching experience awaits you** just as soon as you venture within its walls. From a distance you see the mighty cathedral and the Alcázar and, in their shadows, a host of spires, towers and minarets, palaces and convents. You feel **you have history, legend, art within your reach.**

You may already know that Toledo was a melting pot of Judaism, Christianity and Islam; that for many years the three cultures lived and learnt, tolerantly and fruitfully, together. When you pass beneath Toledo's battlements and enter its narrow streets and alleys you begin to understand that the city is an extraordinary fusion of religions and of attitudes to life. Toledo is an encyclopedia and a museum of the history of art. It is not, however, a succession of exhibits that chronicle the passing of the ages. The rhythm of past civilizations forms a unique whole. Nor is Toledo fossilized in time. It is a living city. **You are re-entering the past as a participant,** not as an onlooker, for Toledo is a gigantic stage where humanity has acted out its changing roles.

Century upon century, stone upon stone, Toledo has seen it all and been it all. An eternal city, Toledo has known heroism and treachery, splendour and ruin, neglect and rebirth. Temporal and spiritual lords, emperors, kings and cardinals strutted through it on the path to triumph and disaster. Romantic love and religious mysticism found their home here. Within Toledo's walls men pursued intellect and reason. In the nooks and crannies of the city's seven cabalistic hills sorcerers and soothsayers plied their trade. Toledo boasted libraries and schools and its peak of tolerance when synagogue, mosque and church stood side by side. And it had its share of inquisitorial dungeons when the age of forbearance passed. Time and again the sensitive spirit was drawn to it. Settling here the restless El Greco captured Toledo's elusive light. The poet Rainer Maria Rilke, nearly 400 years later, found solace in Toledo for his melancholy and renewed inspiration for his lyricism.

In Toledo you can immerse yourself in a pageant of what was once the heart of imperial Europe and of what remains **the soul of Spain.** Those who arrive in the tourist bus avalanche for a four-hour visit will never penetrate the city's mystery. Toledo turns its back on them and keeps to itself. But Toledo beckons travellers who arrive prepared to ride a time machine and to be carried away by bygone passions. These the city welcomes, charms and captivates.

Step out in Toledo and you are meeting history head on. It is not for nothing that UNESCO designated the city a Birthright of Humanity. Toledo's endless array of churches and convents, of synagogues and mosques, of grandiose palaces and humble medieval dwellings is in itself an architectural showpiece. Within, behind the façade, there are treasure troves of fabulous artistic wealth. Down the ages stone and wood have been carved into ceilings and pillars; craftsmen have created beauty out of gold and silver; painters, sculptors and artists of every kind have worked for Toledo's excellence. Every surprise you come across is just a prelude to the one which awaits you. And the museum is a living one for the prized trophies of other ages, the noble Toledo steel sword, the delicate damascened object, remain the bread and butter of today's artisans who have kept up the standards of their ancestors.

Toledo's loveliness and harmony make it magical. Spend time on it and you will always return.

HOW TO USE THIS GUIDE

This guide offers you **everything under the sun**, and everything under the moon and the stars as well, about enjoying yourself, travelling and living in this part of Spain. There's much more here than a listing of hotels and restaurants, monuments and museums: this book contains all the information, tips and advice a visitor will need. It includes suggestions on everything from shopping to sports, trips for the curious and energetic, detailed descriptions for the sedentary, maps and complete city plans, street guides and more.

You'll find an overall description of the city and region, accompanied by basic data, climatic conditions and other general information at the beginning of the guide. The rest of the book is organized **alphabetically** according to topics such as

LODGING

For instance, in a way that makes it easy to find what you're looking for. At the end of the guide's text there are general maps and city maps, as well as a street directory.

Abbreviations

Only the most common abbreviations are used in the guide. Compass directions are given as N, S, E, and W (north, south, east, and west). Common abbreviations for weights and measures are also used.

When addresses are given, the abbreviation *c/* means *calle*, or street (as in c/ Huertas); avenue, *avenida*, is *Av*; highway, *carretera*, is *Ctra*; development, *urbanización*, is *Urb*; square, *plaza*, is *Pl* and building, *edificio*, is *Edif*. When an address doesn't have a street number, it usually is marked *s/n* for *sin número*, without a number.

Cross-References

The guide also incorporates a system of cross-references that refer the reader to other sections or pages where more information on the subject at hand is to be found. The references look like this: ▶ *page xx.* When sites or addresses can't be easily found by address, the guide refers the reader directly to notations in the maps at the back of the book, making getting there simple.

Highlighted Text and Classifications

Throughout the guide you will find words, symbols and complete sentences which are highlighted. The guide has five grades, or levels, of highlighting. The first, in black, indicates anything that is attractive or interesting for one reason or another. The second grade, highlighted in blue, refers to things the visitor should make every effort to see if in the area. The third, fourth and fifth levels correspond to the one, two and three **Miró suns**, which appear alongside the text and always beside an item highlighted in blue. The three grades indicate what the reader should make certain of seeing and experiencing before leaving the area. Their meaning is the following. 🌞 : It's worth making a detour. 🌞 🌞 : Spend a day on this one. 🌞 🌞 🌞 : This alone makes a trip to the area worthwhile.

Prices and Symbols

Generally speaking, this guide doesn't give prices. The reason is
sensible enough: every price printed in any guide in the world is
outdated. It makes more sense, and is more useful to the reader, to use
a gradation of these symbols: from $ to $$$$$.

Hotel equivalencies:	Restaurant equivalencies:
$: up to 2,000 ptas	$: up to 750 ptas
$$: from 2,000 to 4,000 ptas	$$: from 750 to 1,500 ptas
$$$: from 4,000 to 6,000 ptas	$$$: from 1,500 to 3,300 ptas
$$$$: from 6,000 to 8,000 ptas	$$$$: from 3,300 to 5,000 ptas
$$$$$: more than 8,000 ptas	$$$$$: more than 5,000 ptas

Symbols

In **Hotels**

★	category	🏖	beach
🔵	rating	♫	discotheque
$	cost	▥	heated rooms
⚡	postal code	☉	sauna/workout facilities
☎	telephone	≪	view
🛏	number of rooms	🎞	movie theatre/video
⌗	bathroom	↳	children's playroom
✗	hotel restaurant	⚓	skin diving
Ⴤ	hotel bar	⚓	waterskiing
✂	hairdressing salon/beauty salon	⚓	sailing
⚥	access and facilities for the handicapped	🏄	windsurfing
◪	safety deposit boxes	℘	tennis
✔	medical aid	♠	table games
⚘	baby sitting service	⌶	bowling/skittle
📺	television	↳	golf
☏	room phone	🐴	horseback riding
❷	parking	⚐	mini-golf
≋	gardens	⚓	fishing
↕	lifts	✐	hunting
✷	air-conditioned rooms	AE	American Express
⚘	meeting rooms	DC	Diners Club
✸	dogs not allowed	V	Visa
✾	quiet/peaceful place	EC	Euro Card
▬	swimming pool	MC	Mastercard
		CB	Carte Blanche

In **Restaurants**:

☆	category
🔵	rating
$	cost
⚡	postal code
☎	telephone

The guide carries a brief description and commentary on most hotels,
restaurants, discotheques, clubs, bars and similar establishments that
are worthy of note. Information on location is also included in these
sections.

Up-dating the Guide

The book that you are holding in your hands contains more information than any other of its type. It is the product of a team of professionals working up to press time to make it accurate and up-to-date; but should the reader come across any error or outdated information, or have a new aspect or view of a certain topic, **help us to help you** in the next edition. Send any information or suggestions you have to:

Editors
Novatex Ediciones, S.A.
c/ Explanada, 16
28040 Madrid, Spain

Thank you for your confidence in the authors, the editors and the National Institute for the Promotion of Tourism. And now, a final suggestion: **enjoy yourself to the full**.

BASIC FACTS

Climate

The **climate** is characteristic of the entire central region, namely, continental and extremely variable: cold in winter and very hot in summer, though less so than in other surrounding areas. Winters are not as cold as in Castile-León (where snow and frost are more frequent), while the summertime dog days are less fierce than in other flatter parts of La Mancha, thanks to the mountains and the Tagus valley.

Average *temperatures* range from 6.5 to 4.5°C (40-44°F) in December and January, to 27°C (81°F) in July and 25°C (77°F) in August. December and January minimums can, however, drop to below freezing, with July-August maximums rising as high as 35°C (95°F).

Geography and Location

Toledo is located 75km from Madrid, in the centre of the province of the same name (of which it is the capital). Although the province is one of the largest in Spain (with an area of more than 15,000km²), it nevertheless has one of the sparsest populations, barely exceeding half a million. It is divided in two by the **Tagus River**, which runs from east to west. North of the river, the land slopes upward towards the towering granite mass of the **Gredos Mountains**, wherein are found a number of towns and villages. South of the Tagus, the slope is more gentle as it rises toward the low-lying **Montes de Toledo**, or Toledo highlands, a landscape of slate and quartzite covered by rockrose and holm-oak, thyme and other aromatic plants. Between the river and the mountains lies the region of **La Jara** and its diverse geographical features. To the north of the capital lies another flatland area, **La Sagra**, which extends all the way to Madrid. The eastern side of the province is where **La Mancha** begins, with its characteristic landscape and villages steeped in the great tradition of Cervantes —Esquivias, El Toboso, Ocaña, Quintanar, and others.

At the centre of it all stands **Toledo**, atop its mythical rock. With an elevation of only 548m above sea level, the rock has stood almost unaltered throughout the centuries. Although a number of ancient bards may have exaggerated a bit, it is unlikely that the population of the city has ever gone beyond its current 58,000.

How to Get There

By plane: The nearest airport is in Madrid.
By road: When travelling by car, take the direct highway from Madrid (N401), a large part of which has been converted into a dual-lane route, thus avoiding the congested industrial belt around Madrid. Anyone wishing to visit Aranjuez first can take the Andalusia highway, then go by N400 from Aranjuez, which runs parallel to the Tagus all the way to Toledo (a stretch that is not highly recommended).
Distance from Toledo to Madrid: 75km. To Aranjuez: 40km.
By train: The train service between Madrid and Toledo is very good. Schedules may vary according to the season, and should be consulted at any office of RENFE, the Spanish national railway. Travel time between the two cities is approximately two hours. The station in Toledo is located on the Paseo de la Rosa, a short distance outside the walls and below the castle of San Servando.
Public transportation by highway: There are a number of bus lines departing from Madrid's Estación Sur (southern station) at c/ Palos de Moguer. All arrivals come to the new terminal in Toledo, in La Vega next to the new bypass or *Circunvalación* around the city. At this same terminal, you can find regular bus service to all towns in the province.

Language

Castilian, or *castellano*, the Spanish emanating from Castile that is considered *pure* Spanish, is spoken by the entire local population.

People of Toledo

The people of Toledo are good *castellanos*, and as such, good Spaniards, solid as the brick and iron of the Castilian urban landscape,

as austere as the countryside itself, and faithful to its traditions, but with hospitality for its visitors. Not in vain has Toledo opened its doors to a mixture of religions and cultures, to those who look on the serious side, to perfectionists, to those who see the elegance of a city where letting go may well indicate a truly refined spirit.

People Who Go to Toledo

Here you will see busloads of enthusiastic Japanese tourists, long-lensed cameras at the ready, as well as couples or single tourists from around the world, families from Madrid and other Spanish cities, entire schools on a tour, college students who come to study the art, loners, lovers who wander the streets at night seeking out the beauty of an ancient gate, a balcony, or a coat of arms. You will see history buffs and art scholars who leave no stone unturned, and here and there are artists in search of the light immortalized by El Greco.

Telephone

The telephone prefix for the province is **925.** The local phone system is fully automatic for calls to virtually the whole world.

Tourist Information

Provincial Delegation of Tourism, Pl de Zocodover, 11 ☎ 22 14 00; and Bisagra Gate ☎ 22 08 43.

When to Go

Toledo is a city that never closes down. You can visit it when you choose —the choice is yours, whether it depends on the weather, or on the people to be found there. Summer is somewhat like most Saturdays or Sundays, with busloads of visitors on a six-hour whirlwind tour trying to catch all the sights. We recommend that you come at another time, and that you spend a night or two in the city. Thus you will see the tranquil side of Toledo, its pleasant evenings as you stroll about. But even if you arrive when it is at full tilt, you will fall in love with it.

GETTING READY FOR THE TRIP

Baggage

If you are arriving to Spain by plane, it's important to keep in mind the weight limitations imposed by the airlines; more baggage will cost you money. Normally, one adult passenger in tourist class is allowed some 20kg. Over that weight, a supplement is charged. The number of handbags you can carry into the cabin is also limited.

Clothing

Tourists come to Spain from the farthest reaches of the world, and they wear a variety of picturesque clothing. Therefore, when visiting Toledo you may dress as you please —within the limits of decency— bearing in mind that Spaniards are among Europe's leading fashion designers and produce styles that are truly advanced. Anyone strolling through the city's busiest street, c/ Comercio, will notice shop windows chock-full of the most daring and *avant garde* creations.

It is extremely hot here in the summer, so dress accordingly. At the same time, don't forget that Toledo is not a beach resort, and parading through town in a swimsuit, or topless, would be frowned upon. Shorts are not uncommon among tourists but, as is the case in other European cities: remember that **if you are wearing shorts, you will not be allowed into the Cathedral,** nor into other churches open to worshippers. Dress very warmly in wintertime, since the high humidity of the Tagus River and the surrounding valley can make the season rather uncomfortable.

In both summer and winter, you would be well advised to pay particular attention to footwear. High heels will make your going rugged, because the majority of the streets are paved with small and slippery stones. As a general rule, **strive to wear a comfortable type of sport shoe** to make it easier to negotiate the ups and downs of Toledo's cobblestoned streets. Your visit may turn into a punishing, and perhaps even impossible, experience if you neglect this detail.

Going Through Customs

Foreigners arriving in Spain must have a valid passport. Nationals of some countries are required to obtain a visa in advance of arrival; the visa can be obtained at the Spanish consulate in most large cities. The citizens of most European countries need only bring with them their valid identity card. In case of doubt, the best course is to consult your local Spanish consulate.

Tourists need pay no taxes or duties on personal effects like clothes and other articles needed for their stay. There are, however, limits to the amounts of tobacco, alcoholic beverages and perfumes that you can bring with you into Spain which vary according to the country from which you are travelling.

You are also limited to two cameras and ten rolls of film each, one 8mm or 16mm movie camera, one portable tape recorder, one portable typewriter, one bicycle, equipment for golf, tennis and fishing, and two firearms with 100 cartridges a piece for hunting.

To obtain a more detailed list of the articles that are restricted in some way, consult your local Spanish consulate.

Hunting and Fishing

It is helpful to contact the local hunting or fishing federation or association before coming to Spain; they provide a wealth of information about licences, seasons and permits, and also can give good advice about the locale and what to expect.

Insurance

Anything's possible on a trip, so it is wise to purchase health insurance valid for Spain or to make sure your existing policy covers you here. You may also want to consider insurance covering last minute cancellations of a holiday. You can consult the Spanish Tourism Office, a travel agent or your own insurance company: they will also be able to inform you about vehicle insurance. A visitor whose country has reciprocal medical agreements with Spain should not forget to bring his social security documentation.

Toledo is a city that must be visited on foot, even though its ups and downs may prove tiring. Such is the price that must be paid if one wishes to discover the secrets and true aura of a Moorish city; quite clearly no one would think of visiting a *medina* (the old part of an Arab city) or a *casbah* except on foot. A car is useful only for travelling around the city and visiting areas outside its walls. The itineraries that we will suggest in this section should be considered as nothing more than a skeleton guide which should be fleshed out by consulting other parts of the book, such as 'Places of Interest' and 'Shopping'.

Itinerary 1: Outside the Walls

Itinerary by car.

We can begin this trip at la Vega, which is beneath the Cambrón Gate to the right of the *Circunvalación* bypass highway. First off, we have the ancient **Basilica of Santa Leocadia**, or the hermitage of Cristo de la Vega ▶ *page* 110.

From here, we can go on down to the **Roman Circus** located in a park. Excavations began in 1926, and have uncovered a circus similar to the one in Mérida, though not as well preserved. There is the *spina* (central wall dividing the field), the *cárceres* (cages), the *porta triunphalis* (triumphal gate), and the *vomitorium*, among other parts. It had a capacity for 30,000 spectators, which is evidence of the importance of Toledo during Roman times, when the city also had a *naumachia* (site for water-combat spectacles), hot baths, and an aqueduct.

Below the circus is the **Royal Arms Factory** ▶ *page* 128. As we climb back upward, we can visit the Hospital of Tavera, or the *Hospital de Afuera* (Outside Hospital) ▶ *page* 121. A little further and we find the old España hotel, which is now the Garrido Arms Factory ▶ *page* 143, and the barracks of San Lázaro (16C), of which only the walls and a Mudejar apse remain and where a hotel has been installed. Further on we come to the *Plaza de Toros* or **Bullring**, the site of a number of scenes in the novel *L'Espoir* by André Malraux. Even further on, at the exit toward Madrid, there is another Mudejar apse, that of the **hermitage of San Eugenio**. It was constructed in the 12C for housing the relics of the first Archbishop of Toledo. The present apse was built later.

Turning toward the Bisagra Gate, we pass in front of the stretch of wall outside the **Covachuelas** neighbourhood, where potters formerly lived. As we cross the Safont Bridge, we see the Railway Station; behind it are the **Palaces of Galiana** and the *Huerta del Rey* (**King's Garden**) ▶ *page* 126

Returning toward the city, we will be greeted by the **Castle of San Servando** in front of the Alcántara Gate ▶ *page* 124. This is a good place to begin another itinerary, a driving-walking combination that will show us the city's periphery and the Tagus River that has Toledo in its grasp; afterwards, we will climb up amongst the typical country homes, the **Cigarrales**, and marvel at the view of the city.

Itinerary 2: City Periphery and Cigarrales

Itinerary by car.

This is a most appropriate itinerary for an evening, once the museums are closed. It will bring us closer to the city as we take a look at it from the outside in a place that provides a very characteristic view: the southern part, with its jutting *peñascosa pesadumbre* (craggy sorrow) high above the river.

Let us begin with the river. Few others in the world have achieved such literary fame as the Tagus. Originally there was Ovid, one of the first to claim that gold was to be found in the river; it later appears in Berceo, Tirso, and especially Garcilaso. He, as well as Góngora, supported the belief that the river held gold, and both writers populated its banks with nymphs, young ladies, and bucolic characters in their pastoral works (of which the *Eglogas* of Garcilaso is perhaps the most famous). Many other writers have also paid homage to the Tagus, among them Unamuno, Marañón and Miguel Hernández.

The first bridge we find, between the Castle of San Servando and the incline rising up to Zocodover square and the Alcázar, is the **Alcántara Bridge** (a redundancy, since *Alcántara* is the Arabic word for bridge); crossing it, we are at the gate of the same name. Undoubtedly, there was once a Roman bridge at this spot, which was then replaced by a Moorish one. In 1257, according to the Gothic characters on the stone seen on the bridge tower, the river flooded and swept away the Moorish bridge, which was then restored by King Alfonso the Wise in 1259. Its defence, typical of the age, consisted of a gated tower with portcullis at either end; only one tower has been preserved, the other one being replaced in 1721 by a rather uninteresting Baroque arch.

To the left of the bridge, we can see some ruins. This was once the site of the much-acclaimed *artificio de Juanelo* (**Juanelo's Device**), a mechanism built by Giovanni Torriggiano in 1566 for lifting water up to the city, which was a replacement for the destroyed **Roman aqueduct**. The starting point for the aqueduct can be seen in the rocky wall beside the periphery highway, whilst there are also arches beneath Santa Cruz. The mechanism, honoured by such classical writers as Góngora and Quevedo, was later destroyed, which in turn gave the romantic poet Bécquer a location for his legend *Rosa de Pasión*.

Continuing on the Ctra Circunvalación and keeping the river in sight, we arrive at the **Virgin of the Valley**, a small hermitage with one of the classical observation points for seeing the city. A few metres up into the hillside, the head of the Moor Abu Walid has been sculpted into a rock. After losing the battle in an attempt to reconquer the city from the Christians, the Moor asked that he be buried in a place that would give him an eternal view of Toledo; this is now known as the **Moor's Rock**, or **Moor's Head**. On the left is the *parador*, providing yet another majestic view.

Still keeping to the highway, let us drop back down toward the river and the city. Here we are in the midst of the famous **Cigarrales** —whose name means cicada, an insect whose song fills the summer air— a place where the upper classes of Toledo came to escape the dog-day heat. The 17C drama, *Los cigarrales de Toledo*, by Tirso de Molina, describes this idle society of men and women of the court and how they would meet to recite poetry and tell tales, much in the style of the *Decameron*. In the river below, we can see some ruins of windmills, and alongside, the *Embarcadero* (**Dock**) and the *Casa del Diamantista* (**Diamond cutter's House**). In olden times, there was always a boat waiting at the dock, with an occasional trip being undertaken in an effort to prove that the Tagus was navigable all the way to Lisbon. The most famous attempt was by Antonelli, during the era of Philip II. The Diamond cutter's house, directly over the river, owes its name to a clever jeweller who once lived there, with the house being made famous as a trysting site by the poet Garcilaso.

Proceeding onward and passing the hermitage of the *Virgen de la Cabeza* on the right, we arrive at the San Martín Bridge. But first, let us take a look at the so-called **Tarpeya Rock**, which was also mentioned by Tirso ('Red cliffs, the prison walls of the Tagus'). Tradition tells us that the Christians of Toledo were hurled from these cliffs as part of the persecutions ordered by Diocletian.

The San Martín Bridge was thoroughly overhauled in the 14C through the efforts of Archbishop Tenorio. It has five arches, of which the central one is the most outstanding; it, too, has a defence tower at either end. The most interesting from an architectural standpoint is the one farthest from the city, where there is a statue of the Toledan Archbishop San Julián, which has been attributed to Berruguete or Monegro. In the centre of the bridge, on the side facing the lower part of La Vega, there is a worn figurine. Popular legend identifies it with *la mujer del alarife*, the master builder's wife: having learned that the bridge was in danger of collapsing owing to poor design, she set fire to its scaffolding the night before it was to be inaugurated, thus protecting her husband's reputation. In reality, it is an effigy of the Archbishop Tenorio, with his mitre. A little further on, to the left, there is a tower with its base virtually in the water. This is the so-called *Baño de la Caba* (**Caba's bathing spot**), the source of another traditional legend. The tower was a favourite spot of Florinda la Caba, daughter of the Visigothic Count Don Julián, and she used to come here to while away the hours. Rodrigo, the last Visigothic king, was smitten by the girl's beauty and dishonoured her. When she reported this misdeed to her father, who was in Ceuta (on the northern coast of Africa), he promptly took revenge by allowing the Moors to cross over to the peninsula —the legendary beginning of the Moorish domination of Spain. The 16C writer Fray Luis de León put the tradition of the prophecy of the Tagus in verse, whereby Rodrigo is warned of his imminent punishment. The bathing spot was actually the head of a Moorish bridge, destroyed by a flood in 1203, which subsequently led to the construction of the San Martín Bridge.

Itinerary 3: the City Proper

Itinerary on foot.

Though it may prove somewhat tiring to traverse the entire periphery on foot, there is no better way to gain a firsthand look at the wall and its nine gates. Many of these accesses to the city are of a striking beauty, such as the renowned *Puerta del Sol* or Sun Gate.

Let us begin our tour at the largest gate, the *Puerta Nueva de Bisagra* or the New Bisagra Gate. Designed by the architect Covarrubias, it was erected during the final years of the reign of Charles V, during the mid-16C, as a replacement for the inadequate old Bisagra Gate. Altogether, it is composed of two separate elements, joined by side walls and thus creating a spacious central patio. We first come across the outer façade, which is protected by two semicircular towers. The middle of the façade is taken up by a gigantic imperial coat-of-arms bearing the two-headed eagle of the Hapsburg dynasty (Charles V). Above this emblem, sitting atop a pediment, is a statue of the guardian angel of the city.

Entering the patio, we will notice the niche with the statue of Toledo's first Archbishop, San Eugenio, attributed to Berruguete or Monegro.

Above the statue is a commemorative stone with the verses that the Visigothic King Wamba ordered to be inscribed on the gates of the city.

A statue of Charles V stands in the centre of the patio. The next façade is flanked by two towers on which sit two pyramidal capitals separated by a heraldic frieze made of polychromatic stone.

After crossing in front of the doors that lead to the upper rooms and the cellars, we then come to the interior façade, decorated with a new imperial coat-of-arms.

A short walk will give us a look at the stretch of wall built by the Moors as a defence for the Antequeruela area; this part curves downward to join another wall section below the Alhóndiga, which is now a parking lot. There is nothing of particular artistic interest here, though 19C buffs will appreciate its provincial aura reminiscent of the comedy of manners, or the *costumbrista*, genre.

Behind a number of recently-restored Moorish towers can be seen the *Torreón de Albarrana*, visible only from the outside, since its inner area is attached to the neighbourhood courtyards and houses. Dating from the late 12C, it has retained some parapets and loopholes. Its two flanking arches, covered over today, form the **Almofala Gate**. At one time severely punished by the flooding Tagus, they have not been used for centuries. Not far away is an opening in the wall between two towers, which has been given the name *Puerta Nueva* or **New Gate**.

Let us return to the New Bisagra Gate and start walking up the street, the c/ Real del Arrabal. Straightaway we will see a new **stretch of wall from Visigothic days**. This is an expansion that Wamba ordered to be built so as to bring the Roman wall into this area, a wall which ended at the c/ del Cristo, and which had an exit gate called Agilana or Aguilana, that no longer exists.

In this Visigothic wall (previously called the Azor Wall), we find the Gate of Bab-Mardón, or of *Cristo de la Luz* (Christ of Light). Though it is of little artistic interest, its 14C aspect presents one of Toledo's most beautiful scenes; when it was restored, the **Roman sewers** were uncovered, which can be seen in the small garden at its base. The name Christ of the Light came from a nearby mosque. During the Moorish period, the room above the door was a butcher's shop, afterwards becoming the dreaded *Casa de los Leprosos*, or Lepers' House.

If we go through the gate and immediately turn left, we will end up at a small terrace above the wall that leads to the *Puerta del Sol*, from where we get our best view of this famous gate. A look at its construction shows that it belongs to the 12C, perhaps dating from the reign of Queen Urraca or King Alfonso VII. Be this as it may, here we have one of the most magnificent works of Mudejar art in the city. Altogether, the gate consists of two towers —a square inner one and an outer, circular one with parapets, joined by a central structure. The latter has two beautiful arcades with Moorish, or horseshoe, arches; the upper ones are entwined, whilst the lower ones are lobular. Beneath the largest, in a triangle inscribed inside a circle, there is also a relief of the Virgin wearing the chasuble of San Ildefonso, with the overhead sun and moon perhaps being the source of the name, the Sun Gate. The largest of the arcades has a number of rather-worn white marble figures, as well as a head on a sort of tray above them. Legend has it that the figures are of two young maidens who were mistreated by an *alguacil*, or sheriff, named Facundo Gonzalo, who was ordered to be beheaded by King San Fernando. The most likely explanation, however, is that the head is of John the Baptist, since the gate was originally

dedicated to this saint. From the wall terrace, one can pass to the inside of the tower and visit its one-time military quarters and dungeons.

From the Sun Gate, a rather ramshackle gate comes quickly into view, the **Alarcones Gate**, standing alongside the phantasmal convent of the Asunción. Below this edifice, another stretch of wall runs parallel to the highway heading toward the Alcántara Bridge; atop the wall is the Miradero walkway. This was originally the site of the now-disappeared **Perpiñán Gate**, which formed part of the Roman wall.

Whilst the Miradero was being worked on, the old *Alhóndiga*, or **corn exchange**, was revamped. In one way or another, this grain deposit has mostly been associated with misfortune: built in 1575, it collapsed in 1593 and was rebuilt in 1636 for the *pósito*, or grain storage utilized by the city council for aiding poor workers. When the custom of the *pósito* was abandoned, the building was then used as a slaughterhouse, and later a hospital. Just above the building is the hermitage of the Virgin of the Helpless (*Virgen de los Desamparados*), rebuilt in the 16C (now it is a temporary bus station; the future of this structure will not be determined until after the new bus station in la Vega is opened).

Directly in front is a small pillar with a worn inscription: 'Here stood the house in which was born the lieutenant general and poet Eugenio Gerardo Lobo, who died in 1757'.

Let us continue along the street that bears the name of this poet, heading toward the Alcántara Bridge. Above our heads looms the wall with its observation point. Climbing up to it will give us access to a staircase that in turn leads us to the city's best-preserved ruins of a **Roman wall**.

At last we arrive at the Alcántara Gate. This gate has been exceedingly well restored and is a perfect example of a Moorish gate, with its L-shaped, elbow structure. The best view of it can be had whilst coming down from the Pl de la Concepción, along the slope overlooked by the apses of Concepción Francisca.

Keeping to the Ronda de Juanelo, the rampart walk, we can see down below at the riverside the site of the famous water mechanism referred to earlier. High up on one of the walls is an inscription in ceramic of the famed verses of the mystic San Juan de la Cruz.

These verses flow from the heart of the saint, they bespeak his soul that went out on its dark night in search of its loved one... Nevertheless, it was actually San Juan de la Cruz himself who went out from these walls as he attempted to escape from the interrogations and other discomforts of the Holy Inquisition.

The Ronda de Juanelo became the Cabestreros walkway. This will give students of archaeology the chance to decipher and date the various remains of walls and sewers that surround the modest *Puerta de Doce Cantos* (**Twelve-stone Gate**). Going a bit further, the wall ends at the *Jardín del Moro* (**Moor's Garden**) and the **Mozarabic church of San Lucas**.

The following stretch skirting Toledo is truly the backside of the city, scarcely visited by tourists. By following the San Sebastián road that encircles this less-inviting wall section, we arrive at the Mozarabic
🔘 parish church of San Sebastián ▶ page 106. The expanse of sand below is the Alcurnia, where in olden times the **Moorish Gate of Adabaquín** was located. This sandy area was once a luscious garden (the word *alcurnia* is probably a variation of *almunia*, or garden).

This immediately brings us to an austere building, the ancient convent of the **Gilitos**, later a jail, then a firehouse, and now —magnificently restored— it houses the *Cortes de Castilla-La Mancha*, or the parliament of the region's autonomous government. This building alone may well have changed the appearance of what we have labelled the less-attractive side of Toledo. As we draw away from it, we come to the true crossroads of the current flow of tourists: the Paseo del Tránsito. If we go over and look down at the river, we will see that there is no wall here, nor is one needed. We are atop the *Roca Tarpeya*, the steepest cliffside in Toledo. The **Victorio Macho Museum** stands on what was once the site of a feared Roman prison, which jutted out over the precipice. Here was another point where Christians who professed their faith were hurled to their death during the Diocletian persecutions, around the year 303.

Heading onward, we regain the wall and another gate, the **San Martín Gate**, a protection for the passageway to the bridge (referred to in our second itinerary). Above all of this can be seen some recently-renovated **gardens** wherein is found an inscription containing verses by Garcilaso dedicated to the Tagus.

From the nearby and impeccably-restored stretch of Moorish wall, we can look down on the *Baño de la Caba* before we proceed on to the Cambrón Gate.

The original gate was built by the Visigoths and subsequently restored by the Moors. We can get a glimpse of the age in the central patio. However, the construction that meets our eye, with its four towers, dates from the 16C. The name *cambrón* means buckthorn, and was taken from the brambles that used to grow in the area. The outer façade has an entrance arch resting on two small columns that have been borrowed from a previous structure, as can be seen by the Arabic inscription on the right. The façade facing inwardly toward the city has, above its bossed arch, a niche with the image of Santa Leocadia; it is naturally attributed to Berruguete.

Continuing on our way, we can see the *Torreón de los Abades*, or **Abbot's Tower**. Fighting from its parapet in the 11C, the clergy of Toledo led a battle that denied the city to the Moor Alí and his troops as they attempted to retake it. During this siege, the Archangel San Miguel appeared on a lower gate, the **Almaguera Gate** (no longer existent), and with sword in hand, fought on the side of the Christians.

The length of wall we see reinforced by round and square towers and surrounded by gardens was rebuilt by King Alfonso VI after he conquered Toledo, since the Moorish (as well as Visigothic) wall had been severely damaged by the siege. And so we arrive at the last gate on our tour, the *Puerta Antigua de Bisagra*, or Old Bisagra Gate (a name from the Arabic *bab-sahra*, or field gate), and at times known as the Gate of Alfonso VI. Luckily, in the 16C the New Bisagra Gate was built; the old one was not revamped, simply covered over. As a result, we have a rather pristine example of a beautiful, rustic Moorish gate that dates from shortly after the invasion, namely the 9C.

We have two anecdotes that serve to confirm the age of this gate. One concerns the year 838, or thereabouts, when Toledo was in the domain of the Caliph Abderramán II of Cordoba. A rebel, Hixem-el-Atiki, took up arms against the Caliph; soon after the failure of his rebellion, his head was hung on this gate as a lesson and warning.

The other event took place on the very eve of the retaking of Toledo. Outside the city, the troops of Alfonso VI were uproariously awaiting the order to attack. Among Alfonso's captains were Rodrigo Díaz de Vivar (El Cid) and Pedro Ansúrez. The latter, unable to control his impatience, spurred his horse into action and charged toward the gate alone amidst a hail of arrows. The daring soldier reached the gate, ripped loose its knocker, and returned to present the trophy to his King. Soon afterwards, on the morning of May 25, 1085, the besieged Moors surrendered to the Christians, who made a triumphant entry through the gate and proceeded onward to the mosque, the Christ of Light.

Itinerary 4: the Essential Itinerary

Itinerary on foot.

Here we have the **indispensable** tour, the one most tourists take when they can only be in Toledo a few hours —we'll go to the heart of the matter, by beginning in the heart of the city...

...Which, be it in a modern or ancient sense, is the Zocodover plaza. The name comes from *zoco*, meaning livestock market, which formerly was a square or vacant space in front of a fortress. Old documents refer to the large number of *mesones*, or inns, around the Zocodover in Toledo, and as of the 15C, the advent of colonnades and stately buildings. The streets that lead into this plaza —Tornerías, Comercio, etc.— still maintain the narrow, rambling layout typical of the old Arab *zocos*. The illuminated *Cantigas* (poems) of Alfonso the Wise give us an idea of what the buildings used to be like, with their low ceilings and cramped quarters, scarcely larger than a niche or cupboard.

Zocodover Plaza

Today it is still the centre of the city, and the best place to get a feel for the life in Toledo. To the left we see the *Arco de la Sangre* (**Blood Arch**), originally a Mudejar creation. Its name comes from the small chapel of the Christ of Blood overhead —though we can draw an ironic double meaning from it, because condemned prisoners were brought here to pray before being led to the gallows in the corner of the plaza by the street leading up to the Alcázar. Bullfights were once staged here and also plays which were performed in a type of playhouse called a *Corral de Comedias*.

If we pass through the arch and head toward the river, on our right we will see some houses where once stood the famed *Posada del Sevillano*, or Sevillian Inn (later the *Posada de la Sangre*), which was described by Cervantes in his short work, *The Illustrious Charwoman*, which some believe was written here. Close by is the Hospital of Santa Cruz **Museum** ▶ *page* 118.

After visiting the museum, we can go uphill to the Alcázar and visit this ponderous fortress ▶ *page* 85. And next on our list should be the Cathedral and its museum rooms ▶ *page* 97.

We then walk by the *Ayuntamiento* (Town Hall) and cross the Pasadizo del Ayuntamiento, which will take us uphill to the c/ de Santo Tomé. First we will visit the church of Santo Tomé, the church with El Greco's *The Burial of Count Orgaz* ▶ *page* 113, not far from the El Greco House-Museum ▶ *page* 116.

This puts us right in the midst of the *judería*, the **Jewish quarter**.

Close by is the Tránsito Synagogue ▶ *page 132.* A little further on is 　◐ ◐
the other existing synagogue. Santa María la Blanca ▶ *page 130.* 　◐ ◐

Leaving the latter and walking to the right, we immediately come
upon San Juan de los Reyes ▶ *page101* and the Cambrón Gate ▶ 　◐
page 18, thus bringing to an end our tour of the fundamentals.

Itinerary 5: Upper-level Tour 　　　　　　　　　　　◐ ◐

Itinerary on foot.

Do not consider this to be just a supplementary tour, because it
contains some hidden gems that are most often missed by the
hellbent-for-leather tourist. These sights alone are worth a trip to
Toledo. The city's configuration lends itself to a two-part division for the
purpose of our visit: one itinerary will take us to the upper, or northern,
part of Toledo, with our point of reference being the Cathedral and the
Zocodover; the second itinerary will take us down to the lower, or
southern, part of the city.

Once again, we shall start out at the Zocodover, departing by the c/
Nueva in front of the **Blood Arch.** Hidden in a cul-de-sac behind an
enormous neo-Gothic building is the **Palace of Benacazón,** an
interesting example of a Toledan house with its patio and remains of
Mudejar tile and plasterwork. It has been well restored and is currently
the office of a savings bank. A little further on we will find the **church
of San Nicolás,** a church of a more modern bent (1500) and without
excessive artistic qualities (its Mudejar architecture is from the 19C).
Going down c/ Núñez de Arce, we arrive at the **Church and Convent
of San José;** in the patio of the house next to the church can be seen
Santa Teresa's room. In addition to the many **beautiful patios,** both
here and further down we will notice an impressive number of masterly
entrances, often highly artistic, because this is the area where the
hidalgos, or nobles, lived. On the contrary, our tour of the lower level
will show us patios of a more humble stripe.

Let us return to San Nicolás and take c/ Alfileritos, named after a
popular figure of the Virgin located in a niche where young girls
anxious for a suitor used to come and toss pins —*alfileres*— as an
offering. By following Cristo de la Luz street downhill, we will come to
the mosque, after which the street has been named ▶ *page* 114, and
two gates, *Bab-Mardon* and *Puerta del Sol* ▶ *page* 15.

Returning to c/ Alfileritos, straightaway we see a typical cul-de-sac to
our left. Its name is **Agustín Moreto,** after a celebrated 17C playwright
who lived here and who was director of the *Refugio,* a charity house
that operated until the last century.

C/ Alfileritos leads us to the Pl San Vicente, with its **church** of the
same name ▶ *page* 107. In front of it is the **Convent of las Gaitanas**
▶ *page* 98. Alongside, in c/ Plata (another one where the *hidalgos*
lived, with its numerous stonework entrance halls), is the Post Office
(*Correos*), occupying what used to be the 17C Hospital del Bálsamo.

Once again in Pl San Vicente, we can see the neoclassical
University of Lorenzana, almost attached to the church ▶ *page* 107.
But let us leave the plaza, going out to the right of the church toward
the little plaza of Santa Clara. We cross through a covered passageway,
then go down to the plaza of the *Carmelitas Descalzos,* or Barefoot
Carmelites, where we find the **Church and Convent of the
Carmelites.** With a rather plain façade, its main interest is the air of
peace and calm it projects. Retracing our steps, we will pass by one
covered passageway to our left, *Santa Clara,* and through another,

Santo Domingo —here we have a route of silence, a place revered by romantics and writers. We next arrive at the Santo Domingo el Real plaza, brimming with literary memories and dominated by the church of the same name ▶ *page* 112. We will leave the plaza by the far end and take c/ Aljibes; on the right as we come to Tendillas we find the Pl of the Capuchinos and the **Convent** (a 17C building). Baroque altars of multicoloured marble, paintings and frescos by Ricci, Algardi, and others). Going down c/ Merced, we immediately see the provincial council building (*Diputación Provincial*), built toward the end of the last century on the site of a former convent. Going up Vía Santa Leocadia (in front of us), we arrive at the **Church of Santa Leocadia** and the Convent of Santo Domingo el Antiguo, both located in a charming little plaza ▶ *page* 108 and 111.

Facing the door to Santo Domingo, a tiny street bears the name Hospital de San Ildefonso, though the hospital no longer exists. Close to the corner is a commemorative stone on the house where the Bécquer brothers lived from 1868-69 (one, Gustavo, was Spain's most famous romantic poet). There is a small —and romantic— garden.

Retracing our steps down Santa Leocadia and turning into c/ Real on our left, we will come to El Nuncio, formerly a lunatic asylum ▶ *page* 125. A short distance further down this same street we come to the **plaza and Convent of the Carmelites**, dating from 1607, whose prioress was a cousin of Santa Teresa (plain façade, spacious interior, and interesting paintings).

Let us now take c/ Colegio de Doncellas Nobles (**School of Noble Maidens**), and we will soon see the tower and the school itself. Founded in 1551 by Cardinal Silíceo for one hundred blueblooded young ladies, it was remodelled in the 16C and 17C. In the 18C, Cardinal Lorenzana placed the famed architect Ventura Rodríguez in charge of a new restoration; to him we owe the tower and the spacious, two-tiered patio. Inside the church, there is the tomb of Cardinal Silíceo, as well as magnificent walnut chairs at one end of the choir.

Climbing the street that faces the school, a few steps will bring us to the old *Hospitalito de Santa Ana* or the **Small Santa Ana Hospital** with its unpretentious 18C façade, one of the many charity institutions formerly found in the city. Above it, we see the **covered passageway of the Noble Maidens**, which will lead us to the Pl de la Cruz (take a peek at the house and patio at number 3). Then we head to the right until we come to c/ Bulas Viejas, which we follow downhill until we reach a half-hidden house, the *Casa de las Cadenas* (House of Chains). Here is one of Toledo's best-restored mansions, which has been converted into the **Museum of Contemporary Art** ▶ *page* 118.

By following c/ Bulas Viejas, we will arrive at the Pl de Valdecaleros, with house number 14 and its *patio de Cristo* the scene of one of the city's many Jewish vs. Christian legends, in this case the burial of the Christ of Light. On the right is Bodegones (Winecellars), a typical street where 17C students (among them the writer Quevedo) came to live it up. This street leads to Santo Tomé.

· Leaving Valdecaleros by the side opposite to Bodegones, we arrive at c/ San Pedro Mártir, where we will find another **covered passageway**. To our left is a neighbourhood courtyard occupying the former site of the **Armiño mansion** —this being the family of El Greco— with remains of Mudejar plasterwork. At the end of this street, which flanks the courtyard wall, we come out onto Santa Eulalia, where the Mozarabic church of the same name is located ▶ *page* 107.

By taking the Cuesta de Garcilaso, we will find at the end of it another space, where the **Garcilaso mansion** once was. This was the birthplace of the brilliant poet (1501); at one time it must have been a magnficent mansion, because the king of Portugal stayed there. In 1808, a battalion of young soldiers was formed here to fight against the Napoleonic invasion —this was the origin of today's Spanish Infantry.

Above this empty lot is yet another: the **Padilla plaza**. Here lived the famous leader of the 16C *comunero* uprising. When the movement failed, Padilla was beheaded in Valladolid, his house was razed and the ground sowed with salt.

From here, by taking c/ Esteban Illán we will soon arrive at the Mesa House ▶ *page 128*. Going back and circling the block, we come to another of Toledo's vital centres: here there are two connected churches, San Román and San Pedro Mártir; alongside is the Convent of San Clemente ▶ *page 99*. Facing these, in the Pl de San Ildefonso, is the Jesuit church **San Juan Bautista** ▶ *page 100*. This is the highest point in the city, as well as a spiritual and artistic peak.

Let us depart from the Pl de San Ildefonso by c/ Alfonso X el Sabio. Shortly before returning to the Pl de San Vicente, we will turn off to the right in order to reach the Pl de San Ginés. The church here sits on top of a mysterious tradition: the Cave of Hercules. Túbal, or the Egyptian Hercules, had an underground palace dug here, where he taught occult sciences. It housed figures and paintings that would bring great misfortune were they to be revealed. Besides this hermetic tradition —of great significance in medieval Toledo— there is another legend linked to this cave, one concerning the last Gothic king and the conquest of Spain by the Moors. And in turn, other legends have been spawned, that include such figures as the Marquis de Sade in his *Don Rodrigo*, or the *Enchanted Tower*, or *Love Crimes*.

We now proceed by c/ San Ginés to c/ de la Sal, then to Santas Justa y Rufina, where we find the **church** of the same name ▶ *page 108*. This brings us to c/ Comercio, the bustling lifeline which connects Zocodover and the Cathedral and which will serve as the mid-point of our route (see itinerary 6).

Itinerary 6: Lower Level Itinerary

Itinerary on foot.

We will once again kick off from Zocodover, leaving by the narrow c/ Barrio Rey and its terraces, which take us to the **Magdalena plaza** ▶ *page 98* and the *Corral de Don Diego* ▶ *page 127*. Passing in front of the latter and going down c/ Tornerías, we will find the **mosque** of the same name ▶ *page 116*. This street leads to the *Plaza Mayor*, normally the main square in a Spanish city, though here the Zocodover has captured all the glory. To one side is the **Rojas Theatre** ▶ *page 129*, alongside the **market** that stands on the former site of a 15C slaughterhouse. On the other side of the plaza is the Cathedral and the *Hospital del Rey* or *King's Hospital*. Founded either by Alfonso VIII or by Ferdinand the Saint, what was a 15C building has been completely remodelled and turned into a senior-citizens home. There is evidence that as many as twenty-one of these hospitals, or similar charitable institutions, existed during the time of El Greco.

In front of the Cathedral is the *Posada*, or *Cárcel de la Hermandad* ▶ *page 128*. Let us draw away from the Lions Gate in order to descend by c/ Sixto Ramón Parro, named after the writer of one of the first guidebooks to Toledo. At the end there is the **San Justo plaza**, one of Toledo's most evocative plazas, with its trees, fountain, the former San Justo hospital (now a sanatorium), and the Church of Santos Justo y Pastor ▶ *page* 112. At the end of the plaza is the Callejón del Toro, the narrowest street in the city. Leading from one end is c/ Cristo de la Calavera (Christ of the Skull street), the location of one of Bécquer's legends. Close by we can see the **Church of San Miguel**, founded long ago but extensively restored in the last century; the *pasadizo* (alley) of San Miguel, below the church, has a number of paintings; alongside it is the **Templars House**, also known as the *Casa del Duende*, or Ghost's House (a sombre place, linked to a story of a witch and a Jew who held orgies amongst coffins and human bones, part of a cycle of anti-Jewish legends).

Skirting the Mudejar apse of the church of San Justo, we come out onto a tiny plaza. Facing us from the far end is the façade of **San Juan de la Penitencia** ▶ *page* 101.

A descent to the right will take us to the Mozarabic Church of San Lucas ▶ *page* 103. Next to it is the modern *Cigarral de los Doctrinos*, where once stood a famous school, the *Colegio de los Doctrinos*, a refuge for orphans and waifs.

Descending a bit more, on the right we have the **Monastery of the Hieronymites of Saint Paul**. Founded in the 14C, it lumps together a number of periods in an interesting 16C Gothic church housing tombs, altarpieces and paintings. Until the war broke out in 1936, the convent had a knife that was said to have belonged to Nero, and that was used to behead Saint Paul. The novelist Galdós is rumoured to have asked the nuns to lend it to him so that he could sharpen his pencils.

Still heading downhill and taking the Bajada del Barco, we will find ourselves at the **dock** and the **Diamond Cutter's house** (referred to in Itinerary 2) ▶ *page* 14. Going uphill will bring us to the **Convent of Concepción Benita**. Although it was founded in the 15C, its current design is from the 18C —Latin-cross church, dome above the transept, Tuscan columns, and a severe, bare façade.

Higher up is the small *Colegio de Infantes* **(Children's School)** created by Cardinal Silíceo (this one for Cathedral children). Notice its plateresque façade with caryatids, the patio, and the masonrywork in the chapel.

Returning down the street that converges with the one that brought us up, we will arrive at the **Munárriz House**, a stately mansion that belonged to the priest who ordered its *campana gorda*, or fat bell, to be made. It later belonged to the contemporary architect, Chueca Goitia. A little further and we come to a house with an extraordinary plateresque façade, as well as the ruins of the **Church of San Lorenzo**.

The Bajada del Colegio de Infantes ends in the c/ del Pozo Amargo, literally the **Bitter Well street**. A few metres up is a small plaza and well that inspired a popular Toledan legend: a young Christian came nightly to the garden of a rich Jewish girl, whose father eventually had the youth killed; she then returned to the well each night to mourn, until finally she threw herself into it, thinking she had seen her love's face in the water.

Going up to the end of the street, we will arrive at the large plaza surrounded by the Cathedral, the Archbishop's Palace, the Town Hall, and the *Palacio de la Audiencia* or **Court palace**.

At an angle to c/ del Pozo Amargo (which we've just come up) is c/ Santa Isabel; following this street will bring us to a small plaza that contains the Convent of Santa Isabel and a noble house where once

Church of Santo Tomé

was the *Alcázar del rey Don Pedro* (**Palace of King Peter**) ▶ *page* 127. Continuing along the same street, we will arrive at another of Toledo's leading churches, San Andrés ▶ *page* 99. Beside it stands the tumbledown Major Seminary, omissible —however, quite the opposite is true of the Minor Seminary in front, with its *Renaissance patio* and *Mudejar ruins* from the disappeared palace of King Pedro.

Once more orienting ourselves in the Pl de Santa Isabel, and taking the street of the same name to skirt the church, we come to c/ Cristo de la Parra. Here is located the Mudéjar apse of **San Bartolomé** ▶ *page* 99. Descending a bit more toward the river, we come to the Mozarabic Church of San Sebastián on the left ▶ *page* 106. Crossing the Pl de las Mejoras, we can visit **San Cipriano** ▶ *page* 99.

Taking Cuesta de la Reina to c/ Santa Ursula, we begin to climb. On the left is a sort of plaza called *Juego de la Pelota* (Ball Game), indicative of its former use. Take a look at the patios at numbers 9 and 11 on this street. To the right is c/ Ciudad, with a photogenic view of the cathedral tower. At the end, we come to the Convent of Santa Ursula ▶ *page* 109. Here is also the **Toledo house** with its beautiful plateresque door. Going around the apse of Santa Ursula, we emerge on to the Pl de San Marcos where the enormous **Church of San Marcos** greets us. A 17C building, the church connected to the convent formerly belonged to the Calced Trinitarians, who dated from the 13C. After they were secularized, the Mozarabic parish church of San Marcos came to occupy the building. The true original Mozarabic parish of San Marcos, founded in the 7C by a grandfather of San Ildefonso, stood beside the church of Santa Isabel and was burned down by Napoleon's troops.

Facing San Marcos is the **Mozarabic Church of El Salvador ▶** *page* 98. Going along c/ Santo Tomé, on the left we will find the narrow **Alarife** street, which honours the legend of the builder of the bridge of San Martín ▶ *page* 15. Along the right of this street a number of evocative side streets await us —Algibillo, Campana, Bodegones, Soledad... At the end lies the **Convent of San Antonio**, restored in 1874 (ungilded altarpiece with good paintings and altars).

Santo Tomé street narrows down as we reach the convent visible at the end of the street. Changing its name to c/ del Angel, it leads into the Jewish quarter. If, rather than taking this street, we veer to the left, then we end up at the **Church of Santo Tomé ▶** *page* 113, and a plaza where the Palace of Fuensalida is located ▶ *page* 126. Circling this building (whose former stables now house a modern restaurant), we can walk up to the *Taller del Moro* (**Moor's Workshop**) in the Montichel area (also called San Cristóbal). From here, we can see the Gilitos Convent, or the former provincial jail. It was built in 1610 by the Barefoot Franciscans —popularly called *gilitos* because of their convent of San Gil in Madrid; they occupied the convent until their secularization, when it then became a jail. Today, following splendid restoration and expansion, it houses the Castile-La Mancha Parliament. What was formerly the church is now the General Assembly room.

From here we can also see the Tránsito Synagogue **gardens** as well as those of the El Greco House, which we can visit by descending along c/ San Juan de Dios ▶ *page* 116. The house is right by the Synagogue ▶ *page* 132, and in front, above the **Tarpeya Rock**, is the **Victorio Macho House-Museum ▶** *page* 123.

Reyes Católicos street will take us through the Jewish quarter and to the Synagogue of Santa María la Blanca ▶ *page* 131, the *Arquillo del Judío* (a small arch said to be common in Jewish quarters), and the callejón de Jacintos. This brings us to the *Escuela de Artes and Oficios* (**Arts and Trades School**), dating from the past century. We eventually arrive at San Juan de los Reyes ▶ *page* 101, perched by an observation point. opening up a beautiful view of the Tagus and the Cigarrales. On the right are remains of the **Palace of the Dukes of Máqueda** (the legendary residence of Florinda la Caba) and the Cambrón Gate ▶ *page* 18, alongside a school on the site where the parish church of San Martín once was.

CONSULATES

Consulates provide a wide range of services for their nationals. They are there to provide assistance should one encounter difficulties with the Spanish legal system; to advise on local regulations; to act as public notaries for their own nationals; to help out in all emergencies. A consulate can be especially useful in the following cases: **renewing passports** or obtaining other **documents** needed for travel; making **contact with family or friends** —this service can be a lifeline should you need money quickly; **advising** about transfer of funds; contacting next of kin at home in case of **sickness** or **death**.

Unfortunately, there are no foreign consulates in Toledo; one must therefore go to Madrid if such services are required. However, in cases of emergency, the Municipal Police or the Office of Tourism is available for assistance ▶ *page* 152.

CONSUMER RIGHTS

Spanish legislation protects the rights of consumers. Several agencies and groups can help the traveller in this regard; the National Consumer Institute; the relevant *Consejería*, or Ministry, of the regional government; the *Ayuntamientos*, or city halls themselves; and local consumer organizations. Use them if you think a product or service puts your health or safety in danger; if the quality or quantity of what you buy does not correspond to the price of the product or service; or if products or services don't live up to the basic norms of safety and quality.

Before making a claim, you should be quite sure of the facts, checking them carefully. Then decide on the best way to present your claim; personally (many times a simple personal request will solve the problem), by telephone, or by mail. Think specifically about what the problem is and what solution you're seeking.

How to present the claim? It is essential to provide clear facts: your name, address and telephone number; name, address and telephone number of the company or entity against whom you are filing a claim; why you are making a claim; and the solution that you're seeking. You should attach photocopies of all documents relating to the matter when filing claims. Make sure to keep a duplicate of your statement stamped by the office to which you present your complaint.

One particularly effective way of defending your rights in hotels, restaurants, bars, cafeterias, discotheques and so on, is the *libro de reclamaciones*, or complaints book. It is legally obligatory on all establishments to have such a book available to the customer. The simple act of asking for the complaints book —actually loose-leaf forms most of the time— is likely to take care of any problem. The complaint registered in the book is sent directly to local authorities, and the customer retains a copy.

Claims should be made as quickly as possible —if at all possible before you leave the locality; receipts for the object or service against which you are filing a claim should be included.

Complaints and problems may be taken to one of the following places: *Oficina de Turismo* (Puerta de Bisagra); the *Oficina de Información*; or presented by telephone to the *Gobierno Civil* (civil government) ☎ 22 60 00, extension 14 or to municipal offices ☎ 22 28 00. The telephone of the office of consumer rights is ☎ 21 00 26.

CUISINE

From the standpoint of gastronomy, it must be admitted that Toledo has not always had the highest of reputations. In part, this is due to a legacy of a Golden-age literary tradition: the *novela picaresca*, the picaresque novel, liked to depict the streets of Toledo as packed with starving ruffians. This was the other side of the glorious Spanish Empire. At the same time, there is the tourist factor, a great mass of people on the move, visitors whose strongest wish is to see monuments, rather than to eat well. Sadly, there are unscrupulous restaurateurs who take advantage of, and aggravate, this situation.

Yet, changes are taking place quickly, with a desire not only to offer and extol traditional cuisine, but also to redouble efforts in order to adapt tradition to new tastes. A *nueva cocina*, or *nouvelle cuisine*, is being developed, one of high quality and based on traditional elements.

27

Cheeses

No tradition in the region is more deeprooted than that of **Manchego** cheese. Here we have a sheep's-milk cheese that is somewhat buttery, one that can be strong and sharp. Most likely there was a traditional fresh cheese in olden days, or one of another type, but no longer.

In 1986, a national listing of hand made cheeses was issued in Spain. Other than the generally-produced Manchegan cheese, only two regional varieties were recognized: one comes from a small area around **Oropesa**, which produces miniature cheeses packed in oil, whilst another involves a part of the **Toledo highlands**, likewise small, where goat cheese is made.

The custom of submerging the cheese in oil and letting it age is no doubt quite a long-standing one in Toledo, as can be seen in the widespread tradition —still surviving amongst a great many potters in the province— of making *queseras*, or cylindrical pottery pieces of varying heights, with a conical top and small handles. These can hold two, three, or even more of the oil-cured cheeses, though they are now frequently sold as souvenirs.

Cuisine of Toledo

One can place traditional Toledan cuisine within that broad category labelled by the French gourmet Raymond Dumay as *Roman-civilization cuisine*, one that extends from La Mancha to Extremadura. In the case of Toledo, this signifies an essentially Roman inspiration, later enriched by Moorish input, and subsequently by the monastic influence present in cities and castles. It is basically a rural, inland cuisine, one that has apparently turned its face away from the sea. Nevertheless, it has risen to sublime heights as a result of its dishes that incorporate game from the Toledo highlands.

Therefore, the first thing you notice about the cooking from this region are the game dishes which include hare and rabbit, deer, wild boar and, above all, **partridge** and **quail**.

Toledo is a hunter's paradise. The preferred target is most often the partridge, that plump, red bird that blends in with the land and then suddenly bursts forth in its pell-mell flight. The classic way to prepare partridge is in a stew.

The other major dish in the kitchens of Toledo —to the point of being a *cliché*— is ***codornices a la toledana***, or Toledo-style quail. If you consider the partridge to be a palate-tickler, rather than a means of satisfying a great hunger, then the quail, this feisty bird that comes and goes seasonally, as do the tourists, becomes truly a whim. This dish is usually prepared in the same way as partridge, as well as being marinated.

Another game dish that is relatively easy to find in restaurants is **rabbit** or **hare**, especially prepared with garlic, *al ajillo*, or tomato, *con tomate*. The great abundance of these animals in the Toledo highlands accounts for their presence in traditional cooking. If we want other game dishes, then we will have to leave the restaurants in the city of Toledo and head for the highlands. In San Pablo de los Montes, for example, one can savour venison, with sausages from this and other meats available in the off season.

Among the non-game possibilities, you can find in Toledo such typical dishes as mutton, lamb, and suckling pig, roasted *al pastor*, or shepherd style, and seasoned with thyme, lavender and other aromatic herbs. In other words, Toledan cuisine is a sober one which pays tribute to the habits and customs reflected in the cuisines of Castile and La Mancha in general.

Other dishes that are neither meat nor game, yet are completely traditional, include a garlic soup, *sopa castellana*, a common item on every menu; *gazpacho*, mainly a summer treat; *pisto*, a potpourri of stewed vegetables; *gachas*, a type of porridge; *migas*, or fried breadcrumbs; and hotpot dishes. The *tortilla a la magra*, found in almost every restaurant, is a Spanish *tortilla* on which is placed a juicy slice of pork.

Turning to fish, it is only natural that they will be of the river variety, above all, the trout, the wily Tagus trout. The Toledan-style trout, or *truchas a la toledana*, is prepared with vinegar, oil, garlic and a mouth-watering array of spices, though they, too, are representative of the simplicity and sobriety of Toledan cuisine. River crab forms part of another exquisite speciality, the *crema de cangrejos* soup. Fish from the open seas can, nevertheless, be found, such as *bacalao* (cod) and *besugo al ajoarriero* (sea bream), made with egg and garlic, very popular throughout the centre of the peninsula.

This is what we can call the traditional cuisine of Toledo. At the same time, we should add a few dishes from times past that have been well documented in a number of literary sources. These include roast and stewed squab, *fricasséed* or stewed dove, Toledo-style gruel, and a wealth of others that have frequently been pushed aside by the standard tourist fare of *perdiz a la toledana*, *trucha a la toledana* and other similar dishes.

However, the entire country has changed, Toledo as well, and its cuisine has done an about face. The *nouvelle cuisine* or *nueva cocina* is a reality that has arrived in Toledo. Tastes and pocketbooks have changed, and the gastronomic panorama is now on a par with that of any other city that has prospered after a painstaking restoration.

Nowadays, Toledo is home to a good number of elite restaurants. Perhaps because of its status as capital of Castile-La Mancha, not only is the delicate stewed partridge to be found on the menu, along with the other dishes we have mentioned, but it is also possible to choose from an entire range of succulent offerings, including sea food. Here you can dine on *merluza* (hake) or shellfish that rival similar dishes at the most famous seaside restaurants. The traditional offerings have been enriched with a wide-ranging selection of meat, sea food, and vegetables whose origins are as equally varied. Elegance is reflected in menus where you find such items as salmon *en papillón*, an avocado-seafood cocktail, or impeccable French *tournedós*.

There is more. The *nueva cocina* has formed a felicitous partnership with the sombre hearths of Toledo, and there is no small number of chefs who are bent on adapting this cuisine, this new, modern-day taste, to the possibilities that spring from the native soil and traditions of Toledo. One example is *paté de perdiz* (partridge paté), which many restaurants serve to the squeamish who may shy away from coping with the bones of a small bird...

Nor is this the limit: a good many restaurants are searching for new, bold combinations that echo creativity, richness, refinement and novelty, without losing sight of the traditional foundations. Here we can quote the relative frequency of dishes such as venison with mushrooms, *sirloin al cabrales* (with the famous *cabrales* cheese), *tiznao de merluza* (blackened hake, a typical Manchegan dish that is usually made with cod —the substitution with the more exquisite hake is yet another sign of this *nueva cocina*). On goes the list: venison pie, eggplant *au gratin* with shrimp, venison with pears, garlic codfish *glacé*, froglegs, garlic-shrimp omelettes, *ad infinitum*.

Another outstanding aspect of this true rebirth in Toledan gastronomy is the fact that there is a great deal of interest in echoing its history in its cuisine. There are establishments with traditional Arabic and Jewish dishes on their menus —rectifying an inexcusable omission dating from the expulsion of the Jews and Moors (beginning in the late 15C). At the same time, these eastern dishes have now been embellished and transformed by the requirements of a new taste and new society. Thus while dining in Toledo we may come across that most classical of Arabic dishes, **alcuzcuz** (couscous), alongside a Jewish chicken *paté*, almond soup, orange duck, eggplant stuffed with broadbeans, steak with tangerine sauce, oriental sherbets and sweetmeats, to name a few.

Desserts and Pastries

Toledo is one of the top-ranking producers of confectionery items in Spain. It is not only famous for its **marzipan,** but for other even-richer delights as well —not a surprising fact, since Toledo lived for many years under Moorish rule. Other elements of its Arabic heritage have been watered down or uprooted, while here we have a case of a legacy that has been substantially enhanced. As the saying goes, *a sweet never embitters anyone.*

Though you will often see it in the form of figures, this has not always been the case: the oldest-existing moulds are made of beech and walnut and belong to the selfsame San Clemente monastery in Toledo, indicating that they were a type of cake decorated in relief. Used for such purposes was an instrument called a *pintadera*, or painter, a type of tongs for decorating festive bread (which gave rise to the Spanish expression *tortas y pan pintado*, or child's play). The custom of shaping the marzipan into figures may have resulted from another fusion of Christian and pagan rites, since they are related to the bread eaten during certain *romerías*, or local pilgrimages, or in pagan rites celebrating the first fruits of the harvest. All things considered, we are dealing with a rather passionate subject.

The inertia dictated by tradition has led to marzipan being considered as a Christmas sweet, making it impossible to find outside of Toledo during the rest of the year. Here in the city, however, it is available year-round.

The variety of sweets in Toledo is immense, perhaps the largest in all of Spain, and the one with most Moorish influence. The list includes **toledanas, melindres, marquesitas, marquesas** and **duquesas**, as well as an overwhelming selection of pastries (we could easily map out a pastry route that would boggle the mind of the most demanding gourmet). The **melindres de Yepes**, a type of honey fritters, are more tasty and delicate —as well as more expensive— than marzipan. **Sonseca** is a town that should be visited for no other reason than to buy pastries and sweets in one of its many 19C-style shops. Everything is locally made and reflects unsurpassable quality. There are marzipan confectioners who are truly multinational, and who also make *marquesas* and *marquesitas*. Another gourmet visit can be made to **Ajofrín**, where marzipan, *marquesas* and the extremely-famous *magdalenas* are turned out. This town also specializes in *delicias*, with a maddening, tantalizing taste.

CULTURE AND HISTORY

Here let the antiquarian pore over the stirring memorials of many thousand years, the vestiges of Phoenician enterprise, of Roman magnificence, of Moorish elegance, in that storehouse of ancient customs, that repository of all elsewhere long forgotten and passed by; here let him gaze upon those classical monuments, unequalled almost in Greece or Italy, and on those fairy Aladdin palaces, the creatures of Oriental gorgeousness and imagination, with which Spain alone can enchant the dull European; here let the man of feeling dwell on the poetry of her envy-disarming decay...; here let the lover of art feed his eyes with the mighty masterpieces of Italian art... or with the living nature of Velázquez and Murillo...; here let the artist sketch the lowly mosque of the Moor, the lofty cathedral of the Christian...; art and nature here offer subjects, from the feudal castle, the vast Escorial, the rock-built alcazar of imperial Toledo (to) the sunny towers of stately Seville...; let the botanist cull from the wild hothouse of nature plants unknown, unnumbered, matchless in colour, and breathing the aroma of the sweet south; let all, learned or unlearned, listen to the song, the guitar, the castanet; ...(For here,) as Don Quixote said, there are opportunities for what are called adventures elbow-deep.
RICHARD FORD.   *Hand-book for Spain.*

Thus wrote one romantic English traveller in 1845. A century and a half later Spain remains that and much more. Spain's contribution to culture continues to be rich and diverse. Among the highlights are two major 19C novelists, Benito Pérez Galdos and Leopoldo Alas —Clarín—; two famous groups of writers, the *Generation of '98* and the *Generation of '27*, that included Nobel prize winners such as Vicente Aleixandre and Juan Ramón Jiménez, and other names no less universal —Valle-Inclán, Unamuno, Lorca, Machado, Alberti, Cela and Delibes; the philosophy of Ortega and the scientific research of Ramón y Cajal and Severo Ochoa, both of them Nobel Prize winners (Ochoa worked in the United States); the artistic genius of Goya and Picasso, of Dalí, Miró, Gris, and the more recent work of Tapiès, Saura, Ponç and Antonio López; the sculpture of Benlliure, Gargallo and Chillida; the architecture of Gaudí, the world-famous buildings constructed by J.L. Sert and Moneo, the internationally known work of Bofill, the urbanism of Soria, precursor of Le Corbusier; the audacious engineering and the innovative technology of Torroja, Monturiol and Cierva; the work of famous musicians such as Pau (Pablo) Casals, Andrés Segovia, Plácido Domingo and Montserrat Caballé and composers like Falla and Luis de Pablo; the movie-making of Buñuel, Berlanga and J.L Garci (who won an Oscar in Hollywood); the recent fashion of Morago and Domínguez; the industrial design of Ricard and others; the songs of Julio Iglesias —heard today on five continents— and the youngest and hardest rock in Europe; the post-modern *movida*...

Architecture and City Planning

The successive civilizations and empires that have swept across these lands have left an exceptional heritage. They mutually enriched each other by synthesis, first by destroying and then by building on what came before, by a dynamic interrelationship between the traditional and the new.

If there is a melting pot of different cultures to be found in Spain —a spacious showcase of all its architectural trends and styles— Toledo

31

must be the place. No other Spanish city can boast of having virtually the entire range of offerings within such limited confines: from a Roman circus or Visigothic church to an Arab mosque; from a synagogue or Mudejar mansion to a Gothic cathedral, as well as a medieval hospital, a Renaissance palace, a Baroque mansion, or a Neoclassical university.

Prehistoric Remains

Megalithic structures, more than 3,000 years old: the dolmens of Antequera (Málaga); the *talayots* and *navetas*, or tombs, of Menorca; the caves of Guadix (Granada). The Provincial Archaeological Museum in Toledo houses maps and photographs of excavations in the province, as well as many objects discovered at them. Unfortunately, the record of Phoenician, Greek and Iberian cultures is sparse. Our knowledge of the latter is based partially on its constructions, but mainly on its outstanding sculpture and decorative arts. Also to be seen in this museum are some excellent examples of Iberian reliefs and pottery from the province.

Roman (12C BC-4C AD) and Visigoth (5-7C AD) Heritage

Roman legacies include the great aqueducts of Segovia, Tarragona and Mérida (Badajoz), theatres in Sagunto and Mérida, bridges such as the one at Alcántara (Cáceres), innumerable city walls and triumphal arches, the Itálica mosaics (Seville) and those of Ampurias (Tarragona), many of them exhibited in the extraordinary Museo de Arte Romano (Roman Art Museum) in Mérida.

Evidence of the Roman presence in Toledo is considerable, since this

Roman Theatre, Mérida

city was a key to the defence of the central peninsula, located as it was half-way between Caesar-Augusta (Saragossa) and the capital of Lusitania (Mérida). We can admire a splendid circus ▶ *page* 13, the starting point for a vanished aqueduct, remains of hot baths and villas in la Vega, and most of all, a fine collection of mosaics, statues, and other objects on display in the Provincial Archaeological Museum.

The Visigothic heritage comes across more clearly in ideas than in monuments. Not even in Toledo, which was the capital of the Visigothic kingdom, have entire churches or other buildings of that period been preserved. Yet, there are numerous ruins: many of the Mozarabic or Mudejar churches (as well as Arabic mosques) have been built on earlier Visigothic structures, such as Santa Leocadia, the Christ of the Light mosque, or the Cathedral itself, which previously was the main mosque, and before that, the Visigothic basilica. The most-important Visigothic remains still *in situ* are the churches of Santa Eulalia, San Sebastián, Salvador, Santas Justa y Rufina, and others ▶ *page* 97. The Visigoth Museum of San Román has an extensive collection of carved stone (lintels, baptismal fonts), as well as gold and silverwork, including buckles, brooches, and bracelets, though most interesting are the votive crowns found at Guarrázar ▶ *page* 104.

Moorish Architecture, of the Caliph of Córdoba (8-11C)

The arch of the Mosque (*Mezquita*) is in the classical Moorish horseshoe shape, with alternating elements of stone (white) and brick (red). The Mosque's stylised and abundant decoration includes caligraphic inscriptions, geometric drawings and plant motifs. In Toledo

Mosque, Córdoba

there is a mosque from this period, the *Cristo de la Luz* or Christ of Light, a veritable miniature with its nine different domes ▶ *page* 114. Of a slightly later date, but in the same style, is the mosque of Tornerías ▶ *page* 116.

It is strange that there are no Arabic buildings in Toledo other than these two mosques, just a few stretches of wall and some gates, including the Alcántara and the Alfonso VI ▶ *page* 18. Here and there some genuine Arab artifacts do remain (quite easy to confuse with Mudejar ones whose only difference is that they were produced later), such as in the Archaeological Museum or the Moor's Workshop.

Pre-Romanesque Architecture (8-10C)

Using Visigothic architecture as a basis, Asturias developed a type of building that was a precursor of the Romanesque style: simple, austere churches, without ornaments and made of solid stone with semicircular arches. Santa María del Naranco and San Miguel de Lillo are two examples.

Moorish Architecture, of the Almojades of Seville (11-13C)

Almoravids and Almojades built austere mosques and minarets of brick, replaced the Moorish horseshoe arch with a more oriental version, a pointed arch, and introduced wooden coffered ceilings and those made of *azulejo* (a blue and white tile) as in the Giralda and the Torre del Oro of Seville. The only evidence of this style in Toledo is seen amongst the Mudejar master builders, since the city was retaken by the Christians in 1085.

Romanesque Architecture (11-13C)

The Christian kingdoms of the north consolidated their power as they faced their Arab neighbours to the south: Christian architecture was solid and made of stone, as opposed to Moorish delicacy of form and of materials such as brick, wood and plaster. The earliest Romanesque, in Catalonia, is represented by sober churches with severe lines, barrel and ribbed vaults, flat walls, and narrow and elongated windows as in the monasteries of Ripoll and San Pedro de Roda. The religious fervour of the Medieval world together with the flood of European pilgrims travelling the route to Santiago de Compostela were later responsible for a succession of churches that were marked by their softer lines, greater ornamentation, capitals, arches and religious lockets sculpted with absolute freedom by the artists. The cathedral of Santiago —which nestles within a Baroque façade that was added later— is the period's greatest work. In Toledo, so thoroughly impregnated with the Arabic element, the Romanesque style is the only one that did not take hold, the only one that left no notable monuments in the city —unless we associate it with the so-called brick-Romanesque style, or in other words, Mudejar.

Mozarabic and Mudejar Architecture (11-15C)

The Mozarabs —Christians who lived in Moslem territories— combined the architecture of the Visigoths with that of the Caliphate: an example is San Miguel de la Escalada (León). However, the best examples of this Christian art in Moslem territory are to be found in the city and province of Toledo. In the city, the Mozarabs continued to worship in seven churches, some of which have preserved at least a part of their Mozarabic design: Santa Eulalia, San Lucas, San Sebastián, and El Salvador.

The Mudejars —Arabs who lived and worked under the Christians— extended the use of brick and refined ceiling work in wood and *azulejos*, an art that has lasted to the present: there are numerous examples in Aragón and the Alcázar of Seville. In Toledo, the Mudejars were to create one of their fundamental provinces. Whilst in the rest of Spain (and Europe) construction was to follow Romanesque —and later, Gothic— lines, the Mudejar style would prevail in Toledo. Even at the dawn of the Renaissance and at a time when great palaces and mansions were being built, Toledo would maintain the tradition of the oriental palace, with its coffered wood ceilings looking down upon large, tile-decorated rooms with their plasterwork, surrounded by smaller chambers and gardens ▶ page 38.

The list of Mudejar structures in Toledo is virtually endless: synagogues, such as Santa María la Blanca and Tránsito; churches such as Santiago del Arrabal and dozens more; mansions, such as the Moor's Workshop mentioned earlier, the Palace of King Peter, Trastámara, and the Mesa House; convents, such as Santa Isabel and Santo Domingo el Antiguo; gates, doors and walls; tombs such as those in the Cathedral, and on and on.

Nasrid Architecture of Granada (14-15C)

The Alhambra in Granada is the great monument to Moorish architecture, the fruit of long and rich traditions of design, decoration and the arrangement of open spaces, delicate columns, sculpture and water.

Gothic Architecture (13-16C)

The Cistercian abbeys of Catalonia —Poblet, Santa Creus— helped spread Gothic influences in Spain. Buttresses, up to then simple pillars leaning against walls, now became distinct flying buttresses that supported lofty barrel vaults. Ogival arches and fine stone carvings with

Church of San Juan de los Reyes

filigree details became apparent; large columns rose stylistically toward the ceilings; enormous rose windows and others of multi-coloured glass lit church interiors and gave an incomprehensible lightness to the structures: the cathedrals at Burgos, Toledo and León are three Gothic jewels. Later Gothic cathedrals (Seville) strove for immensity and returned to a strict floor plan in the shape of a cross that contrasted with the richer ornamentation of the Arab influence. The castle of Coca and the palace of the Generalitat (Barcelona) are Gothic examples of civic architecture. Toledo has a splendid religious example from the late Gothic: San Juan de los Reyes. On a smaller scale is the transept of San Andrés, a number of vaults, and other elements (generally speaking, the persistence of the Mudejar style was so tenacious that it continued to assimilate and adapt successive styles almost up to Baroque times).

Architecture of the Renaissance (16C)

The Isabeline style of the Catholic Monarchs embraced the Gothic —adding sculptured details to Gothic façades— in a new style known as the *plateresque*. This form, which took its name from the work of silversmiths, featured profusely ornamented surfaces —as in the university of Salamanca. Another, more classical, tendency was seen in the works of Gil de Hontañón in the university of Alcalá (Madrid), of Siloe in the university of Granada and of Machuca in the palace of Charles V (Granada).

When considering the shift from Gothic to Renaissance, special mention must be made of Toledo's Hospital of Santa Cruz ▶ page 118. A number of *façades*, interiors, and exteriors reflect the purest and most florid of plateresque styles (San Clemente el Real; the chapels of the New Monarchs and the Treasury, in the Cathedral; the main façade of the Alcázar, and others). Going beyond classicism is the *herreriano* style, named after Juan de Herrera, Philip II's architect, whose *tour de force* was El Escorial. This building is a palace with the austerity of a monastery and the functionality of a royal residence. Its clean, rectangular form with a severe and rectilinear monumentality marks a fortress at the service of Counter-reformational orthodoxy, an emblem of imperial psychology. In Toledo, this stern approach is echoed in several buildings of note: the City Hall, the Hospital of Tavera, the Archbishops Palace, a part of the Alcázar (here Herrera himself worked) and a great many patios and churches.

Baroque Architecture (17-18C)

In the middle of the *Siglo de Oro*, Spain's Golden Age, there was an exuberant explosion of voluptuous lines and curves, of exaggerated reliefs and motifs drawn from nature. Architecture, sculpture and painting blended together to decorate façades, retables and retrochoirs —the area behind the choir. The style at its most sumptuous may be seen in the wreathed columns of the ornate *churrigueresco* fashion initiated by the Churriguera brothers, as in the Plaza Mayor of Salamanca and the *Transparente* of the cathedral in Toledo. But Baroque architecture was different in every Spanish province as seen in the façades of the cathedral of Santiago, and those of the palaces in Ecija (Seville), of the grand houses in Jerez (Cádiz), of the palace of San Telmo (Seville) and of the sanctuary of the Cartuja (Granada).

At this point in the Baroque, a highly-important —though not exclusive— phenomenon was to occur in Toledo: the old Mudejar churches were reconstructed, their interiors were plastered over and then refurbished with new altars with their image-laden contortions. Yet entirely-new churches and mansions (*palacios*) were also designed, the

most outstanding of them perhaps being the monumental Jesuit church.

Neoclassical Architecture (18-19C)

Coexisting with the Baroque, the classicism of Herrera was continued by Gómez de Mora (Plaza Mayor, Madrid) and Herrera the Younger (Basílica del Pilar, Zaragoza). As a reaction to the excesses of the Baroque period, there was also a return to the Greco-Roman classical world of columns, cupolas and similar features. Charles III promoted the new style and neoclassical landmarks in Madrid such as the Prado Museum, the Botanical Gardens, the Cibeles Fountain and the Alcalá Arch were built in his reign. Pertaining to this period and style in Toledo are such buildings as El Nuncio, the design of the main façade of the Cathedral, the Royal Arms Factory, and others.

Modernism and Contemporary Tendencies (19-20C)

Gaudí was a leading representative of the extravagant *Modernist* style, a singular combination of Catalonia Romanticism and the pre-Raphaelite world of John Ruskin: Gaudí used curved forms, plant motifs and earth colours, his lintels appeared to flow over doors and windows and his towers and balconies melted into heavy curves (houses of Batlló and Milá, Güell Park and neighbourhood, Church of the Holy Family, Barcelona).

Rationalism, in line with Le Corbusier, was propounded by GATEPAC, García Mercadal in Madrid and Sert (dean of Harvard University architecture faculty since 1958) in Barcelona. As dean at Harvard, Sert was succeeded by another Spaniard, Rafael Moneo, whose most recent work, integrating classicism and the most advanced present-day architecture, is the Roman Art Museum in Mérida. During the 1960s, realism was advocated by many (Bohigas, Mila, De la Hoz, Fernández Alba and others). The latest *avant garde* tendencies crystallize in Bofill in Les Halles (Paris) as well as various works in Barcelona.

In Toledo —perhaps fortunately, perhaps not— art seems to have come to a standstill in the 18C, or at least by the 19C (if we accept as art certain doubtful structures such as the neo-Gothic buildings in c/ de la Sillería and the Pl del Consistorio, or new ones such as the train station, the *Escuela de Artes y Oficios* or the numerous 19C examples along c/ Comercio or nearby). There is an on-going controversy as to whether good 20C architecture should be allowed to have its say, as has been the case with other styles of other periods, or if vacant spots should continue to be filled with reproductions —frequently quite risky— of a no less risky typical Toledan style.

Traditional popular architecture

It is not easy to comment on this type of architecture, owing to the great variety that has existed over the years. Nevertheless, what may be called a typical Toledan house is a dwelling characteristic of the Golden Age. These are houses adapted to the narrow streets and, consequently, they have no exterior display of their inner richness, at best presenting a simple stone façade. Inside, however, there is a difference. One may find a spacious, sumptuous and elegant patio surrounded by columns, in the case of an elegant mansion, or a simpler one, if it is a more modest house.

Traditional Mudejar elements are still used; above all, this means brickwork, quite a bit of tile, wooden coffered ceilings, and at times even plasterwork, a tradition that was kept alive until very recently.

Houses and patios of this type are extremely common in Toledo. The more noble examples are to be found in the upper part of the city (some marvellous ones in c/ Sillería, c/ Núñez de Arce, c/ Alfileritos, and c/ de la Plata), whilst the more popular ones are in the lower section. Amongst the first type, which often have been extensively restored and even embellished, are the El Greco House and the House of Chains ▶ *page* 116.

Cinema

The burst of Spanish cultural activity over the last ten years is perhaps most obvious, and has the most markedly individual features, in the cinema. The mass market Spanish film-makers serve an audience which is largely between 25 and 45 years old, and the viewers' attitudes seem to mirror closely those of the directors —a happy situation for those behind the camera. The film-makers and their audience are both attentive to the changes shaping and reshaping Spanish society.

Spanish **cinema** is basking in the warmth of heightened popularity inside the country and increased prestige in international film circles. Luis Buñuel —*The Exterminating Angel, Viridiana, Belle de Jour*— is a landmark in the history of Spanish cinema, and he strongly influenced film-makers like Carlos Saura —*La Caza, Blood Wedding, Carmen*—, scriptwriters like Rafael Azcona and producers like Elías Querejeta.

Juan Antonio Bardem —*Death of a Cyclist*—, Luis Berlanga —*La Escopeta Nacional*— and Victor Erice —*The Spirit of the Beehive*— have completed a body of work that lies somewhere between political commitment social satire and poetic metaphor. This line of work and Spanish film in general achieved a new dimension of international fame culminating with the Oscar awarded for *Volver a Empezar*, a film by

José Luis Garci, and the two Golden Bear awards, given at the Berlin Film Festival, awarded to Manuel Gutiérrez Aragón for *Habla Mudita* and *Camada Negra*.

A different view of life is reflected in the work of Pedro Almodovar —*What Have I Done to Deserve This?*, *Matador*— which constitutes at once an exercise in black storytelling and a sardonic comedy of manners determined to *épater les bourgeois*.

Design, Crafts, Fashion and Decorative Arts

Things, those domestic objects with which human beings live so closely, are a testimony to the habits and culture of a people. Spain's is a history of things. This part of Spain is full of such objects, reflections of the history and the way of life of the men and women who have lived here.

Of particular interest amongst the scant inheritance from the Visigothic period is its delicate **gold and silverwork**, discovered in Toledo, which we can admire in the Museum of Visigoth Culture. The so-called Guarrázar Treasure is a prime example of this production.

During the Moorish period, the kingdom of Al-Andalus ▶ page 42 contributed Eastern techniques and sensibilities derived from Arab **ceramics**. This began in the 10C in Elvira (Granada) and continued during the 11-12C in Málaga. The products included cups, plates, pitchers and flower vases decorated with metallic glazes and relief patterns. The *azulejo*, an ornamental tile that still today reflects a profoundly Spanish style, appeared with the Almojades in Triana, Seville, in the 12C ▶ page 43. Under the influence of the Italian Renaissance during the 16C, more floral patterns were added to the geometric motifs of the Almojades design.

Arab craftsmen built the principal ceramic workshops of the Middle Ages: the Levantine **Paterna** during the 13C first produced green and white ware and later blue and white products; **Manises** has been famous since the 14C for its ceramics decorated with reflecting metallic glazes and with botanical motifs and characters.

The 15C brought the rise of the ceramics centre of Talavera de la Reina (Toledo). This town's pottery replaced the Arabic themes with those from Christianity, bringing a Renaissance spirit to the work and blue and yellow colours to the kiln.

As the 18C unfolded, the porcelain plant of the Buen Retiro, founded by Charles III, became the leading manufacturer. In the 19C, the Sargadelos ceramics, lovely to look at and resistant to fire, and later, the glazed earthenware and *azulejos* of Pickman (La Cartuja of Seville), decorated with vivid colours and drawings, developed worldwide reputations that have lasted to the present day. At the start of the 20C the tile factories of Triana were working in the Arab-Andalusian tradition as the Catalans to the north began to experiment with tiling in a more Modernist style.

This long tradition continued into the contemporary period with the ceramic work of Picasso, Miró, the Serró brothers, Sert, Llorens Artigas and Cuixart. It continues still with the work of Durán-Lóriga and many other young artists and craftsmen.

Spain's **fine metal works** show their Moslem influence in the copper vases that are popular to this day in Andalusia. The genius of these works of art is found in the clocks, instruments and the Hispano-Arab **automats**, or robots, of the court of Alfonso the Wise. Their zenith came in the **monstrances** of the 16C, enormous and conical towers built replete with columns and statues embossed in silver in which the host is shown in processions. The Gothic monstrance in Toledo and the Renaissance monstrances of Santiago and of Seville are the most important in Spain. Iron, just as much as silver, was used with stylized delicacy in the **wrought ironwork** seen in the iron gates of the gardens and courtyards of Seville and the balconies of Ronda (Málaga), modest, secular inheritors of the **grillework** that encloses the chapels and choirs in Toledo's Cathedral and churches, as well as in those of Avila, Jaén and Granada. Fray Francisco de Salamanca, Juan Francés and Francisco Villalpando are some of the masters of this technique.

Furniture-making in Spain has produced some extremely popular styles: the Castilian, sturdy and austere, to be expected of an empire based on religious faith and asceticism; the embossed Moroccan leathermaking from Córdoba; and the *bargueños*, the portable, multi-drawered cabinets with collapsible door to be placed on a table and used as writing desks, that come complete with inlaid ivory and mother-of-pearl incrustations and mouldings, all rendered in the Mudejar style. The name for this last item comes from the town of Bargas, not far from Toledo. A modern-day equivalent can be found in the many young and prestigious Spanish industrial designers.

Spanish **fashion** is in fashion. It is competing vigorously with the most important fashion centres of Europe: Dusseldorf, Paris and Milan. Clothes have become something of a national obsession in Spain, from *prêt-à-porter* and sportwear to very expensive and fashionable garments, and including a wide range of accessories: shoe enthusiasts should consider the stylized design of Sara Navarro and Teresa Ramallal, and the product range of Selec Balear, Yanko, Lotusse and Camper; Joaquín Berao and Puig Doria are trend setters in jewelry and costume jewelry; Llongueras and Blanco are leaders in hair creations; Elena Benarroch's fur line is very successful; the Loewe leather goods need no introduction.

The Spanish fashion industry has built on the solid foundations of *haute couture* brand names such as Balenciaga and has found its place in the contemporary designer clothes market. Pedro Morago, Adolfo Domínguez —with shops in Paris, London and Japan—, Elena Benarroch, Sybilla, Jesús del Pozo, Agatha Ruiz de la Prada and Manuel Piña are fashion market makers that reflect the present creativity in Spain.

The background is a Spanish **textile** tradition that also goes back to prehistory. This tradition includes the line of work that evolved from the Royal Textile Workshop of Abd al-Rahman II in Córdoba (822 AD); Hispano-Arabic weavings with their geometric decorations, dating from the 10C to the 15C; the technique of the Spanish knot, to which 12C references have been found; the splendour of the richly coloured art produced in Granada for the Holy Week processions in the 14-15C; the workshops at Chinchilla and Cuenca; **tapestry** factories including the Santa Isabel factory in Madrid —dating to the 17C, and masterfully painted by Velázquez in *Las Hilanderas*— and the Royal Factory of Santa Bárbara, founded in Madrid by Philip V. In the 18C Goya painted patterns for tapestries here, and the factory continues as a private enterprise to the present day.

It is the same long history of things that underlies Spanish **design**. Since the middle of the last century Spanish designers have shown a flair. Some highlights: Monturiol, the submarine engineer; the *modernism* of Gaudí who, in addition to his architectural achievements, created furniture and wonderful iron fittings that continued a tradition

established by Herrera, Villanueva and Ventura Rodríguez centuries
before; painters like Casas and Rusiñol who designed posters for
beverages like *Anís del Mono* and *Codorniú*; graphic artists like Apel.les
Mestres, Gual and Opisso; the jewelry of Masriera and, from the 1920s
up to the Civil War, the furniture of the architects Luis Feduchi and
Sert; the perfume bottles of Myrurgia; the drawings for the magazine
Blanco y Negro by Rafael de Penagos; the aeronautics of Juan de la
Cierva with his autogiro; and the posters of Renau and Miró during the
Civil War. More recently, Spain has advanced rapidly toward a
post-industrial state, and so the **latest designs** are not only artistic but
also functional and industrial. The high-speed train known as the *Talgo*,
designed by Goicoechea; the chairs of Oscar Tusquets; the lamps and
other objects of André F. Ricard, Mila, Coderch, J. Carvajal, Pep Cortés
and C. Cirici; the bookcovers of Daniel Gil; and the general graphic
design of Alberto Corazón, Enric Satué and Cruz Novillo; the industrial
design of Moneo, Riart and Miralles —these are but some of the better
known names that enjoy an international reputation.

History

Spain is an old country, with more than 3,000 years of rich history to
boast of; at the same time it is young, modern, forward looking and
freedom loving. It is an open country, for milleniums a melting pot of
peoples —much like the United States— and the cradle of adventurers
and emigrants to the five continents of the world.

In the makings of this country, in the birth and death of towns and
cultures, reigns and empires, one name stands out as an everpresent
theme: Toledo. This is not surprising if we consider the Spanish writer
Galdós' words, who wrote that *Toledo is a history of all of Spain*.

. This rich history is reflected in its buildings, streets and interesting
sites about many of which the reader will find ample details in this
guide. See 'Places of Interest' ▶ *page 85* and 'City itineraries'
▶ *page 13*.

Chronological Table

	Origins
-10,000 BC	Upper Paleolithic period. The world-famous cave paintings of Altamira (Santander) and those at La Pileta (Ronda, Málaga).
9,000-4,000 BC	End of the Old Stone Age. Decadence of hunting communities.
4,000-3,000 BC	Neolithic Period. The beginnings of modern agriculture in the peninsula.
-1,100 BC	Bronze Age. The Phoenicians found Cádiz and other manufacturing posts along the coast.
900-400 BC	Celtic tribes from northern Europe make their way into the north of the Iberian Peninsula, mixing with the Iberians and giving rise to the Celtiberian race.
2C BC	Arrival of the Carthaginians from Africa.
230 BC	The Carthaginians make Cartagena the capital of their colonial empire.
	Roman Spain
218 BC	The colonization of Spain by the Roman Empire begins with the arrival of Publius Cornelius Scipios' legions at Ampurias.
214 BC	Hannibal attacks Saguntum, a Roman ally. The Second Punic War.

2C BC	Toledo, defended by a coalition of Celtiberians, Vectons and Vacceos, is attacked by the Romans. Marcus Fluvius Nobilior lays siege to the city and conquers it. Toledo becomes capital of Carpetania, within the province of Ulterior, then in Carthage. Originally a stipendiary town, it becomes a Roman colony with all privileges, including that of coining money.
1C AD	A prolonged period of Romanization. The economy flourishes as the subjugated inhabitants adopt Roman engineering, culture, law and architecture, even the Roman currency and language. Iberia —or Hispania— becomes an important part of the civilized world, making up three provinces of the Roman empire. It produces philosophers and writers and gives two great emperors to Rome: Trajan, who rules the empire from 98-117 AD, and Hadrian, 117-138 AD. Impressive monuments and public works are built.
2C	Extension of Christianity in Spain. San Eugenio preaches in Toledo and establishes the Episcopal See.
3C	Crisis of the Roman Empire. Toledo has its first martyrs, among them Santa Leocadia. Vandals and Burgundians invade the peninsula in mid-century.

Visigothic Spain

5C	The Visigoths, allies of the Romans, come to defend Spain against invasions of Vandals, Germanic peoples and others.
5-7C	The Visigoths establish a relatively weak kingdom, with its capital in Toledo. The history of Spain cannot be separated from that of Toledo. The Visigothic monarchy pours all its energy into developing this centre and under it Toledo achieved the full bloom of its political, cultural and religious splendour. The task of compiling the *Fuero-Juzgo* (the code of laws that enriches Roman law) is undertaken. A number of illustrious prelates and writers begins to flourish, including San Isidoro. Grandiose basilicas and monasteries. The *Concilios de Toledo* (Councils of Toledo) meet at the basilica of Santa Leocadia ▶ *page* 110. During the Third Council, Recaredo renounces Arianism and changes the destiny of his nation. The last period of the Visigothic monarchy enjoys a co-existence of Hispano-Romans, Goths and Jews. The discontent of the latter, along with that of certain nobles, facilitates the Moorish invasion.

Moorish Spain

711	The Moors cross the Straits of Gibraltar from North Africa and defeat the Visigoths at Guadalete. In seven years, the invaders conquer the peninsula, and they are not fully driven out again for eight centuries. Tarik appears before the walls of Toledo and easily captures the city. Christians are victorious at the battle of Covadonga. The kingdom of Asturias is founded.
8-11C	Al-Andalus, heart of the Moorish kingdom and the southern region later to be known as Andalusia, flourishes economically and culturally. Toledo, having remained faithful to Damascus, surrenders to Abd al-Rahman, who forms the independent Omeya emirate.

	Continuous rebellions, during one of which four hundred noblemen are beheaded, known as the *Toledan night*.
10C	Modern Spanish develops as a language.
11C	The Caliph disintegrates into competing kingdoms, known as *taifas*. In Toledo, Ismail-Dilmun establishes the foundations of a dynasty destined to flourish, especially under his son Al-Mamún, in whose court Alfonso VI will take refuge whilst fleeing from his brother Sancho.
1085-1086	Christians conquer Toledo. Almoravids invade Al-Andalus. The royal court will remain in Toledo until moved by Philip II.
1095-1099	The famous Castilian warrior El Cid —*lord*, in Arabic— conquers Valencia.
12C	Tension rises between the Christians of the north and the Moors of the south. The Christian Reconquest, or *Reconquista*, is a time of war, but also of peace and mutual influence. Moorish authority is re-established in Al-Andalus by the Almojades. Alfonso II unites the kingdoms of Aragón and Catalonia.
13C	By the middle of the 13C, half the peninsula is under Christian domination. The kingdoms of Castile, León, Asturias and Aragón are growing ever more powerful. 1212: The Christians win an important victory at Navas de Tolosa. 1236 and 1248: Ferdinand III conquers Córdoba and Seville. The Reconquest peters out for the moment. The Moorish kingdom of Granada will enjoy another two centuries of prosperity. Alfonso X presides over a cultural flowering in Christian Spain. Toledo is at the peak of its cultural splendour.
14C	A dark period marked by the apocalyptic preachings of Vicente Ferrer and popular attacks on Jews and converted Moors. The Crown of Aragón continues its expansion into the Mediterranean: in addition to Sicily, conquered in the 13C, Aragón acquires part of Greece and consolidates its Mediterranean empire.
15C	The Catalan claims to the throne of Aragón end with the Compromise of Caspe and the accession of Ferdinand I. Castile emerges as a European power largely due to its cereals and its wool trade with the Low Countries.

The Catholic Monarchs and the Modern State

1469	Marriage of Ferdinand V of Aragón —the model for Machiavelli's *The Prince*— and Isabel I of Castile, uniting the two greatest Christian powers in Spain.
1492	The Conquest of Granada completes the Christian unification of Spain. Columbus discovers America. The Inquisiton is begun and the expulsion of 400,000 Jews ordered.

The Golden Age of the 16C

| 1500-1512 | Reconquest of the kingdom of Naples by Gonzalo Férnandez de Córdoba who was popularly known as *El Gran Capitán*. Spanish dominion in North Africa: Melilla, Orán, Tripoli, Mazalquivir. 1503: The Casa de Contratación in Seville is awarded the monopoly of Spanish trade with the Americas. 1512: Navarre is annexed. The *Leyes de Burgos* legislation protects Indians in America. |

1513	Núñez de Balboa discovers the Pacific. Two hundred years of glory begin for a completely unified Spain, the first modern and centralized European state and now the pre-eminent power in the world.
1516-1556	Reign of Charles V. 1519: Cortés conquers Mexico. 1519-1522: Juan Sebastián Elcano becomes the first man to circumnavigate the world. 1532: Pizarro conquers Peru. 1536: Almagro explores in Chile. The Spanish empire stretches from Sicily and Naples in the Mediterranean to the Americas, and includes most of present-day Germany, France, Austria and the Low Countries. Spanish galleons arrive regularly at Seville laden with gold and silver treasures from the New World. Several wars in Europe. Toledo takes a strong position against the Emperor. The Spanish church declares itself an enemy of Martin Luther's Protestant Reformation in Germany.
1556-1598	Philip II rules over the largest empire under one man yet known to history. His domain extends to four continents. 1561: Philip II moves the royal court from Toledo to Madrid. 1571: A Spanish fleet defeats the Turks at the Battle of Lepanto. 1580: Unification with Portugal. The Escorial is constructed. It is the start of the *Siglo de Oro*, or Golden Age, in art and literature. But Spain is already squandering her treasures, brought from the New World, in European wars. The Inquisition and the struggles against Protestantism known as the *Counter-reformation* sap the creative energies of the country. 1588: The powerful Spanish Armada is sunk in a disastrous confrontation with Elizabethan England. English naval power is on the upswing. Spain's decline from imperial power has begun.

Decadence

1598-1621	Reign of Philip III, a period that sees the end of Spanish world hegemony and the beginning of its post-imperial decadence. 1605: Cervantes' *Don Quixote* is published and in many ways perfectly reflects the transition from imperial splendour to decline. Spain is momentarily at peace with her neighbours, but an economic crisis has begun.
1609-1648	Expulsion of the converted Moors, or *Moriscos*. 1609: The Low Countries declare their independence. 1618-1648: Thirty Years' War. Independence of Portugal. Loss of territories and European hegemony.
1700-1715	War of the Spanish Succession between Philip of Anjou (supported by Madrid, Alicante and France) and the Archduke Charles of Austria (supported by Valencia, Aragón and England). 1707: Philip V accedes to the throne, the first of the Bourbon dynasty in Spain. Loss of the Low Countries, Menorca, Gibraltar, Italy, Sicily and Sardinia.
1716	Philip V issues a Decree called the *Nueva Planta* which abolishes local privileges and dissolves the once-great kingdoms of Valencia and Catalonia. Castilian laws emanating from Madrid replace traditonal local statutes. It is a decisive moment in the creation of a central

	Spanish state. The Bourbon regime is stabilizing rapidly.
1759-1788	Reign of Charles III. Aided by competent ministers (Floridablanca, Aranda), Charles III enacts sweeping reforms under the banner of the *Enlightenment*. The monarchy's prestige grows as the economy and culture flourish. In Toledo, Cardinal Lorenzana promotes the enlightened spirit. Construction of the university and the insane asylum ▶ *page* 125. Last remaining swordsmiths are gathered to work in the Royal Arms Factory.
1789-1805	The French Revolution. 1793: Charles IV goes to war with revolutionary France after Louis XVI is guillotined. 1804: Napoleon becomes Emperor. 1805: Spain collaborates with Napoleon in the war against England. Disaster strikes at *Trafalgar* with Admiral Nelson's victory, and Spain sees the last vestiges of its maritime power wiped away.

Romantic Spain: The Turbulent 19C

1808	Popular pressure against the powerful minister Godoy and Charles IV forces the abdication of the monarch and his heir, the future Ferdinand VII. Napoleon foists his brother, Joseph Bonaparte, as king on Spain. On May 2, citizens rise up against the French, in Madrid, and the *War of Independence*, or Peninsular War, against the French occupiers is underway.
1812-1813	The parliament at Cádiz proclaims a liberal Constitution. 1813: Several American colonies declare their independence from Spain: Colombia, Chile, Paraguay, Uruguay and Buenos Aires (La Plata).
1814-1877	With the aid of the British and after a pitched guerrilla war, the Spanish forces finally succeed in expelling Napoleon following the Battle of Vittoria. Ferdinand VII regains the throne and promptly repeals the Constitution of 1812, an act that serves to mark the start of the Romantic period, a turbulent era of struggle between the *absolutism* of the ancien régime and the new *liberalism*. 1820: Riego, a charismatic, young officer stages a liberal insurrection. 1821: Mexico wins its independence. 1821-1824: Venezuela and Peru gain their independence. Spain is administratively organized into its present day provinces. 1830: Isabel II is crowned. 1833-1839: The First Carlist War breaks out between supporters of Don Carlos and Isabel II. French, English and German romantic writers discover Spain. 1835: Suppression and expropriation of the religious orders. 1840: A keynote military rebellion, led by Espartero, decided at Valencia. 1843: Revolution and rising of Narváez. 1847-1849: Second Carlist War. 1850: End of the economic crisis and beginning of prosperity under Queen Isabel II. 1868: Prim's insurrection forces the abdication of Isabel II. 1869: Progressive Constitution adopted. 1870: Amadeus of Savoy is elected constitutional king. 1872-1876: Third Carlist War. 1873: Amadeus of Savoy abdicates. The First Republic is proclaimed. 1874: Pavía dissolves the *Cortes*, Spain's parliament. Peasant and worker rebellions break out and the middle classes pin their hopes on a restoration of the

	monarchy. A military coup brings back Alfonso XII, Isabel II's son, as king.
1898	Spain loses colonies of Cuba, Puerto Rico and the Philippines in the Spanish-American War. An intellectual resurgence gets underway ▶ page 51.

The 20C

1902-1921	The reign of Alfonso XIII, crowned at the age of 16, coincides with the growth of socialist and republican movements, as well as of trade union organizations like the socialist UGT and the anarchist CNT. Pablo Iglesias, the founder of the Spanish socialist party, is elected to the *Cortes*. 1914-1918: Spain remains neutral throughout World War I and prospers economically as a result. 1917-1921: A nationwide general strike begins in Valencia; other peasant strikes and conflicts between tenant farmers and their landlords follow. There is discontent in the armed forces, tension in Catalonia and military defeats in North Africa.
1923-1930	The Catalan Captain General, Primo de Rivera, installs a *military dictatorship* as a critical report on the army is about to be released by parliament. Spain enjoys seven years of prosperity due to peace in Morocco and a huge public works plan. But the international financial crisis of 1929 and the restiveness of the opposition brings Primo de Rivera's resignation. There is a renewed surge of cultural activities ▶ page 51.
1931-1935	Republican supporters of democracy in Spain win municipal elections. Alfonso XIII abdicates when army officers tell him the army will not support him. On April 14, 1931, the Second Republic is declared; but revolutionary pressure exercised by peasants and workers shakes the new regime. An abortive right-wing coup is followed by a centre-right victory in the 1934 elections and worker insurrections.
1936-1939	The Spanish left, running as a united front, wins the elections; Manuel Azaña is prime minister. On July 18, 1936, Generals Franco and Mola lead a right-wing military insurrection, sparking the three-year *Spanish Civil War*. The conflict involves untold cruelty and destroys the nation. On April 1, 1939, the war ends and many choose to go into exile.
1939-1975	Franco's dictatorship. The early years are especially hard. Spain remains neutral in World War II, but sends a volunteer division to help Hitler on the Russian front. 1953-1955: American bases are set up in the country and Spain is admitted to the United Nations. 1959: An economic stabilization plan opens Spain's closed economy to the world. The tourist boom begins, accompanied by a decade of growth and modernization.
1975	Franco dies. Juan Carlos I is proclaimed king. The transition to democracy begins in 1977 under centre-right prime minister Adolfo Suárez. Political parties are legalized.

Modern Spain: The Democracy

1978-1981	The modern Spanish Constitution is adopted, a liberal document that allows for political power at the regional

level. 1980: Statutes of autonomy for Catalonia and the Basque country are approved. On February 23, 1981, a military coup attempt is aborted with the king's intervention.

1982   Socialist Prime Minister Felipe González takes office.

1986   Spain enters the Common Market on January 1. The Socialists win again in general elections. Forty-six million tourists a year are visiting Spain.

1992   Seville hosts the Universal Exhibition and Barcelona hosts the Summer Olympics. It is the 500th anniversary of Columbus' discovery of America.

Literature

Like a multi-coloured fabric, Spain's pre-Golden Age literature is woven with threads of at least three colours: Latin, Moslem and Hebrew. The towering Christian intellectuals, King Alfonso the Wise and the anonymous author of the *Cantar del Mio Cid* take their place in the rich pantheon of Spanish literature alongside captivating Arab poets, sagacious Moslem scholars and the great Jewish writer and royal physician, Moses Ben Maimon, better known to the world as Maimónides. Spain's 20C intellectual giants include Federico García Lorca, José Ortega y Gasset, Miguel de Unamuno and Antonio Machado.

A quick checklist of contemporary Spanish Letters includes mature writers such as Cela, Delibes, Mercé Rodoreda, Juan Goytisolo, Martín Gaite and Marsé; poets, among them, Gimferrer, José María Alvarez, Martínez Sarrión and Leopoldo María Panero; and novelists such as Guelbenzu, Eduardo Mendoza and Jesús Ferrero. Political themes are no longer predominant as was the case during the Franco years. In fact, the political decentralization that has accompanied the restoration of democracy in Spain has meant a new literary vigour in the country's several, distinct regions.

But to start at the beginning.... Seneca the Elder, known as the Rhetorician, and his son, Seneca the Stoic, were revered for the purity and grace of their Latin. Christian literature, coming with the Roman adoption of Christianity, was less creative in Spain for the Moorish invasion in 711 severed it from western European currents.

The Moorish kingdoms on the Iberian peninsula were however rich in literature and scholarship. They produced a wealth of classical Arab poetry, Moslem religious tracts, and Maimónides (1135-1204) who has been compared to St. Thomas Aquinas for his attempts to reconcile reason and faith.

The Galician and Catalan languages had rich literary traditions, but Castilian began to achieve predominance with epic poetry in the 12C. The *Cantar del Mío Cid* (*Song of My Cid*), which recounts the heroic deeds of Rodrigo Díaz de Vivar, the great hero of the Christian Reconquest, is the greatest work to survive. Alfonso X, the Wise, made Castilian the language of the court and of scholarship, replacing Latin. He also created the *Escuela de Traductores*, which undertook translations from Arabic into Latin and from Latin into Spanish. This was a priceless endeavour that made the treasures of classical antiquity available to the western world. In the 14C his nephew, the Infante Juan Manuel, followed with a wonderful collection of tales in prose, while the archpriest of Hita wrote a brilliant satirical work, *El libro del buen amor*, in verse.

47

Early Spanish theatre reached a peak with the *Tragicomedia de Calixto y Melibea*, better known as *La Celestina* after its bawdy central character, by Fernando de Rojas (about 1500).

At the dawn of Imperial Spain's Golden Age, a period which was to be exceptional in the history of world literature, we find Bartolomé de las Casas, a Sevillian member of the Dominican order and later a bishop, who was a tireless literary champion of the Indians in the New World and a critic of the often brutal excesses of the conquistadors.

The Golden Age, which extended through the 16C and part of the 17C, coincided with the reigns of Charles V, Philip II and Philip III and was both Spain's and the world's literary heyday, especially in the theatre. After a period of Italian influence, the Salamanca school —Friar Luis de León (1527-1591)— and the Seville school —Fernando de Herrera (1534-1597)— began to make their mark in theatre. Renaissance drama, however, reached its peak with Lope de Vega (1562-1635), one of the world's most prolific playwrights and a poet who excelled in beautiful imagery and musical cadence. Tirso de Molina (1584-1648), who created Don Juan, the mythical lover, and Pedro Calderón de la Barca (1600-1681) were well-known colleagues and fellow dramatists. Francisco de Quevedo y Villegas (1580-1645) was famed for his all-round literary personality and for his virulent temper. At one time or another, all of these figures either lived in or passed through Toledo, leaving their mark on its life and culture. The *églogas* (pastorale poems) of Garcilaso were centred around the Tagus; Tirso de Molina was to write *Los cigarrales de Toledo*, set in the country homes of this name; other poets of the Golden Age, such as Góngora, found inspiration here, as did the mystic San Juan de la Cruz, who wrote his *Cántico espiritual* whilst imprisoned in a cell above the Alcántara Bridge.

Certainly the most famous author of the *Siglo de Oro* was Cervantes (born in Fuentetodos, 1547-1616). He wrote what has been hailed as the world's first modern novel, *Don Quixote*. Shakespeare, among others, has acknowledged his debt to the Spaniard. Cervantes would doubtless have won great fame as the author of the *Novelas Ejemplares* —one of them, *The Illustrious Charwoman*, was written whilst staying in the Posada del Sevillano, an inn close to Zocodover— in the absence of *Don Quixote*. But that world-famous book, anticipating literary forms by several centuries, has extended Cervantes' influence to the present day, as may be seen in the work of modern writers as diverse as Fyodor Dostoyevsky, James Joyce and Vladimir Nabokov.

The Golden Age set the ground for literary creations to be produced within the next centuries. It is not farfetched to state that all Spanish classics are in one way or another connected to Toledo, which was the capital and site of the royal court at the time.

Decadence and a loss of energy in the arts marked the end of the Golden Age, at the close of the 17C, and was accompanied by the nation's preoccupation with a growing French influence that made itself felt in the Spanish arts. This uninspired era lasted from the death of Calderón until the advent of Romanticism at the start of the 19C. The memorable lyric poetry of Gustavo Adolfo Bécquer (1836-1870) was post-Romantic rather than Romantic. He had a deep-seated love of Toledo, as seen in the fact that no less than six of his *Leyendas* (Legends) take place in its streets and secret places. Several outstanding writers rose to prominence in the first half of the 19C: Pedro de Alarcón (1833-1891), author of *The Three-Cornered Hat*, the revolutionary José de Espronceda (1810-1842), who fought at the barricades in Paris in 1830, and the deeply sceptical journalist Mariano José de Larra (1809-1837) were foremost among them. Zorrilla and the Duke of Rivas utilised popular legends and beliefs from Toledo, turning them into melodramatic romantic dramas of the cape and sword variety.

Toward the end of the 19C, the realistic novel, acidly critical and chronological in its storytelling, made its appearance in Spain. The leading novelist of the time, Benito Pérez Galdós (1843-1920) —who wrote his novel *Angel Guerra* in Toledo's Hotel Lino— rejected the social injustice he saw around him, as did his contemporaries, Countess Emilia Pardo-Bazán (1852-1921) and Leopoldo Alas, better known as Clarín. The Valencian, Vicente Blasco Ibáñez, also belonged to this group, and his writing has been compared to the great naturalism of the French novelist Emile Zola. One of his works of lesser literary interest, though with incalculable value as a reference in getting to know and understand Toledo, is *The Cathedral.*

The *Generation of '98* was the name given to a group of writers who faced the moral crisis and general break-down of the Spanish spirit in the aftermath of Spain's humiliating defeat in the Spanish-American war of 1898 and loss of her last colonies (Cuba, the Philippines and Puerto Rico). The group was deeply critical of Spanish decadence and sought the regeneration of the nation. The most famous member of this group, which was very diverse but was bound together by a common commitment to a reborn Spain, was the Basque Miguel de Unamuno (1864-1936). His copious output included philosophical works, essays, novels and volumes of poetry. An austere intellectual, Unamuno had a profound impact on his own and on succeeding generations of Spaniards.

Other members of the Generation of '98 included Ramón María del Valle Inclán (1869-1936), who became famous for his four *Sonatas;* José Martínez Ruiz, a critic and essayist who wrote under the pen name Azorín, the novelist Pío Baroja and the historian Menéndez Pidal.

The philosopher José Ortega y Gasset (1883-1955) was a key intellectual whose *Invertebrate Spain* and *The Revolt of the Masses* achieved lasting notoriety in Europe. Salvador de Madariaga (1886-1978) was another influential critic and essayist. Like many intellectuals, Madariaga went into exile during the Spanish Civil War.

Modern Spanish poetry achieved outstanding lyricism with the work of Antonio Machado (1875-1939), who though a Sevillian born was principally inspired by the landscapes of Castile, and Juan Ramón Jiménez (1881-1958), who is best known for his book of lyric prose *Platero and I,* and who won the Nobel Prize for Literature in 1956.

Federico García Lorca (1898-1936) deserves special mention. A member of the so-called *Poetic Generation of '27,* Lorca developed his own form of lyric poetry, based on the folk poetry of his native Andalusia and the songs of the Gypsy flamenco singers so prominent in his home town of Granada. His chief poetical works are *Gypsy Ballads* and *The Poet in New York; Blood Wedding* and *The House of Bernarda Alba* are his major plays. His genius was cut short soon after the outbreak of the Spanish Civil War when he was executed in Granada by rebel Francoists.

The Civil War had a terrible impact on the country's artistic renaissance. Another singular casualty was the young poet Miguel Hernández, who wrote haunting verses of great beauty. He was strongly identified with the Republic and did not survive the prison term that the Franco regime imposed on him. Manuel Andújar, Ramón J. Sender,

Rosa Chacel, Corpus Barga, Rafael Cansinos-Asséns and León Felipe were other writers of the period. Among the essayists of the time, Américo Castro and Claudio Sánchez Albornoz stand out. The latter's reflections on the unrepeatable historical experiment of medieval Toledo is required reading if one wishes to penetrate to the core of the city's secrets. Sender, who wrote *La Tesis de Nancy*, the tale of an American student in Spain, spent most of his life in exile in the United States. Ramón Pérez de Ayala, Republican ambassador in London until 1936, and Ramón Gómez de la Serna went to Argentina.

A generation of new novelists appeared after the war. Many of them, and the many poets belonging to the *Poetic Generation of '36* who began writing then as well, attacked the Franco regime or dwelled on themes of human rights and oppression. Among the more important novelists were Miguel Delibes, Camilo José Cela (who founded the school of *Tremendismo*), José María Gironella and Ana María Matute.

Martín Santos and Benet are authors who belong to the generation of the fifties. Juan Goytisolo is one of those who followed the forms of the *nouveau roman* and North American writing. Cela, Sánchez Ferlosio and Torrente Ballester are leading novelists of the time. Ballester and Alvaro Cunqueiro were leaders of a trend of magic realism.

In theatre, the century has produced the high comedy of Benavente, winner of the 1922 Nobel Prize. A famous follower is Buero Vallejo. The plays of Antonio Gala, like Buero Vallejo's, have combined literary merits with wide ranging popularity.

One should finally mention the influence of essayists such as Aranguren, Laín Entralgo and María Zambrano, who have become national institutions. And a younger group of philosophers, spearheaded by Fernando Savater and Javier Sádaba, has started to emerge over the last few years.

Music

Spain is a musical country, a place where the people both sing and dance, and where an array of styles and types of music coexist. It is a music above all marked by a joy of living.

Lyrical Music

Montserrat Caballé, Plácido Domingo, Alfredo Kraus and José Carreras are opera names that have gained international fame and prestige. Nevertheless, the great popular tradition of Spanish music owes more to the **zarzuela**, a form of operetta that is genuinely Spanish and has its roots in the 18C, than it does to opera properly speaking. The Spanish court in those days was much taken with hunting. After the hunts, it was normal to sleep out in a tent surrounded by brambles, somewhere in the countryside around Madrid. There, the evening's entertainment was enlivened with theatrical presentations accompanied by music and song. This was the birth of the *zarzuela*. The form was much influenced by Italian opera until the 19C. Subsequently the **género chico** —the genre comprising zarzuelas and one-act comedies— lost ground to the great German operas. Spanish work returned to prominence, however, with Tomas Bretón's *La Verbena de la Paloma* in 1894, which was purely Spanish and Goyaesque in its aesthetics. Torroba, Sorozabal and Guerrero are also in the front line of major *zarzuela* librettists.

Classical Music

Music schools and composers flourished during the Visigoth heyday. Several antiphonaries contain **hymns** by San Ildefonso, San Eugenio and San Julián, 7C bishops of Toledo. There are 38 Mozarabic liturgical manuscripts, many of them with music corresponding to the centuries of Moorish domination. There are references to Abdul Husaih, a very famous Arab musician in Toledo. The leading centre of music at the time was Andalusia.

The *Cantigas*, written by Alfonso the Wise —musician, poet, mathematician, astrologer—, is an impressive legacy of the Middle Ages. During the *Siglo de Oro*, when the guitar became a highly popular instrument displacing, in the process, the more courtly vihuela (an ancient type of guitar), Tomás Luis de Victoria won international renown for his beautiful religious choral music.

This developed into a glorious age for Spanish music, for it included such brilliant composers as the great Cristóbal de Morales, choirmaster in the city of Toledo, as well as Francisco Guerrero, Flecha and Juan Vázquez. Music for keyboard instruments reached its peak during the first half of the 15C, thanks to the outstanding genius of Antonio de Cabezón. The second half was to produce a composer on an equal level with Morales, Tomás Luis de Vitoria, the most widely-respected of Spanish musicians in his day.

As Romanticism laid down roots in Spain so did that most Spanish of all instruments, the **guitar**, spread its influence. Modern guitar-playing is largely based on the work of Tárrega (1852-1909). The aficionado will recognize one of his most beautiful pieces, *Recuerdos de la Alhambra*, played with Indochinese instruments for the soundtrack of the movie *The Killing Fields*.

Romanticism developed into what critics term musical nationalism through the work of Turina (1882-1949), Albéniz (1860-1909) and Manuel de Falla (1876-1946). Turina's compositions reveal solid technique and descriptive rigour. In *La Procesión del Rocío, Mujeres Españolas* and *Danzas Gitanas*, perceptible French influences are balanced by Turina's pronounced Spanishness.

In Albéniz's suite *Iberia*, a collection of 12 highly original piano pieces, Spain's musical nationalism reached its zenith. The influence of Albéniz, together with that of French impressionism, can be traced in the refined and colourful work of the Andalusian Falla, who wrote *El Amor Brujo*, the *Concerto for Harpsichord and Five Instruments* and *Atlantida*, which was completed by his disciple, Ernesto Halffter.

The musical renewal of the 20C was a mixture of classicism and newer movements. The synthesis was apparent in the work of Frederic Mompou, a fine pianist and composer of works for a range of instruments —*Suburbios* (piano), *Becquerianas* (voice) and *Suite Compostelana* (guitar). Joaquín Rodrigo, author of the world-famous *Aranjuez Concerto*, and Xavier Montsalvage are the best-known postwar composers.

Contemporary Spanish composers no longer cultivate nationalism. Instead, they have immersed themselves in the more advanced Western tendencies, such as **electroacoustics**. Luis de Pablo, C. Halffter, Bernaola, Guinjoan and Tomás Marco are among the prominent musicians of this genre.

Spain's major musical interpreters are the guitarists Andrés Segovia (1894-) and Narciso Yepes (1927-). The most revered was the late Pau (Pablo) Casals who in the course of a career that spanned the first half of this century became an international musical institution. Casals composed the *Hymn to the United Nations*. Teresa Berganza and Victoria de los Angeles are firmly established sopranos, and López-Cobos is unquestionably Spain's leading conductor.

Flamenco

Flamenco is a music whose origins are little known and much debated —in Roman times writers such as Martial discussed the dancers of Cádiz. Truly flamenco **folk songs** and **dances** have blended with Andalusian popular singing to the point where it is difficult to mark out the precise boundaries of this exotic and picturesque art form.

Whatever flamenco's origins, there is no doubt that the genre constitutes *an entire people's form of expression*. Flamenco is the art form of Spain's gypsies who remain a tightly-knit race. Over the centuries gypsies have been socially proscribed and more or less clandestine in their rituals according to the degree of prevailing social benevolence.

When Charles III decided in 1783 partially to ease the persecution of the gypsies, who lived alongside pockets of Jewish and Moorish communities, a large group settled in the area between Seville and Cádiz. The first reports of flamenco came from this area in the late 18C.

The ancient roots of flamenco are an amalgam that mixes Byzantine liturgical chants with Arab and Hebrew melodies. As it came increasingly into the public domain in the middle of the 19C when it began to feature in *cafés cantantes* —music halls— flamenco began to embrace all types of Andalusian and Mediterranean influences. Modern-day professional flamenco performances take place in the *tablao*, a form of cabaret devoted exclusively to the genre.

Basic, primitive flamenco singing is called *cante jondo*. The purest and profoundest jondo is the *tonás* (variants include the *martinete, debla* and *carcelera*) and the *siguiriyas* and *soleares*.

Direct descendants of these folk forms include the *caña, polo, corrida, saeta, liviana, serrana, tango, tiento, cantiña* and *bulería*. Less orthodox are the *alegrías, romeras, mirabrás, caracoles* and the many different renderings of the *fandango*, such as the *malagueña, verdiales, jabera, rondeña, tarantas, cartageneras, granaínas* and so on. Other folk themes based on flamenco, but of a different and folkloric line, are the *peteneras, farrucas*, the extremely popular *sevillanas* and the *nanas, trilleras, guajira, rumba* and *garrotín*. Flamenco's hall of fame includes the names of Antonio Chacón, Antonio Mairena and the Niña de los Peines. Young, contemporary flamenco singers take the extremely successful Chiquetete as their model.

As to **flamenco dancing**, the primitive *zapateado*, literally stamping, which is austere and dramatic, has given way to a commercial style known as *festero*. Distinct dances have been developed according to the different variants of singing like *alegrías, tangos, bulerías* and *sevillanas* where the singers and dancers perform together. Antonio Gades is probably the best known today among the top class dancers.

Spanish Popular Music, Rock and Pop

Apart from traditional and classical music, Spain produces some of the most wild, aggressive and sometimes even sinister rock and roll in Europe. In melodic composition, there is a series of soloists and well-known groups whose recordings include the more or less involved ballads of Joan Manuel Serrat, Mocedades, Ana Belén and Victor Manuel; the songs of urban sentiment and indifference of Luis Eduardo Aute and Joaquín Sabina; the beautiful tones of María del Mar Bonet which recall musical forms with deep roots in Majorcan and Mediterranean tradition; and the voice that is known on five continents, that of Julio Iglesias. All styles coexist in what is broadly known as the *Spanish song*. This is not to be confused with flamenco, although there are sometimes common melodic and rhythmic roots.

Painting and Sculpture

Spanish painting spans the period from the prehistoric Altamira cave-paintings to the 20C genius of Pablo Picasso. In between lie the haunting faces of the men before the firing squad in Goya's *Executions of the Second of May*, the mystical, elongated paintings of El Greco, the magnificent canvasses of Velázquez, a painter of truly global importance, and Murillo's religious works. From the old master to Picasso's contemporaries Salvador Dalí and Joan Miró, Spanish painters have always been in the front rank. There is something about the country that has always prompted its people to paint and to paint well.

Prehistoric Legacies

The bisons, deer and wild boars of the Altamira caves (Santander) are Spain's most impressive cave paintings. Executed with great naturalness and force in several colours —they've been called the *Sistine Chapel* of rupestrian, or cave, art— they are believed to be over 10,000 years old. The paintings and engravings of the cave of Parpalló, also Paleolithic, and the Mesolithic art of Bicorp (Valencia) are extraordinary for the surprising sense of movement in their monochromatic hunting scenes.

Roman, Visigoth and Romanesque Influences

The Romans and Visigoths left behind a rich harvest of statues, busts and sarcophagi, or stone coffins. Only when Moslem culture began to mix with pure Catalan Romanesque after the Moorish invasion in 711 —as at Taüll (Lérida) and in the paintings of Vic and Ripoll— did strong new influences on Spanish art come into play.

Gothic Art, 13-15C

Gothic painting in Spain is derived from three major sources: France during the 13C; Siena and Florence, especially in Catalonia (Ferrer Bassa) during the 14C; and the Flemish school, which made itself felt in the courts of Aragón and Castile during the 15C. Nonetheless, the naturalism and picturesque details of these works was entirely Spanish. In sculpture, this was the time of the great retables, altarpieces with numerous fantastically carved scenes which reached heights of 15m. Sculpture grew more delicate and its relief more accentuated than in the Romanesque era. This was a period of fine work in the porticos and sepulchres of many cathedrals. A good example is the *Doncel* in Sigüenza or the many sepulchres to be seen in the Cathedral of Toledo, as well as in many of its convents and churches (Santo Domingo el Antiguo ▶ page 111).

The 15C brought increased vitality to Toledo —all the main painters and sculptors of the time in Spain passed through its gates, leaving their imprint on the city.

Renaissance Art, 16C

Several Spanish sculptors studied in Italy, including Diego de Siloé —cathedrals of Burgos and Granada— or Alonso Berruguete whose countless works in Toledo include the *sepulchre of Cardinal Tavera* and a number of *retables* (such as the Visitation and Santa Ursula). His crowning glory, however, is his own *Sistine Chapel*, the Cathedral choir, with its magnificent reliefs and sculptures imbued with tortuous movements that transcend the limits of classicism and herald the Baroque, a style whose maturity and strength can be compared with the best of Michelangelo. Juan de Juni —works in Valladolid— used a more theatrical style. It was during this period that the famous Milanese bronzesmiths Leone and Pompeo Leoni were at work on the monastery of El Escorial for Philip II.

The Renaissance deeply influenced the study of perspective, the glorification of the human body and clarity in composition. Fernando de Llanos and Fernando Yáñez de la Almedina worked in the style of da Vinci, while Vicente Masip followed Raphael. Masip's son, Juan de Juanes, known as *the Spanish Raphael*, was one of the great painters of the period. In Castile, the great master of the late 15C was Pedro Berruguete.

However, transcending all other styles or schools of the age is the work of Doménico Teotocopuli, El Greco. After settling down in Toledo in 1577, he was to produce his most outstanding work here: the *Disrobing of Christ, The Burial of the Count of Orgaz, San Mauricio,* and others. The lengthened figures, the vibrant and original colouring (blues, yellows, ochres, penetrating greens, mauves and violets), and the geometry of his compositions impart a personality to his work that is unique in the world of painting. Many of his works are still to be found in Toledo ▶ *page* 113 and 117.

Baroque Art, 17-18C

The Baroque era, a period that unfolded during the *Siglo de Oro*, or Golden Age, produced an extraordinary wealth of painters in what was truly one of the high moments in European art. The sculptors of the time were also a rich and diverse group: Gregorio Fernández, of Valladolid; Martínez Montañés and his excellent disciple Juan de Mesa of Seville ; Alonso Cano of Granada, known for the unusual grace and delicacy of his *Inmaculadas*, while his disciple Pedro de Mena was known for his realism. In Murcia, Salzillo was already extremely famous.

The exceptional Spanish paintings of the 17C began with the penetration of an Italian influence which is obvious in the assimilation of Caravaggio by the Valencian Francisco Ribalta. José de Ribera stands at the head of the schools of painters established in both Valencia and Naples. He was the painter of martyrs, saints and ascetics.

The Sevillian school also produced several masters of painting. Zurbarán painted cycles of religious exaltation (monastery of Guadalupe) and still life. Murillo was another Sevillian, a painter of intense realism who was famous for his *Inmaculadas*. Valdés Leal painted macabre profiles —*Las Postrimerías de la Vida*— and sacred compositions such as *San Jerónimo*, which hangs in the museum of Seville. The painter, sculptor and architect Alonso Cano worked in Granada. In Castile, Claudio Coello, Carreño and Carducho painted, like Murillo, in a carefully realistic style.

The greatest painter of the epoch was doubtless the Sevillian Diego Velázquez, court painter to Philip IV. His work included portraits —*Felipe IV, Conde Duque de Olivares, Inocencio X*—, history —*Rendición de Breda*—, mythology —*Fragua de Vulcano, Los Borrachos, Las Hilanderas*—, and landscapes —*Villa Medicis. Las Meninas* is painted with a stroke so skilful that it puts Velázquez alongside the twin giants of Spanish painting, Goya and Picasso.

Neoclassical Art, 18C

The Bourbon monarchs in this period founded the San Fernando Academy and brought foreign painters, such as Mengs and Tiepolo, to teach there. But head and shoulders above these and others was a man of complete genius who was to lead the way into the Romanticism of the 19C. Francisco de Goya, a multi-faceted, dynamic and sarcastic man, broke with all the academic principles of painting and anticipated in his work artistic trends characteristic of 20C contemporary art. In 1799 he became principal painter to Charles IV, whom he depicted in a painting (hanging today in the Prado Museum) that is now

world-famous for its subtle mockery of the monarch and his family. His two paintings of the rebellion in Madrid against the French —*The Charge of the Mamelukes and the Imperial Guard in the Puerta del Sol* and the chilling *Executions of the Second of May*— haunt the imagination. No less interesting are the series of engravings *The Disasters of War*, the suggestive and erotic pair of paintings *The Maja, Clothed* and *The Maja, Unclothed*, the terrifying lines of *The Insane Asylum* and the bright tenderness of *Children Playing*, one of a series of joyful and colourful paintings of daily life. His so called black period works must be seen as well. A *Goyesca* school followed him: Eugenio Lucas was the best of his disciples.

Art in the 19C

The shadow of the great 18C painters reached into the 19C, affecting profoundly the character and attitudes of its painters and sculptors. Some developed a dark cast to their work, such as Rosales; others were airy, cosmopolitan and almost frivolous, like Fortuny; there were portraitists like Vicente López, and those who revelled in depicting the bourgeoisie, like the Madrazo family.

In Catalonia, the work of such artists as Casas, Nonell, Rusiñol and Mir was clearly related to the currents of European art, while the Valencian Sorolla brought a Mediterranean brightness to French impressionism in his paintings of beaches bathed in light. In sculpture, naturalism and an impressionist cast also feature in the work of the Valencian Mariano Benlliure, especially in his bullfight scenes. Aureliano de Berveta and others gained renown for their landscapes, now exhibited in the Museum of Modern Art in Toledo.

Art in the 20C

Pablo Picasso, the great painter and sculptor of Málaga, was, in a sense, the embodiment of the history of Spanish painting and sculpture. His work —from his early blue, pink and Cubist periods to the depiction of the horror of the Civil War bombing of *Guernica* (The Prado Museum, Madrid)— ranged over a wide variety of themes but was executed with the same consummate skill everywhere. He was one of the most productive painters in history. Along with Picasso, the 20C also produced the great Spanish Surrealist painters Salvador Dalí and Joan Miró, who was also a skilled muralist (Cincinatti, Harvard and Barcelona), ceramicist and sculptor. Their works made Surrealism known around the world. Juan Gris was an analytical Cubist, while Solana and Zuloaga painted everyday life with careful realism. J.M. Sert was known for his large frescoes.

After the Civil War, several schools of painting and sculpture developed. They included the Catalan group Dau al Set formed by Ponç, Tapiès, Cuixart and Tharrats; the landscapes of Benjamín Palencia; the Neo-figurative group which brought together Clavé, Pancho Cossío and Vázquez Díaz; the informal work of Guinovart and Feito; and the Madrid group called El Paso which included Millares, Saura, Canogar and Viola. The period's better-known sculptors included Llimona, Clara, Chillida, Hugué, Pablo Serrano, Mallol, Gargallo, Picasso, Ferrant and Subirachs. The Toledan Alberto Sánchez, a banned artist during the Franco years, is worthy of special mention. He was exiled to Moscow after the Civil War but most of his work is found in the Museum of Modern Art in Toledo.

Antonio López, a hyperrealist, has become internationally famous. Now, new values are making their appearance in present-day Spain. Artists such as Barceló and Pérez Villalta already have, despite their youth, solid reputations.

ENTERTAINMENT

More than anything else, the tourist activity taking place in Toledo is cultural. This makes it difficult to cook up entertainment for visitors especially since most of them only visit the city for a few hours. With the exception of an occasional play or concert, such as during the October Music Festival (*Semana de Música*), most entertainment is intended for the residents of the city; because the city is not all that big, offerings are therefore limited.

Bars, Cafeterias, Terraces, Pubs and Similar Establishments

The visitor looking for the best chance to fraternise with the natives should simply choose one of the countless open-air terrace cafés and participate in the timeless Spanish custom of the *copeo* (which may be interpreted as sitting with a drink as long as you wish, or engaging in more extensive pub crawling) and *tapeo* (which involves eating one or more of the bar snacks or *tapas* available in all of these establishments ▶ page 144). Let us not forget that a great deal of Moorish blood still pumps through Toledan veins; we should therefore not be surprised at the love of open spaces and fresh air. Whether it is a case of sitting and having a leisurely chat on a terrace, or simply strolling through the streets with a group of friends, either activity is dear to the oriental hearts of the Toledans.

As has virtually always been true, the lifeline of the city begins at Zocodover. Here is where Toledans spend their spare time, standing around, sitting in the terrace cafés, coming and going. Looking for someone? Just come here and wait —they'll quite likely pass through the plaza.

The arcades and narrow streets that surround Zocodover have regained their liveliness, and here the most fashionable bars and *mesones* can be found. The focal point is in Callejón Barrio Rey (*tapas*) and Callejón and c/ Sillería, the favourites of the *movida*, Spain's new youth and *avant garde* generation, whose home territory ranges between here and c/ Alfileritos.

The farther one goes from this area, with the endless strolls along Comercio street, the harder it will become to find entertainment in the way of bars and open-air cafés.

Bullfighting

Spring and summer is the bullfighting season, especially during the Corpus Christi Fair, when Spain's leading *matadores* are billed. The architecture of the bullring or *Plaza de Toros* is very much in keeping with the city's style (and French novelist André Malraux used it as a backdrop for his novel *L'Espoir*). Dates and times of bullfights will be billed all over town.

Cinemas

Despite the tradition dating back to the Golden Age, when there were quite a few *corrales*, or playhouses, there is currently only one theatre in town, the **Rojas** ▶ page 129. It serves as a cinema for the most part, although national travelling theatrical companies are beginning to appear here more frequently. Other cinemas are the following: *Candilejas*, c/ Alberche, 38.

59

Impero, Cuesta del Aguila, 7 (near Zocodover).
María Cristina, c/ Marqués de Mendigorra, s/n (next to the Hospital de
  Tavera). In summer: Paseo del Miradero, s/n.

Discotheques

Youth is the keynote at the city's **discotheques** (*discotecas*). There are
only three in Toledo proper:
Edén, c/ Cascajoso, s/n.
Jam's, Galería del Miradero, local 222 (the most popular and the most
  crowded).
Sithon's, c/ Lucio, 4.
  A new disco —also a target of the *movida* and other beautiful
people— has opened up on the outskirts of Toledo:
Gris, Ctra Toledo-Avila, km2.5.

Games of Chance

Gambling is immensely popular all over Spain, and Toledo is no
exception. Apart from lottery and horse racing punts, bingo is widely
played. One may try one's luck at various **Bingo parlours**, with the one
most centrally located being in the *Antiguo Casino* in the Pl de la
Magdalena; for the modern touch, try the one on the Madrid highway,
in front of the Hospital of Tavera.

EXCURSIONS

As a general rule, visitors to Toledo rarely have enough time to see
even the standard sights of the city. It is not possible to take in
everything in a single day, and to do so in three or four days is also a
rather tall order ▶ page 85.
  Nevertheless, for those who have the time, or who are able to make
several trips to the city, we will set up some itineraries for excursions to
nearby towns and other places in the province. These will serve to add
a touch of landscaping to what some may consider to be the
overwhelming sensation of lofty splendour seen in Toledo's art and
history.
  Some of these excursions will be brief —perhaps a few hours or an
afternoon (Guadamur, Santa María de Melque)— whilst others may
require a more relaxed day or two spent in enjoying the countryside
(the Toledo highlands, the route of Cervantes, Talavera and the
ceramics route).

Guadamur Castle: the Castles Route

This is a short excursion, since Guadamur lies only 15km from Toledo.
Leave the city via the new bypass (*Circunvalación*) bridge which lies
alongside San Martín and goes toward Navahermosa. With the city still
in sight, take the branch road to the right, which leads to the *Ermita de
la Bastida* (**La Bastida Hermitage**). Here we have a nostalgic and
picturesque spot surrounding the hermitage, a place where people
come from Toledo to picnic during the summer.
  Returning to the Navahermosa highway, we soon arrive at the town
of Guadamur. The town proper is rather undistinguished; its focal point
is the castle. Although it is posted as private property belonging to the

current Marquis and Marquess of Campoo, tourist visits are permitted.

The architecture of the fortress, with its romantic aura of neglect, is particularly interesting. The castle was built between 1444 and 1464 by Pedro López de Ayala, and it was last restored in the 19C. In spite of this, it has been well preserved. The castle keep is particularly impressive, with its toothless battlements, its parapets and parapet walk, its moat, drawbridge and escarpments.

The interior is less interesting, though there are a number of artistic highlights and objects of considerable value to be found throughout. Here lived Juana la Loca (Juana the Mad, daughter of Ferdinand and Isabel) and her husband Felipe el Hermoso (Philip the Handsome), as well as Cardinal Cisneros and Charles V among others, and here the Princess of Eboli was imprisoned upon the death of Escobedo.

Not far from this castle is another, Guarrázar, close to the ruins of the ancient monastery of Agaliense. Here one can see the fountain where marvellous Visigothic crowns were found (now in Madrid's National Archaeological Museum, with a copy in the San Román Museum in Toledo). A Museum of Toledo Highlands Traditions and Popular Arts has recently been opened in the ancient hermitage of San Antón. On display is hunting equipment —snares, traps, and so on— and tools used in everyday life, such as for farming, masonrywork, and weaving, as well as pottery, furniture, common utensils, and other artifacts from the area.

Any visitor especially interested in castles should take notice that a number of splendid examples are to be found in the province of Toledo. By following this castles route, you will find some very pleasant surprises. The following are the most picturesque: in the northern part of the province, the photogenic Escalona Castle, next to the Alberche

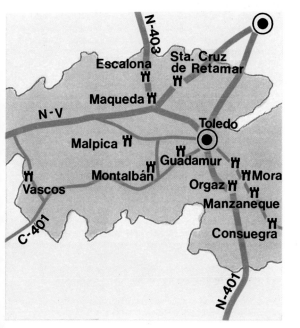

River; the castles of **Santa Cruz of Retamar** and **Máqueda**. In the west-central part (in addition to Toledo's **San Servando** castle which overlooks the Alcántara Bridge), we have the Malpica castle, with its magnificent location overlooking the broad, green Tagus; the castle of **Guadamur**; the castle of **Oropesa**, now converted into a *parador*; the Spanish-Moorish fortress of Vascos (forming an entire town) at Navalmoralejo, and the castle of **Montalbán**, only a few kilometres from La Puebla de Montalbán. Recommended visits in the south include the castle of **Almonacid de Toledo**, the **Mora** castle, as well as those of **Manzaneque, Orgaz, Consuegra**, and **Guadalerzas**. This is only a brief list, for there are more than fifty other castles scattered throughout the province, though perhaps less well-preserved than the ones we have just mentioned.

Illescas and La Sagra

The star of the La Sagra region is Illescas. Its easily-recognisable features are the *Mudejar tower* and the *Giralda de la Sagra* (weathertower). In addition to its tower, the church has interesting Mudejar graves. There are five famous El Greco paintings on display in the *Hospital de la Caridad*, (Hospital of Charity) which was built by Cisneros. Illescas appears continually in the classical literature of Spain, since it was the half-way point between the old and the new court, that is between Toledo and Madrid. The nobles of Illescas can be seen at least twice yearly: in the Corpus Christi processions in Toledo, as well as in the annual chapter, or investiture of new knights in their own hometown.

Many towns in this area bear the surname *de la Sagra*, for example, Alameda de la Sagra, Cabañas de la Sagra and Numancia de la Sagra, among others. Roast suckling pig and the custards of Numancia are local gourmet treats. The asparagus grown in **Añover de Tajo** easily competes with that of Aranjuez, while one of its natives, Casimiro Gómez Ortega, was the founder of the Botanical Gardens in Madrid. **Sorox** is also well-known for its farm products, especially its onions, and for barbel and other fish caught in the nearby Tagus. A rather well-preserved castle with moat is to be found at **Seseña**.

At the other end of the highway to Madrid there are a number of wine-producing towns whose fermentations need not take a back seat to the wines of Yepes or Noblejas, especially the wine bottled at **Fuensalida**.

Along with its fine wine, **Casarrubios del Monte** has a quite interesting brick castle (though it is not in the best of conditions). Here, too, is a pillory, whilst its huge, decaying church houses several valuable paintings. There used to be a hospital, but only the façade remains. An ailing Philip III was once a patient here —a cure was attempted by fetching the body of Madrid's patron saint, San Isidro.

Another castle that adds a note of delight to the landscape is at **Bargas**. This town is essentially a neighbourhood of Toledo, and is one of the places that has best preserved the Moorish character of its inhabitants. Here the name *bargueño* originated, one of the most typical pieces of furniture in all of Spain.

La Puebla de Montalbán and Santa María de Melque

This is a longer excursion, and will require at least one full day, especially if you wish to visit the ruins at Melque.

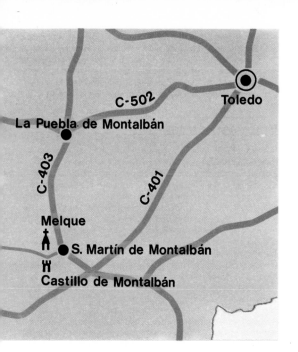

There is a distinctive charm to the mid-town streets, especially the main square, in **La Puebla de Montalbán**. Dominating the square is a huge house, the Palace of Cardinal Pacheco y Guevara, a native of the town. Another famous local figure, honoured on a plaque here, was Francisco de Rojas, the author of *La Celestina*, a novel that perhaps ranks alongside *Don Quijote* at the apex of Spanish classical literature. Christopher Columbus' son, Diego, died here, and Santa Teresa de Avila came to visit her aunt and uncle here before she became a nun. In the Soledad Hermitage, we can see two paintings by Ribera.

Twelve kilometres outside La Puebla de Montalbán, on the road to San Martín de Montalbán, there is a side road to the right and another to the left. By taking the first, we arrive at the **castle of Montalbán**, whilst the second brings us to the **Melque ruins**.

Situated 2km from the road and perched on craggy rocks above the Torcón River, the **castle** presents a stunning site, from the standpoint of both its architecture and its picturesque location. Built by the Templars in the 12C, it later belonged to Alvaro de Luna, and then to the Duke and Duchess of Frías. It was a decisive bastion in defence of the Tagus, and its architecture reflects elements from the 12C to the 14C.

Taking the left-hand road, we come after 4km to the so-called Melque Hermitage, a true gem of Mozarabic art that stands here lonely and deserted. The church most likely dates from the mid-9C. Of greatest interest is its rustic construction and odd-shaped blocks (ashlars) that give the impression of a small fortress —a use to which it was probably put in order to take advantage of its strategic location between two rivers.

The floor plan is that of a Greek cross, with barrel vaults, apses and a central tower dome that rises above the transept. The irregularly-shaped Moorish arches are formed by courses of granite ashlars, emplaced without mortar, and with a cyclopean appearance. Having practically fallen into ruins, the church has recently been restored. Moreover, archaelogical diggings have uncovered what may well be a pre-Roman town.

The Ceramics and Embroidery Route

Talavera (65,000 inhabitants) is the largest city in the province of Toledo, and is more populous than the capital. However, this factor —along with its industries and role as a modern financial centre— is of less interest to the tourist, who will be attracted to the ceramics produced here. Along with Puente del Arzobispo, Talavera is Spain's best-known and most abundant source of pottery. Out of these two places pour the items that flood shops far and wide throughout Toledo and all of Spain, hence the need for a sharp critical eye when it comes to making a judgement based on tradition and good taste. Here we have indeed a true route of ceramics.

From Toledo, we can reach Talavera via La Puebla de Montalbán ▶ page 63 or by the town of Torrijos.

Torrijos is one of the oldest towns in the province. The **Collegiate church**, with its plateresque façade, reflects a grandeur easily on a par with the church in Yepes. Nuns from the old Monastery of San Francisco, which now lies in ruins, have taken a mummified body to their new convent, and therein lies a curious story. The body is that of Teresa Enríquez, *La Loca del Sacramento* (The Madwoman of the Sacrament), as she was called by Pope Julius II. She assisted him in preparing the Mass, squeezing grapes for the wine and kneading dough for the communion wafers. Whenever a priest spat after saying Mass, she would light a candle by the spittle and kneel alongside it until it dried, then proceed to clean the spot.

After Toledo (58,000 inhabitants), Talavera de la Reina is the second city of importance in the province. Once it was strongly-walled, though of its original seven gates, only two now remain. It is located in an extremely rich valley, therefore it is known for such crops as cotton and tobacco, in addition to its pottery and other industries. On the first and fifteenth of each month its famous livestock fairs are held.

A good portion of time should be reserved for a visit to the Gothic Collegiate Church, a testimony to the importance of Talavera in the church hierarchy during the 12C. Students of Spanish literature will recall the amusing episode of the Talaveran priests in the *Libro de Buen Amor* (*Book of Good Love*) by the Archpriest of Hita, as well as *Corbacho* by the Archpriest of Talavera. Another famous name from the olden town is the Jesuit historian, Padre Mariana. Besides the collegiate, also deserving of a visit is the church of San Prudencio (the ancient Hieronymite monastery of Santa Catalina, later an Augustine school), which dates from the late-16 and early-17C. There are also parish churches: Santiago (Mudejar, 14C) and the Romanesque Salvador church (12C). King Philip II called the hermitage of *La Virgen del Prado* (Virgin of the Fields), on the outskirts of the city, the *queen of the hermitages*. Decorated with the famous ceramics of the olden town, it is the site of the unique *Fiesta de las Mondas* on Shrove Tuesdays. In this Christian version of a pagan rite, natives from five villages in the area —Mejorada, Pepino, Segurilla, Gamonal and

Cervera— carry baskets of bread as an offering to the Virgin of the Fields ▶ *page* 74.

Visitors should not miss the **Ruiz de Luna Ceramics Museum**. (See the 'Shopping' section for comments on Talaveran pottery ▶ *page* 138).

Also open to visitors is the birthplace of Francisco de Aguirre, a lieutenant who served under Pedro de Valdivia, the conqueror of Chile. Aguirre founded the Chilean city of La Serena, where he died in 1580.

There are a number of highland towns to the east of Talavera, as well as a beautiful landscape that rises up toward the Gredos Mountains. On Easter Sunday the town square in **Montesclaros** is decorated with eggshell wreaths. **Mejorada** has preserved its castle, and also a native dance, the *rondeña*. **Alendral de la Cañada** was the birthplace of Santa Ana de San Bartolomé, secretary to Santa Teresa, an illiterate who miraculously learned to write. **Navamorcuende** is a livestock-raising town, with clean and crisp air that makes it a popular spot for summer holidays. At an elevation of 1315m, there is **El Piélago**, with its sparkling waters and impressive scenery. In the nearby mountains is the cave of the martyr-saints —Vicente, and his sisters Sabina and Cristeta. On the road to La Hinojosa are the ruins of the castle of San Vicente. **Real de San Vicente** is another possible summer vacation choice. It, too, has a *soldadesca* and groups of dancers. **Bayuela** is known for its castle, flogging post, Roman ruins, *verraco ibérico*, and a ceramic altarpiece by Ruiz de Luna that stands over eight metres high..

Leaving Talavera and heading toward Extremadura (in a southwesterly direction), we arrive at Oropesa, capital of the so-called *campana de Oropesa* (Oropesa Bell), the group of

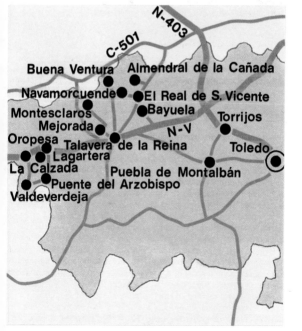

surrounding towns whose common denominator is their embroidery and openwork. Oropesa (3,500 inhabitants) has a walled-in area and masterful ruins that bear unmistakable witness to its past glories and the days when it lent its support to Ferdinand and Isabel in the conquest of the Moors at Granada —the parish church, the ruins of the Jesuit church, the palace of the Counts, and others. Yet, looming high above all of this is the **castle**, which has been converted into one of the most stunning *paradors* on the Iberian peninsula.

Only a few minutes away is Lagartera, a town world-famous for its embroidery, an art that has been honoured in the *zarzuelas* (light opera) of Guerrero and the paintings of Sorolla. Any wedding that involves natives of this town will bring a host of photographers to take pictures of the women dressed in their typical skirts, aprons, short capes, slit-sleeved shirts, multicoloured stockings, exquisite silk cloth, and coral necklaces with pearls and charms. The women use no pattern when embroidering, only their imagination.

Another town in the Oropesa bell is **La Calzada**, with its fine church and Moorish patio in the Augustine convent. In **Torralba**, there are two *verracos ibéricos*.

We now proceed to Puente del Arzobispo, a name derived as follows: The *puente*, or bridge, was ordered to be built by a 14C *arzobispo* (archbishop) so that pilgrims on their way to Guadalupe could cross the Tagus —the good archbishop also imposed a toll, payable at the gates to the bridge. In addition to this architectural work, the city is also renowned for its ceramics, a sister-product to that in Talavera, which is characterized by its greenish tones. A curiosity of the place is that it has no municipal boundary —there are the bridge, the houses, and nothing more, though we can mention its pillory, its small hospital (remindful of the days when pilgrims passed through), and a garlic fair, where thousands of baskets of the bulbs are sold.

Near Puente is Valdeverdeja, one of the most beautiful towns in Toledo. The place has something of an Extremaduran touch, with attractive houses typical of the highlands. There is also a strange type of pottery that has been miraculously preserved ▶ page 140. Lastly, it is the birthplace of the Jesuit Juan de Loyola, one of the first in Spain to spread the cult of the Sacred Heart.

The Route of Cervantes

This itinerary will take us through that part of La Mancha lying in the province of Toledo.

We depart from Toledo by the Orgaz highway, shortly turning off onto the road toward **Mora**. Before arriving at this town, we pass through **Almonacid**, with castle ruins here, then **Mascaraque**, also with similar ruins. In addition, Mora has a stately fortress atop a hill surrounded by olive trees, which is the site of its famous Olive Festival.

At last we arrive at Consuegra, the ancient Roman town of *Consaburum*, with a current population of some 10,000 and where ruins of a Roman aqueduct and circus can be seen. Nonetheless, the town's greatest attraction is its typical Manchegan look: outlined against the sky on Calderico Hill is its *castle* and the remains of a Moorish fortress; following the line of the ridge, we see a row of windmills. From the top of the hill, we can see the rooftops of the town, while spreading out beyond us is the infinite horizon of La Mancha.

The castle was built by order of the Knights Hospitalers of St. John in the 12C, after Consuegra had been named the Priory See of the order.

Olive groves abound, along with saffron and excellent wines. Here the famous Saffron-Flower Festival is held each year ▶ *page* 74. There is also an age-old tradition of potterymaking ▶ *page* 39, as well as a confectionery industry that is a legacy from Moorish times.

A few kilometres north of Consuegra is **Turleque**, which boasts a magnificent church designed by Juan de Villanueva.

Our arrival in **Madridejos** puts us in the midst of a town with a true Manchegan air. Passing through it is the national highway to Andalusia, and from this point we begin to steep ourselves in the La Mancha rendered famous by Cervantes: *Alcázar of San Juan*, **Campo de Criptana**, and El Toboso with its *Dulcinea House*, which, being the residence of Don Quijote's legendary lady love, has been made into a museum.

If we don't wish to stray too far from Toledo, another choice is to take national highway NIV toward Madrid, which leads us to the town of Tembleque. Here we will be treated to the sight of one of Spain's most original and beautiful plazas, one surrounded by colonnades and triple-tiered rows of balconies and exquisitely-wrought wooden galeries. In olden times, this was a site for jousting and bullfights, and we are readily reminded of the gay, festive atmosphere of the Spanish Golden Age.

By returning to Mora from Tembleque, we close the circle on our excursion; if we wish to extend it, we can proceed north to **La Guardia**, where we can visit the strange *Sanctuary of the Holy Infant*, a true monument to Christianity. Our next stop will be **Ocaña**, also with a masterful plaza, which has been called Spain's third most splendid square, after those in Salamanca and Madrid (though the visit to Tembleque may have produced doubts).

67

Windmills, Consuegra

The tomb of the poet Ercilla is located at the Carmelite convent in Ocaña, whilst an interesting choir can be seen at the Dominican convent. There is also a marvellous *fountain*, with ten spouts feeding into a basin that measures over 50m across, reputed to be the work of the architect Herrera. The town has its own potterymaking tradition ▶ *page* 140, as well as one of the best-known May festivals in La Mancha ▶ *page* 72. This festival is celebrated in honour of the Holy Virgin of Remedies. It is characterized by processions and singing.

Lying close to Ocaña is **Yepes**. This is the site of another work by Herrera, the *church*, which most closely resembles a cathedral (an anecdote tells of a bishop who asked: *Here's the church —but where are the people?*, in reference to the small population having been swallowed up by its immensity.) Inaugurated by Cardinal Silíceo, it houses six paintings by Luis Tristán, a student of El Greco, as well as the remains of the Manchegan Saint Dubio, in whose honour Calderón de la Barca wrote *The Prodigious Magician* in 1637.

Nothing more logical than to wrap up our Route of Cervantes tour by going to **Esquivias**. It has been said that had this town not existed, *Don Quixote* would never have been written. Here is the church wherein is kept the marriage licence issued to Miguel de Cervantes and Catalina Palacios. You can visit the *Cervantes House*, now turned into museum, as well as the large house that was the home of Alonso de Quijano, the uncle of Catalina who served as the model for Don Quixote himself.

La Mancha, land of windmills and beautiful *pueblos*, is, as Don Quixote said, a place where *there are opportunities for what are called adventures elbow-deep*.

The Toledo Highlands

The entire southern part of the province is sheltered by low-lying mountains with their nostalgic aura so often expressed in songs whose themes run from love affairs to the exploits of highwaymen. Since they are not high mountains, only the deepest-entrenched towns manage to take on a mountainous appearance; the rest have the characteristic landscape of mid-elevations, namely, a mixture of farm plots and heather, holm-oaks, cork trees and rockrose. It is an area propitious for hunting, with big game found at the uppermost heights. There are also fascinating prehistoric archaeological ruins throughout.

A great many towns near **Puente del Arzobispo** bear the name *Jara*, which pertains to the entire region through which flow the Pusa, Huso and Frío rivers, along with other lesser tributaries of the Tagus. In **Navalmoralejo** are the singular ruins of the city of **Vascos**, the only Spanish-Moorish city known of prior to the discovery of Medina Azahara. A visit to this phantom city is a separate excursion and one of the outstanding highlights of the entire central region. A whole day should be set aside for it. In **Robledo de Mazo**, from whose enchanting valley the Guadalupe mountain range can be seen, villagers retain the tradition of *sombreros de paja* (straw hats) and their adornments, including tiny mirrors. Here are also found the *pingas*, or weavings made by hand on rustic looms, which incorporate an array of old rags that are compressed and woven into colourful striped pieces.

Sevilleja is the site of an old spa, *Los Baños del Boticario* (The Chemist's Baths), where people in the 19C came to seek a cure for their rheumatism. Wild boar and wolves still occasionally roam the mountain passes of **Collado Raso**, **Risco Gordo** and **Torrozos**. The church at **Mohedas de la Jara** is given special mention in the

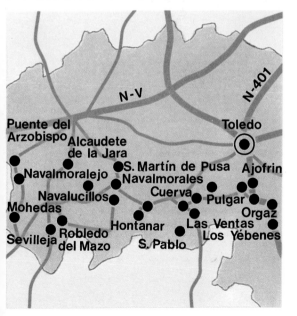

Catálogo Monumental, or Monumental Catalogue of the Count of Cedillo. In **Torrecilla**, there are two figures of the *verraco ibérico*, a series of statues in Spain dating from pre-Roman times (although *verraco* means boar, there is a certain controversy as to whether they represent this animal or a hornless bull).

San Martín de Pusa boasts a splendid church and the castle of Santisteban. **Villarejo** has a Roman bridge and the castle where Don Juan de Austria was trained in the use of arms. He was eventually to send the town a statue of the Virgin of Victory, a gift from Pope Pious V.

Alcaudete de la Jara has a magnificent church, along with a military fortress, *la Torre del Cura*. For the Candlemas festival on February 2, the *soldadesca* (soldiers' group) performs an amazing dance in the streets ▶ page 74. In **Bilvís de la Jara**, with its fertile lands, the *quintos* (conscripts) perform the Ring-around-Judas and roosters are chased through the town. In addition, marriageable young ladies wash their faces with water that has been placed outdoors on the night of San Juan, precisely at the time when a beautiful Moorish girl is said to have come out of her enchanted rock alongside the Tarunjoso River to bathe in its waters.

Navalmorales was originally two sister towns that were united in 1833. It has a large, somewhat ramshackle 17C church with a nice Baroque altarpiece. On the edge of **Calancho** there are interesting *prehistoric remains*; it is recommended that someone in the village be asked to serve as a guide in order to make finding them easier. There are several attractions: The *pocilgas* (pigsties), a group of strange, cyclopean caves that farmers have utilized for their animals; the dolmen of *La Cobertera*; the village and cemetery of **El Palomar**; as well as megaliths. Our prehistoric route continues in **Navalucillos**, where there is a large number of *lucillos* or small tombs carved in the slate. In a place called **Malmoneda (Hontanar)**, there are ruins of buildings and a cave cemetery with almost one hundred graves. Also to be seen here are the 16C church and the Malmoneda castle, built in the 12C atop Roman hot baths.

There are two religious processions that depart from Hontanar and **Navahermosa** simultaneously, then meet at Cruz del Milagro. This is the *Romería de la Milagra* (The Miraculous Pilgrimage), a local celebration that echoes the original one carried out by these two towns in 1780 as they prayed for rain —when the two processions met, the skies opened up in copious rainfall ▶ page 75. In celebration of *La Milagra*, a week-long cultural festival is held in Navahermosa, which is also a favourite vacation spot for those in Toledo who don't wish to trek to the beach in the summer. Amongst other festivities amidst its highland setting are traditional music and dances, such as the *jotas*, *rondeñas* and *seguidillas*. Not far away is **Valdezarza**, with its 12C castle of *Dos Hermanas* and its burial sites.

In **Menasalbas**, there are Roman ruins and graves alongside the Torcón River, as well as a 16C Gothic-Renaissance church. On the first of February, the *Fiesta de la Encamisada* (Masquerade Festival) is held. Riders on horses decked out in elegant caparisons traverse the town; the traditional *bandera* is danced, and the streets are filled with the *calayos*, natives dressed in white with red sashes and carrying large pitch torches.

From Menasalbas, you can proceed to **San Pablo de los Montes**, a beautiful highland town known for its venison sausage, as well as its 16C church and the ruins of an Augustinian convent built in the 15C on the site of a Visigothic monastery. On the edge of town, there are rupestrian graves. Nearby is **Las Ventas con Peña Aguilera**, with its houses clinging to the cliffside. The strange name of this town —The Inns with Eagle Cliff— reflects a combination of two circumstances: in olden days, its inns provided shelter for muledrivers and travellers; secondly, there is the tradition of the tiny Virgin of the Eagle, a small 12C metal figurine that an eagle once plucked out of a niche in the cliff. Nearby, the Chorrito Valley has menhirs and graves, as well as wolves, lynxes, foxes and wild boar. The *Torre de los Moros* (*Tower of the Moors*) is the ruins of a castle. Hunters take note: there are a number of equipment shops around the plaza, as well as outside the town. One of the most widely-known in Spain is *Angel Gutiérrez Serrano*, whose quality products are sold in many stores, including Loewe's.

Cuerva has a monumental church and castle ruins, in addition to beautiful traditional potterymaking ▶ *page 140*.

Pulgar has a church that once was a feudal castle; in the sacristy, the dungeon transoms can still be seen. **Mizarambroz** also has a castle with its *rollo de justicia*, a type of flogging post.

Sonseca is a large town with major furnituremakers and confectioners, though it is best known for the latter, which is also a feature of **Ajofrín**, the site of a splendid Renaissance church.

Orgaz (3,000 inhabitants) boasts of one of the largest and most beautiful churches in the province. Of Baroque design, it was planned on such a grandiose scale that it was never finished, being left with a single tower. There is also an extremely well-preserved **castle**, a fortress utilized during the 16C *comunero* uprising. It is a town of tidy streets and houses, of thousands of olive trees and millions of grapevines. The first mayor and Count of Orgaz was none other than El Cid.

Los Yébenes, a little to the south, is a focal point for the entire region, which is a veritable paradise for the hunters who flock to its mountains: Yébenes, los Torneros, Rebollarajo, Comendador, Retamar, Piedras Blancas, Morrones, Oso, etc. VIP hunting parties from Spain and abroad come here in search of deer and wild boar. Also to be found in the foothills are wolves, foxes, martens, polecats, and that terror of hencoops, the weasel. In the Guadalerzas Valley is located the late-Roman *Puentes Secas aqueduct*, with its twenty-four arches, as well as the *Castle of Guadalerzas*, standing in defence of the Congosto pass. The Gothic-Renaissance church of Santa María de la Real y de San Juan in Los Yébenes has a thorn from the crown of Christ. **Urda** is a town in the Calderina highlands, the uppermost elevation in the province. The valour of its inhabitants was praised by Alfonso VI, who said: *They are the tallest peaks in my kingdom*.

FIESTAS AND FESTIVALS

The Corpus Christi day procession in Toledo, framed by the city's uniquely splendid location, is one of the most solemn, colourful and famed events in the entire calendar of Spanish festivals. There are, also, other celebrations throughout the province that are no less deserving of our presence. These include the splendid Corpus in Camuñas, with its ancestral and impressive dances of Virtues and Sins; the fascinating *Fiesta de las Mondas* in Talavera, a relic from the pagan worship of Ceres; the Saffron Harvest festival in Consuegra; the Olive Festival in Mora, among others.

◉ ◉ Corpus Christi

Declared to be of tourist interest by the Ministry of Culture, the Corpus Christi procession takes place on the Thursday of the ninth week following Holy Week. Heading the solemn procession is the Cardinal-Archbishop of Toledo (the Primate of Spain) and government officials. The procession leaves through the *Puerta Llana* of the Cathedral shortly after having displayed the Holy Sacrament on the ◉ ◉ ◉ marvellous *custodia de Arfe*, or monstrance, underneath a large white canopy in the presbytery. The monstrance is then carried out into the street just a few minutes after 11.30 a.m. The route taken is Cisneros, Pl Mayor, Martín Gamero, Comercio, Zocodover, Sillería, Alfileritos, Pl de San Vicente, Alfonso X, Jesús y María, Trinidad, Arco del Palacio and Pl del Generalísimo, then it re-enters the Cathedral through the same door. The walls of the Cathedral are draped with Flemish tapestries, twenty of them, all from the 17C. The procession represents a tradition that has been carried on for eight centuries. Whilst everything about this celebration is admirable, a number of features deserve special mention. The cross at the head of the column is of embosssed and gilded silver, a gift from Alfonso V the African (16C). Participants include the nobles (*infanzones*) of Illescas, with their red habits; the Mozarabic knights, in blue habits; the knights of the Holy Sepulchre, in white; a recently-created group from the Latin American chapter of the Knights of Corpus Christi, wearing green habits; and the oldest Brotherhood in Toledo, the *Santa Faz y Caridad* (Holy Face and Charity, who attended condemned prisoners), dating back to the 11C. Also look for the guide-cross of Cardinal Mendoza, present at the conquest of Granada in 1492, when the Moors were driven from the city, as well as the officiant prelate's superhumeral (vestment worn over the shoulders) laden with emeralds and other precious stones from the rings of the Primates of Spain. The final group in the procession is an honour company from the Infantry Academy. Covering the streets are old awnings from the guilds of ancient weavers and silkmakers in the city (who were formerly required to furnish them), whilst the streets are strewn with thyme, marjoram and other wild herbs. On Corpus afternoon, a bullfight is traditionally held. The week-long festivities also include plays, music, and dances.

La Mancha May Day

The *mayos de la Mancha* is celebrated in Ocaña (51km from Toledo via highway N400) in honour of the *Santísima Virgen de los Remedios*. At the stroke of midnight on April 30, the Pl San Juan is filled. A richly-dressed image of the Virgin amidst branches, flowers, and flags is placed in a brightly-lit niche in the door of the church. Then, proceeding from c/ Cisneros, lively groups of young serenaders make their way through the crowd to the niche. A young girl sings the *mayos*, and afterwards the people file in procession to other places throughout the town where there are similar niches and images.

Olive Festival

The *fiesta del olivo* is celebrated in the village of Mora de Toledo on April 27. Declared to be of tourist interest, this *fiesta* represents the culmination of the olive harvest. It begins with the *pregón* (the call to celebrate) and selection of the queen. There are expositions of livestock farm machinery, olive oil and its derivates, as well as knotted rugs,

72

classical Spanish furniture, and cowbells, the latter a long-standing traditional handicraft in the village. A mass is said in the countryside, followed by a parade with floats, bedecked *burros*, minstrels, and folkloric groups from various towns in the province. Prizes are awarded for the best floats, best olive-grower, oldest olive-grower, and for olive-tree trimming.

Saffron Flower Festival

Held in the village of Consuegra on October 26, the *fiestas de la rosa del azafrán* are also of tourist interest. The celebration begins in a typical potter's workshop with the *pregón* by an illustrious Spanish literary figure. Afterwards comes the *monda de la rosa* (Saffron clipping) in front of the gathered crowd. There is also singing and dancing, and a mass is said in the countryside on the Crestería Manchega, next to the windmill and castle atop Calderico hill. Typical Manchegan food is served, with bullfights and visits to wineries.

Various Festivals Elsewhere in the Province

January 25, in San Pablo de los Montes: **La Madre Cochina** (Mother Pig), whereby for one day a man dressed as a woman has licence to hoist the ladies' skirts.

February 2, in Alcaudete de la Jara: *La Soldadesca* (Soldiers Troupe), consisting of a general, a colonel, standardbearers, drummers, halberdiers, and others, who parade through the village streets following a High Mass; then come typical dances in the town square. Beginning on this day, there is a parade each Sunday and holiday until Shrove Sunday.

Holy Week, in Ocaña: **Good Friday** and the articulated images —Jesus falls three times, Veronica wipes his face, and the Virgin of Solitude weeps and wipes away her tears with a handkerchief.

Shrove Tuesday, in Talavera de la Reina: *Fiesta de las Mondas*. Unlike the celebration in Consuegra, this *Monda* is related to worship of the goddess Ceres in pagan times (the Roman *Munda Cereris*), with the tradition of presenting the first fruits of the harvest as an offering.

March 11, in Illescas: **Festival of the Miracle of the Virgin of Charity**. Fair and bullfights.

March 30, in El Carpio del Tajo: **Festival of the Virgin of Ronda**. *Romería* bearing the image of the Virgin from her sanctuary in the hermitage of Ronda, on the banks of the Tagus, to the parish church. Festivities and popular dances.

March 31, in Puente del Arzobispo: **Pilgrimage to the hermitage of Our Lady of Welcome**.

April 14, in Yepes: Blanket-tossing of the **pelele**, or rag-doll —see the Goya painting in the Prado museum—, by young girls from the town, whilst singing typical songs.

April 27, in Maqueda: **Festival of the Virgin of the Fingers** with the traditional *Moors and Christians*.

April 30, in Santa Cruz de la Zarza: *Festival de la Rondalla*, with singing of the *mayos* throughout the village.

May 2, in Almorox: **Patronal Festival** honouring the *Santísimo Cristo de la Piedad*. The image of Christ is brought down in a procession from the hermitage to the parish church, accompanied by a band and with singing at different points along the way. *Dianas*, public and private dances performed in the street.

May 2, in Noblejas: *Fiestas* of the *Santísimo Cristo de las Injurias*, with bullfights and fireworks.

3rd Sunday of May, in Navahermosa: Typical *Romería de la Milagra* to a sanctuary in the Toledo highlands, two kilometres from the village. Celebrated since the 13C, it features riders on elegantly bedecked horses. This *romería* joins up with another proceeding from Hontanar at la Cruz del Milagro, in remembrance of one in times past that ended a drought. Dancing of the typical *rondeñas*.

Thursday of 9th week following Holy Week, in Camuñas: *Fiestas* of the Corpus Christi Dancers and Sins. Declared of tourist interest. A celebration well worth travelling the 40km from Toledo on Corpus morning. This *auto sacramental*, or mystery play, is done as mime accompanied by thunderous music, whereby Divine Grace frees each of the Virtues from evil in a final dance called *la Danza del Cordón*. During the procession with the monstrance, the *Pecados* (Sins) race through the streets whilst screaming wildly, until they fall at the feet of the Crucifix and remove their strange masks.

Sunday closest to the day of San Pedro, in Poláu: *Fiesta* of the Absent, in honour of the natives of the village.

July 15, in La Puebla de Montalbán: Festivals honouring the Holy Christ of Charity. Pamplona-style running of the bulls, bullfights, popular dances, *dianas*, fireworks, and *gigantes y cabezudos* (giants and bigheads with monstrous figures).

July 25, in El Carpio: Geese and Horses (for want of a better term), namely, a rather gory spectacle in which horseback riders attempt to rip off the head of a live goose hanging from a rope as they dash by. Parade of *cofrades* (brotherhoods) in the morning; on the following day, the running of the *vaca del aguardiente*.

August 15, in Escalona: Patronal Festivities. Popular dances. The traditional *la guerrilla*, dating from a siege at the hands of the Moors (Almojades) in the 12C.

August 18, in Esquivias: *Fiesta* in honour of the *Virgen de la Leche*. Bullfights, fireworks and sporting events.

August 21, in Orgaz: *Fiestas* of the *Santísimo Cristo del Olvido*. Fireworks, dances, concerts and bullfights. Halberdier company and the typical *juego de la bandera*.

August 25, in Illescas: Festival of Our Lady of Charity. Major livestock fair, bullfights, *dianas* and public dances.

September 1, in Torrijos: San Gil Abad festivities. Fireworks, dances, spectacles, procession.

September 7-16, in Guadamur: Festivities honouring the *Santísima Virgen de la Natividad and the Santísimo Cristo de la Piedad*. A fervent, traditional procession and typical dance of the *bandera*. Manchegan *jotas* and *seguidillas*. Also bullfights.

September 8, in Consuegra: Patronal *fiestas* in honour of *Nuestra Señora de la Blanca*. Dances both public and folkloric (Manchegan *jotas* and *rondeñas*). Procession, bullfights, fireworks.

September 10, in Santa Cruz de la Zarza: *Fiestas* in honour of the Holy Virgin of the Rosary. Procession bearing the image in a lighted float. The festivities include a ploughing contest, with furrows over 5km in a straight line to the tower where the Virgin is kept. Bullfights, public dances and *dianas*.

September 21, in Bargas: *Fiestas* of the *Santísimo Cristo de la Sala*. Procession that includes the ladies of the town decked out in their typical dresses and jewelry. A long-standing and celebrated tradition in the region. Of particular interest is the fairground set up in the Las Eras neighbourhood, which is a Moorish village within the town. Bullfights.

October 6, in Lagartera: Traditional *fiestas* of **Our Lady of the Rosary**. Regional dances. Typical costumes. Traditional auctioning of the *banzos*, the portable platform that is used to carry the image of the Virgin.

Various Other Festivals in Toledo

During Holy Week there is the impressive **silent procession**, with a beautiful 18C woodcarving paraded through the streets.

The **fairs and festivals of Our Lady the Virgin of the Chapel** are held August 14-20. Honoured by Calderón in one of his plays, they include bullfights, popular festivities and fireworks. Upon the conclusion of the religious ceremonies, it is a tradition to drink water from one of the *botijos* or waterjugs placed in the cathedral cloister, entreating the Virgin for protection during the coming year.

On May 1, there is a local pilgrimage, the **Pilgrimage to the Virgin of the Valley**, with a picturesque procession in which the Virgin is borne through the countryside.

On August 24-27, there is a festival in honour of **Our Father Jesus the Nazarene** with bullfights, dances, *gigantes y cabezudos*, concerts, bicycle races, greased-pole contests, balloons, and more.

FIRST AID

There are three cardinal rules in dealing with emergencies: **Don't panic**. Panic cannot help anyone and can worsen the state of the victim. **Think before acting**. Don't worsen what may already be a major accident. **Act sensibly**. Forget what you've seen on TV. You are not a hero in a movie script.

Burns

Any clothing or other articles near a serious wound should be removed: watches, necklaces, rings and so on included. Then try to cool down the affected areas as quickly as possible. Apply ice water and an ice compress for at least ten minutes. Do not make the mistake of ending this treatment too soon: prolonged freezing decreases pain and reduces the spread of damaged skin. After this, cover the burnt area with clean and dry clothing and get medical attention.

Fainting or Unconsciousness

Any fainting or swooning spell should be taken seriously. If the victim remains unconscious, do not put anything under his head or give him anything to drink. Position him so his mouth faces down. Extend one of his legs and bend the other at the knee. The arm on the same side as the straightened leg should also be straight, extended forward. The other arm should be bent at the elbow, with the hand positioned low, corresponding to the bent leg. The victim's head should remain tilted downward, with the mouth open and free of dirt or any other obstruction. If the victim isn't breathing, ignore these instructions and immediately apply artificial respiration. Keeping the victim's nose pinched shut, put your mouth directly on the victim's, making a seal, and blow with enough force to inflate the victim's lungs.

General

Try to keep curious onlookers away from the scene of an accident. Help the victim by acting calmly and reassuringly.

Hemorrhages

Do not apply tourniquets if you are not a professional —it is an extremely dangerous procedure. With the victim lying down and the wounded limb held high, try to close the wound with pressure from your fingers. Or hold the wound closed until you are able to get gauze or a compress to cover it. If the bleeding does not stop while you are pressing on the bandage, apply another compress and reapply pressure to the wounded area.

Shock

Shock can be suffered as easily by the victim of a major traumatic accident as by one who undergoes a seemingly much less violent experience. It is advisable to seek medical treatment if shock is suspected, since symptoms are not always obvious. Profound shock can cause death, though normally in such a case symptoms would be evident. The shock victim perspires, trembles or turns pale. His breathing becomes faster and his pulse weakens. His mouth is usually dry and he will show signs of thirst, but he must be given no liquids. Treat any wounds that have been suffered and keep the victim warm, but not hot.

HEALTH

The **sun**, that great attraction for vacationers and in many ways the enduring monarch of Spain, can present a serious danger if adequate precautions are not taken, particularly on your first days in the country. Protect your eyes with sunglasses, preferably polarized. Don't make the mistake of buying a cheap pair; they are usually very fragile and may not be good for the eyesight. Take the sun slowly when you first arrive, staying out a little longer every day. Remember: by the time your skin starts to feel like it's burning it's already too late. Protect your skin with products recommended at your local pharmacy.

Spanish **water** is in general good; in many places, it is excellent. But it has distinct characteristics in every region; consequently, some local waters may not suit the palate and stomach of every visitor. As an alternative, there is a wide range of mineral waters available in Spain, some claiming therapeutic qualities. It is served bottled *sin gas* —without bubbles— or *con gas* —with bubbles.

Health Food

Keep in mind that Spaniards use oil in their cooking and that they season with garlic and use plenty of salt. If you have any special diet needs that conflict with this you should advise your hotel or restaurant.

Those who must follow a special diet, for example **macrobiotic, whole-grain or vegetarian**, will find specialised establishments for such purposes in Toledo. One is *Casa Santiveri*, c/ Chapinería, s/n (next to the *Puerta del Reloj* of the cathedral); others are located in c/ Núñez de Arce and in the Galerías del Miradero.

LODGING

For the typical tourist, Toledo represents a one-day visit. As a result, guidebooks, travel agencies and sightseeing companies often have little to say about lodging. Nevertheless, Toledo is a marvellous place to spend the night, a must if you wish truly to experience the city and break away from the standard fast-paced visit. The beauty of the twilight and the illuminated skies that inspired El Greco's world-renowned painting, the vision of Toledo at night, the chance to stroll through its nooks and crannies without the crush of people attempting to adhere to an unbending schedule —all of this can be yours simply by spending a few nights in this city of infinite wonders. The traveller who decides to do so will find a number of splendid choices.

State-run Paradores

Located far and wide throughout Spain, the *paradores* (state-run hotels) represent a hotel chain whose originality and value are unequalled anywhere else in the world. These hotels and inns have been created in the lesser-visited areas that have an unquestionable tourist appeal. Ancient castles, palaces, and convents have been faithfully restored and they combine a maximum respect for tradition with modern services in order to meet present-day demands. Some cases involve a totally new construction. All official government tourist lodgings are located in peaceful sites of incomparable scenic beauty. Guests are served by a staff of specialised, highly-skilled and conscientious personnel. These conditions have allowed the *paradores* to become pacesetters for modern hotelkeeping.

Parador Conde de Orgaz

★ ★ ★ ★ H (Open 1/1-31/12) Paseo de los Cigarrales, s/n ☎ 22 18 50 ⇤ 57 ✆ ✕ ♟ ⌷ 📺 🛜 ℂ 🅿 ♨ ‡ ✽ 🍴 ⛷ ⌔ ⚓ ▥ ≪ AE, DC, EC, MC, V $$$$$.

Occupying an exclusive location on the *Cerro del Emperador* (Emperor's Hill), amongst the *Cigarrales* (country houses) and with a commanding panoramic view of the city, between the Alcántara and San Martín bridges. Modern architecture with a Toledo flavour and refined decoration. Cuisine reflecting the area of Castile and Toledo. Rooms with mini-bar.

Parador Virrey Toledo

★ ★ ★ ★ H (Open 1/1-31/12) Pl del Palacio, 1 ☎ 43 00 00 ⇤ 44 ✆ ✕ ♟ ⌷ 📺 ℂ 🅿 ♨ ‡ ✽ 🍴 ⛷ ⌔ ▥ ≪ ✉ AE, DC, EC, V, MC, CB $$$$.

Located in Oropesa, occupying a castle-palace in this small town with its medieval charm. Converted into a *parador* in 1930, the castle represents a blend of the impeccable and elegant surroundings of the period of its founding and the modern comforts of present-day hotelkeeping. Its cuisine includes typical dishes of Toledo: partridge, quail and the *suspiros de monja*, a type of fritter. About 117km from Toledo, it is a restful spot, ideal for sightseeing or hunting.

Hotels, Hostels or Inns, and Boardinghouses

Hotels are officially classified from ★ to ★★★★★. The rating is indicated on a light-blue sign, under the letter H, and is based on the number and category of services and installations. Prices are regulated by tourist authorities. Should you have any queries, ask at the reception desk. Regulations require that rates be visibly posted at the desk and in each room, normally behind the entrance door. Hotels are legally required to adhere to these rates; however, there are certain variables —such as VAT— that some hotels may reflect in their room prices, whilst others may add the extra charge to the bill. If a single room is not available, you must not be charged more than 80% of the price of a double. The charge for an extra bed may not exceed 60% of the price of a single room, or 35% of a double. Children are usually given a reduced rate based on their age. And lastly, don't be surprised should you find no relation between official rates and your total bill when you are travelling with an organized tour, or on a package deal that includes transportation, lodging, and perhaps other services. The rates may be much lower, or more or less the same.

★ Installed heating. Lift when there are more than four floors. Lobby. Shower, washbasin, and toilet in 25% of the rooms; washbasin in 50% of them; common bath available for every seven rooms. Laundry service available. Telephone on every floor.

★★ Installed heating. Lift when there are more than three floors. Lobby. Bar. Complete bath in 15% of the rooms; shower, washbasin, and toilet in 45% of them; washbasin in 40% of the rooms; common bath available every six rooms. Laundry service available. Telephone in all rooms.

★★★ Installed heating. Lift. Lobby. Bar. Complete bath in 50% of rooms; shower, washbasin, and toilet in 50% of them. Laundry service available. Telephone in every room.

★★★★ Air-conditioning in all common rooms and bedrooms, unless climatic conditions make it necessary to have only central heating or cooling. Lift. At least two lobbies. Bar. Garage (in cities). Complete bath in 75% of rooms; shower, washbasin, and toilet in 25% of rooms. Laundry service available. Telephone in every room.

★★★★★ Air-conditioning in all common rooms and bedrooms. Central heating. Two or more lifts. Several lobbies. Bar. Garage (in cities). Hairdressers. Complete bath in all rooms. Several suites including reception rooms. Laundry service available. Telephone in all rooms.

Alfonso VI
★★★ HR (Open 1/1-31/12) c/ General Moscardó, 2 ☎ 22 26 00 ≙ 80 ⌨ ✕ ♀ ⚓ ✓ 📺 ℃ ‡ ✽ ♠ ✻ Ⅲ AE, DC, EC, MC, V, CB $$$.
Located opposite the Alcázar. Peaceful surroundings, decorated in Castilian style, with convenient mid-city location. Shopping area with souvenirs and photographic supplies.

Carlos V
★★★ H (Open 1/1-31/12) c/ Trastamara, 1 ☎ 22 21 00 ≙ 55 ⌨ ✕ ♀ ◻ ℃ ‡ ✽ ⑤ Ⅲ AE, DC, V $$$.
Tucked away just off the Zocodover square, with a relaxed, family atmosphere.

◉ Cardenal
★★★ HR (Open 1/1-31/12) Paseo de Recaredo, 24 ☎ 22 49 00 ≙ 27 ⌨ ✕ ♀ ◻ ℃ ᵐ ✽ ⑤ Ⅲ ≪ AE, DC $$$.
Close to the Bisagra and Alfonso VI gates, located in a 17C palace that belonged to Cardinal Lorenzana, and virtually a part of the city's monumental walls. It has a romantic garden, and is in one of Toledo's outstanding landscaped areas. Its restaurant enjoys a well-deserved and long-standing reputation in the city. Elegant and distinguished atmosphere.

María Cristina

★★★ H (Open 1/1-31/12) c/ Marqués de Mendigorria, 1 ☎ 21 32 04 🛏 43 🖃 ✕ ▢ 📺 ℄ ↕ ❊ 🐾 🅿 AE, DC, V, EC, MC, CB $$$.

Recently installed in what was in olden-day the *Hospital de San Lázaro* between the Tavera Hospital and the Bullring. Exquisite atmosphere and decoration, with an air of elegance. A monumental and stately exterior, with the interior tending toward an *avant-garde* style that balances colour and traditional elements. Above all, comfortable and peaceful. A number of meeting rooms with capacity for up to 500 people. Honeymoon suite in the dome of the original church. Restaurant in a Mudejar apse with *nouvelle cuisine*, as well as Moorish and Sephardic dishes.

Almazara

★★ HR (Open 15/3-31/11) Ctra Toledo-Arges and Guerva, km3.4 ☎ 22 38 66 🛏 21 🖃 ▢ ✈ 📺 ℄ ❊ 🐾 ≪ $$$.

Maravilla

★★ H (Open 1/1-31/12) c/ Barrio Rey, 7 ☎ 22 33 04 🛏 18 🖃 ✕ 🍷 ✈ ℄ ↕ ❊ 🏛 $$.

Los Cigarrales

★★ H (Open 1/1-31/12) Ctra Circunvalación, 32 ☎ 22 00 53 🛏 29 🖃 ✕ 🍷 ♿ ▢ ℄ ❊ 🐾 ≪ $$.

Imperio

★ HR (Open 1/1-31/12) c/ Cadenas, 7 ☎ 22 76 50 🛏 21 🖃 ℄ 🏛 $$.

Lino

★ HR (Open 1/1-31/12) c/ Santa Justa, 9 ☎ 22 33 50 🛏 29 🖃 🍷 ℄ ✈ 🏛 $$.

The novelist Galdós wrote his novel *Angel Guerra* while staying at this hotel.

Miraltajo

★ H (Open 1/1-31/12) Ctra. de Madrid, 1 ☎ 22 36 50 🛏 12 🍷 🏛 ≪.

Hostels and Boarding-houses

Like the hotels, hostels are officially classified on a scale from ★ to ★★★. This rating will appear on a light-blue sign under the letters Hs. The minimum requirements of the *hostales* or inns are the following:

★ Washbasin in all rooms, with cold water; common bathroom every twelve rooms. A public telephone.

★★ Installed heating. Lift when there are more than four floors. Vestibule or small lobby. Washbasin in all rooms; common bath every ten rooms. Public telephone.

★★★ Installed heating. Lifts when there are more than three floors. Lobby. Complete bath in 5% of rooms; shower, washbasin, and toilet in 10%; shower and washbasin in 85%; common bath every eight rooms. Laundry and ironing service available. Telephone in all rooms.

Boarding houses (*fondas* or *pensiones*) —indicated on a sign under the letter P— offer low-priced accommodations that usually include family-style meals and laundry service. They may be of interest not only from the financial standpoint, but also because they offer closer companionship, and you may also be able to practise your Spanish in the informal atmosphere. Some guests may find the limited privacy to be a disadvantage.

Hostería Madrid

★★ P (Open 1/1-31/12) c/ Marqués de Mendigorria, 6 🛏 10 $$.

Labrador
★★ HsR (Open 1/1-31/12) c/ Juan Labrador, 16 ☎ 22 26 20 ⌂
40 ✐ ⦀ $$.
Las Armas
★ HsR (Open 1/1-31/12) c/ Armas, 7 ☎ 22 16 68 ⌂ 20.
Los Gavilanes
★★ HsR (Open 1/1-31/12) Ctra de Madrid, km65 ☎ 22 46 22 ⌂
6 ✐ ∞ ✹ ⦀ ↩ $$.
Los Guerreros
★★ HsR (Open 1/1-31/12) Av de la Reconquista, 8 ☎ 21 18 07
⌂ 16 ✐ ♡ 📺 ☏ ✱ ⦀ $$.
Madrid
★★ P (Open 1/1-31/12) c/ Covarrubias, 4 ☎ 22 11 11 ⌂ 10 $$.
Santa Bárbara
★ HsR (Open 1/1-31/12) Av Santa Bárbara, 8 ☎ 22 02 98 ⌂ 14
⦀.

MAIL

Post offices are open from 9.00 a.m to 1.00 p.m. and from 5.00 to
7.00 p.m. Facilities include a *poste restante*, in Spanish *lista de correos*,
for mail sent care of the post office in question. You need to present an
identity document or passport to pick up your *poste restante* mail.
Private agencies like Thomas Cook and American Express have similar
services, though the latter company only serves cardholders or
purchasers of its traveller's cheques.

Normal letter boxes are painted yellow, with two red, horizontal
stripes. The letter boxes for express mail are red. Stamps can be bought
in the *estancos*, or tobacconists, as well as at the lobby counters of
most hotels.

To send *telegrams*, you can go to the post office in person —easiest
if you don't speak the language— or dial a special telephone number
and send the message by phone. Telegrams may also be handed in at
most hotel lobbies.

To send a *telex* you must go to the post office or to the lobby of a
hotel with telex facilities.

The following addresses and telephones may be of use in case a
letter or telegram is to be sent from Toledo:
Post and Telegraph Office, c/ de la Plata, 1, next to Pl San Vicente.
Telegrams by Telephone ☎ 22 20 00. From 8.00 a.m. to 10.00 p.m.
Telephone Company, c/ de la Plata, 18 ☎ 004. Information ☎ 003.
Long-distance ☎ 009.

MASS MEDIA

Local Press

The only daily newspaper for Toledo (city and province) is *La Voz del
Tajo*, which gives good coverage of local events. It has offices in
Talavera ☎ 81 24 00 and in Toledo ☎ 22 81 00.

There are also two national newspapers that print a special edition
for Toledo, with information concerning the city: one is *El Alcázar* ☎
22 16 66. This newspaper started life during the civil-war siege, as a

ew mimeographed sheets. It is now a nationwide tabloid, and its bent
s unquestionably ultra-right wing. The second is *Ya* ☎ 21 11 50.

Magazines, Periodical Publications and Books

There is one regularly-published magazine, *Castilla-La Mancha* ☎
22 34 50, a monthly that covers this Autonomous Community (whose
capital is Toledo).

The Academy of Fine Arts and Historical Sciences of Toledo
publishes a magazine from time to time, the rather erudite *Toletum* (the
Roman name for the city).

There is also the *Zocodover* publishing house (c/ del Comercio,
s/n), mainly involved in re-editing guidebooks and classics dealing with
Toledo, as well as specialist books on ethnology, legends, traditions,
and the like.

The *Instituto de Estudios Visigóticos y Mozárabes San Eugenio* also
turns out an occasional publication.

Anyone looking for rare or old books relating to things Toledan is
especially urged to try *Balaguer*, a bookseller on c/ Cardenal Cisneros,
in front of the Puerta de los Leones of the Cathedral.

ORGANIZED TOURS

Toledo has no agencies that specialize in organizing tours. Groups
arriving in town normally proceed from agencies and offices in Madrid
or other cities, both in Spain and abroad. However, if one wishes to
hire the services of a private guide, the *Oficina de Turismo* at the Puerta
de Bisagra can be of help.

A number of outside travel agencies have opened branches in
Toledo, and may be consulted when problems arise, or for obtaining
tickets to travel to other points in Spain or abroad ▶ *page* 153.

PHOTOGRAPHY

Spain is a beautiful country. Furthermore, it is photogenic, owing to its
landscapes, its monuments and its people, as well as its light.

There is no better place to verify this fact than Toledo, for this may
well be the most photogenic city in central Spain. It has always been
the most-painted, the most-drawn, the most-sketched city in the country
—and long before photography was even invented! Thus the 19C
travellers, steeped in Romanticism, came to Spain and found
themselves dazzled by its cities. Their drawings and engravings suggest
that Toledo, this city with its teeming mixture of exotic cultures they had
never seen before, was the place that captivated them above all others.

This power to fascinate has not waned, though today's visitor is more
likely to carry a camera than a sketchbook. Today, as yesterday, Toledo
is most of all a landscape, a presence that is almost unreal as it sits
atop its rocky dome capped by clouds. Words, as well as cameras,
have also captured this city. Rilke saw it as one crushed beneath a sky
of biblical torment; Kazantzakis has spoken of the clouds charged with
divine lightning.

But there is more than the overall panorama: each rock is eloquent,
suggestive. Just around the streetcorner may stand a filigreed column,

or a Visigothic stone sunk in a decaying façade, thus producing a pang that can only be alleviated by taking a picture. Whatever the reason, the possibilities are infinite, much more so than will ever be shown in books and postcards. Only the imagination limits what can be taken away in the camera. Finally, there are the people, the daily life of the Toledans that offers another entire harvest of suggestions.

Helpful Hints

A cloudy day? Don't be upset —here is an excellent opportunity to capture the age-old Toledo, the one painted by El Greco and penned by Rilke, Bécquer and Unamuno. By the same token, on a sunny, hot day, remember that the city can become almost desert-like, so take care with your film and camera. Don't leave them in the sun, in your car, or near a window.

If your film gets stuck and won't advance or rewind, don't force it. First of all, make sure you have finished the roll (for example, was it a 36 or a 24-frame roll?). Cameras should never be loaded in direct light, but in the shade. You may wish to request the services of a camera shop ▶ *page* 85. Bear in mind, however, that repair services in Spain can be as slow as anywhere else in the world.

Intense summertime light can affect the quality of your pictures. There may be reflections, overexposure, unwanted shadows and the like that can produce unsatisfactory results. Again, camera shops can offer advice as to film sensitivity and proper filters. As a rule of thumb, remember that the best time for shooting is early morning or late afternoon. An ultraviolet filter will protect your lens, whilst a polaroid filter will help to avoid unwanted reflections, making your pictures cleaner and the colours more natural, especially when the sky is included, with its blues, and the warm hues of the stone. In general, ASA 64 film is recommended for Toledo; for late afternoons, try ASA 200 (at other times, don't forget to shutter down). With ASA 400, you'll need a reflex camera with F-stops of at least 16 or 22.

Bear in mind that most of the indoor places you will visit —the cathedral, museums, and others— will not allow photography unless you obtain written permission (which can take a great deal of time and bother). Some places will charge a small fee. Thus, when purchasing your film, it is best to think of outside shooting, since indoor opportunities will be minimal.

Ideal Spots and Moments for Picture-taking

The classic view of Toledo —with or without clouds— is from the Peña del Moro (next to the *parador* Conde de Orgaz; go by car). You will see why the Moor Abu Walid was changed to stone here as he gazed upon his lost city.

If you wish to define the city in some rather effective shots, one idea is to go down to the river near the bridges, perhaps the Alcántara or the San Martín. Here you can take in the cliff and a number of monuments at the same time.

If your target is the Alcázar and the cathedral, and you wish to break away from the postcard-syndrome, then head for the southern, or lower, part of the city toward late afternoon ▶ *page* 23. At San Andrés, for example, you will get a virtual sociological explanation of the contrast of the spiritual power of the church and the worldly power of the Alcázar as they loom over the motley array of houses and rooftops.

84

Perhaps less of a monumental site, the southern part of the city is nevertheless arguably more evocative and more apt to preserve the essence of the old oriental city. This is especially the case if you are more interested in people than in monuments.

If you are a true photographic expert forgive this rather elementary explanation —by all means turn to the **Upper-level** or **Romantic itinerary** ▶ *page 21*; pay this part an evening visit and attempt to capture the unsettling mystery of the covered walkways and the lights shining in front of a large cross against the wall. Or else, take a night-time drive around Toledo and choose a spot where you can best capture its magnificently-lit gates, walls or bridges, with a lighting rarely seen anywhere else.

Useful Addresses

Burbur, Pl de Zocodover, s/n. You can get one-hour developing service.

There are also many other shops in Toledo that both sell film and offer rapid developing service.

PLACES OF INTEREST

Alcázar

Visiting hours: 9.30 a.m. to 7.00 p.m. (March-August); 9.30 a.m. to 6.00 p.m. (September-October).

From wherever you view Toledo, two structures always stand out: the Cathedral and the Alcázar. This is no mere coincidence. The two, the fortress and the church, symbolize the two powers, face-to-face, that subject everything to their indisputable authority, one divine, the other earthly and secular. In addition to this symbolism (easy to photograph, with the most appealing views being from San Andrés or down from Barco), the Alcázar has recently taken on certain emotional and patriotic tones as a result of the Spanish Civil War (Spanish visitors now far outnumbering foreign ones). Nevertheless, this magnificent palace that the Emperor Charles V built atop the former royal fortress is worthy of non-sectarian respect for at least three reasons: its history, its architecture, and its significance.

The path taken by its history has been most irregular; it is as if the Alcázar was jinxed. It appears that the Romans established a *praetorium* here (a residence for a provincial ruler) somewhere around the 3C AD. During Visigothic times and the Moorish domination, it continued to be utilized as a fortress. Alfonso VI had it remodelled and promptly turned it into his royal residence as well. At the time it was nothing more than a modest-sized castle, though quite capable of housing sufficient forces to safeguard the royal power from any outside threat and even from an internal situation that was often tumultuous. Successive monarchs —especially Alfonso VII, VIII, and X, Ferdinand III, John II, and the Catholic Monarchs Ferdinand and Isabel— expanded and improved the castle. The Emperor Charles V wanted to convert it into a palace worthy of his Empire; consequently, the architect Covarrubias produced the design that is seen in the structure today, being assisted in the task by artists such as Vergara, Vega, and Villalpando. Upon the death of Charles V, the project was finished by his son, Philip II, who had the northern façade (designed by Juan de Herrera), as well as the staircase and certain outbuildings built.

The Alcázar has had its share of glory. Its first governor was the legendary El Cid, after Toledo had been retaken by Alfonso VI. Later, Queen Berenguela of Castile and León successfully defended it against Moorish attack (legend has it that the Moors refused to do battle upon hearing that their adversary was a woman). Here Alfonso VIII pursued a celebrated love affair with a young Jewish girl called Raquel. This was the residence of María de Padilla, the mistress of Pedro I (the Cruel), and also the jail of the king's wife Blanca de Borbón. The defence of Toledo during the 16C *comunero* uprising was directed from here, and it was here that Charles V convened his Court amidst great pomp and splendour.

Yet, the jinx would not take long to make its presence felt. In the mid-16C, Philip II moved his court to Madrid, and never again did the Alcázar house a monarch. In 1643, it was made into a national prison. It suffered its first fire in 1710 during the War of Succession. The fire was the work of the allied German, British and Portuguese troops as they were forced to retreat. In 1771, Charles III gave the building over to Cardinal Lorenzana to create the Royal House of Charity, and it was restored under the guidance of the architect Ventura Rodríguez. Then came the War of Independence. On January 31, 1810, as the French garrison departed from Toledo, they also set fire to the Alcázar and virtually burned it to the ground, leaving only the outer walls, the patio and the staircase. A new restoration was begun in 1867, and in 1883 the General Military Academy was founded. However, in 1887 another fire gutted the building. The year 1890 saw another restoration, with the Military Academy continuing to occupy the premises. Then came the 1936-39 Spanish Civil War. For the first three months of the war, the Republican army submitted the Alcázar to fierce bombardment. The siege was successfully resisted by the Nationalist General Moscardó and the 1,000 or so inmates who included women and children as well as troops. The Alcazar became a Nationalist symbol of resistance, and it was reduced to rubble. At the conclusion of the war, existing drawings and photographs were used to initiate yet another reconstruction. Currently there is considerable discussion concerning the future use to be made of the building.

Symbolism aside, the most important feature of the Alcázar lies in the structure itself. Its most grandiose and harmonious façade is the main façade. This side faces north, toward Zocodover (owing to the military garrison there, however, it can only be seen from a distance). It is the work of Covarrubias, done in the plateresque style, and to a certain degree its serene grandeur may be said to redeem the overall bulkiness. Moving around the building, plateresque decorations are sparse on its western side. On the other hand, the southern façade is of greater significance: it is the only original side, in that it was the least damaged by the 1936 siege. The Juan de Herrera design is noteworthy for its restraint. The eastern façade reflects the oldest design, since it was modelled after a 14C wall. This is the most-visible side, with its battlements and towers, and it is here that the visitor enters the fortress. The stairs leading up from the basement rooms —which are currently filled with siege memorabilia— bring the visitor to a splendid patio, designed by and built under the hand of Covarrubias. The feeling one gets here is of an elegance and serenity that are truly imperial. The vestibule faces the northern (Covarrubias) façade; above it is the **Throne Room**, or *Salón del Trono*, formerly decorated with murals painted by Saus and surrounded by sumptuous Moorish antechambers. From one end of the patio rises the magnificent staircase, created by

Villapando and Herrera. The two sides form a central landing onto which three doors open; these provide access to the **chapel**, yet another work by Herrera. In the centre of the patio stands the **Statue of the Emperor**, a copy of the statue of Pompeius Leoni that is exhibited in the Prado Museum, Madrid.

The museum-room displays at the Alcázar currently revolve around the Civil War bombardment. Upon entering the building, you go directly to the basement, which served as a shelter for women and children, as well as an infirmary. Alongside the cisterns, a **medieval jail** has been reconstructed, similiar to the one that held Queen Blanca. In front, there is a crypt that contains the bodies of some of the defenders. On the main floor, accessible by continuing up the stairs, the office of General Moscardó has been preserved intact. This was the scene of the famous telephone conversation the general held with his son, who was a captive of the Republicans —Moscardo refused to surrender in exchange for the life of his son. On this same level several rooms house exhibits lent by the Military Museum in Madrid: The Arms Room, the Model Room, the African Room, the Uniform Room, and so forth.

The **basement** holds a certain archaeological interest, in the area where the bread ovens were installed during the Siege. There is a crypt that tradition considers to be the Roman prison in which Santa Leocadia was kept. The Visigoth King Sisebuto ordered a church to be built on the site, and Alfonso X had the tombs of Recesvinto and Wamba installed in it. In the 17C a Capuchin convent was established here which later became an annex to the Military Academy although the crypt was preserved. Nowadays, it can be reached by the so-called **curved patio**; the Moorish arch through which you pass represents the oldest ruins in the Alcázar.

Lastly, we can visit the *Museo del Asedio*, the **Siege Museum**, installed in three basement rooms and containing a number of exhibits of that traumatic event.

Outside, on the esplanade, stands the Monument to the Martyrs of the Alcázar, a work by the sculptor Juan de Avalos. It is grandiloquent, and of rather dubious taste.

🟠 🟠 🟠 Cathedral

Visiting hours: 10.30 a.m. to 1.00 p.m. and 3.30 to 6.00 p.m.; in summer, open until 7.00 p.m.

This is the foremost cathedral in Spain. Its artistic and material riches have led it to be called the *Dives Toletana*, while the novelist Blasco Ibáñez labelled it *La Giganta* (Giantess). The cathedral is one of those privileged places, one eternally consecrated to the glorification of the divine. It rises above the site of the original Visigothic basilica, built around the pillar onto which, tradition has it, the Virgin descended to bestow a chasuble on San Ildefonso. This prelate had defended the virginity of Mary in his writings; thus she came down to Toledo to reward him with the garment as he made ready to say Mass. Over the centuries, this deed has become a deep-rooted and indelible tradition in the city.

Following the Moorish invasion, the main mosque (*mezquita mayor*) was built here. As in Córdoba, it also made use of Visigothic, and even Roman, capitals and columns. When Alfonso VI took Toledo (11C), one of the conditions of the Moorish surrender was that Moslem places of worship would be respected. This was the case until the time came when the tolerant Alfonso happened to be away from the city.

Constanza, his French wife, in cahoots with the Archbishop Bernardo de Sedivaé, also French, took advantage of the King's absence to convert the mosque into a Christian church.

Both the king and the Moslems were infuriated by this trick, and a riot was soon in the making; however, thanks to the intervention of Abu Walid, (the *alfaqui*, or Moslem priest), the Moors were placated and the deed was accepted as a *fait accompli*. In 1222, a papal bull authorized the construction of a new cathedral, and Ferdinand III solemnly laid the cornerstone in 1226.

The Cathedral, measuring 120 by 60m, is one of the six largest in the Christian world. It is a marvellous example of Gothic art, although stylistically it incorporates a rather wide range of designs. The original architect was probably a man called *maestro* Martín, and not, as commonly thought, Patrus Petri. The latter simply followed previous drawings in finishing the Mudejar ambulatories and triforia. The naves were built in the 14C. Two towers were originally planned, though only one was ever erected; the base of the second was utilized by Cardinal Cisneros to found the Mozarabic chapel, topped off by a lantern designed by Enrique Egas and a dome designed by the son of El Greco. The last vaults to be finished were the work of Juan Guas, or his successor Egas, and date from 1493. The ensuing centuries have seen no end to the work both inside and out, as we shall subsequently note.

Cathedral Exterior, Doors and Stained-glass Windows

The main façade opens onto a peaceful square highlighted by an impressive cluster of buildings, including the City Hall, the Archbishop's Palace, and the Provincial Court. This façade, located between the tower and the Mozarabic chapel, has three doors: *Juicio Final* (Final Judgment), *Perdón* (Pardon), and *Infierno* (Hell), as we look from right to left. Only the doors with their archivolts are original 15C Gothic structure; the rest of the façade is the result of the 18C Neoclassical reform under the guidance of the architect Durango, and inspired by Cardinal Lorenzana. The *Last Supper* and other sculptures on the façade are by Mariano Salvatierra.

Of the other doors, the oldest is the *Puerta del Reloj,* also called the *Feria* (Fair), *Chapinería* (Cork-shoe), or the *Ollas* (Pots) portal; this area offers one of the best glimpses to be had of medieval Toledo. The small patio is closed off by a fine *reja*, or grille, designed by Juan Francés. If we go around the sanctuary of the church, we arrive at the *Puerta de los Leones,* also called the *Puerta Nueva* or *Puerta de la Alegría.* Artistically, this one is the most interesting. It was created around 1460, sketches by Hanneguin de Egas being used, and it represents the work of three sculptors —Pedro and Juan Guas, and Juan Alemán. The figure of the Assumption is by Salvatierra, as are the other Mudejar sculptures incorporated to the designs by Durango during the 18C. The *bronze doors* by Villalpando are magnificent (their exterior side is protected by wooden screens). The next door, cold and simple, is appropriately called the *Puerta LLana,* or Plain Door, and dates from the time of Lorenzana. You enter the cloister through the small *Mollete* (Soft Bread Door), next to the tower base (where admission tickets are purchased). Upon entering the church, one is greeted by the stately pillars on which the vaults of its five naves sit. Here, in the muted, polychromatic light filtering through the stained-glass windows, we may well experience a shudder somewhat like the feeling captured by Bécquer in his tale *The Golden Bracelet,* which takes place in the cathedral.

The *stained-glass windows* represent a unique collection begun in the 14C and extended through the 18C. Amongst the oldest are the rose window in the north transept and certain ones above the apse aisle. Those in the main chapel are all from the 15C, and are the work of Jacobo Dolfín and Gusquim de Utrech. Also dating from the 15C are windows by Pedro Bonifacio and *maestro* Cristóbal, located in the southern transept, as well as those by the German Fray Pedro on the side of the evangelist. The rose window over the *Puerta de los Leones* is probably the work of Nicolás de Vergara, an enormous task that was continued through the 17 and 18C.

Chapels (*Capillas*)

Let us begin with the Mozarabic Chapel, or *Capilla Mozarabe*, which occupies the place originally intended for the second tower. This chapel was founded by Cardinal Cisneros in 1504, on top of the original Chapter Room. The Cardinal also obtained permission from the Pope to perpetuate the ancient apostolic, or Isidorian, rite in this area. The rite, preserved by the Mozarabs whilst under Moorish rule, had been practised in Spain since the 4C though following the conquest of Toledo it was replaced by the French, or Roman, rite. This *Mozarabic mass* is still said on Sunday mornings, which is the only time the chapel can be seen from the inside. It is enclosed by an extraordinary *grille* (Juan Francés), with the *Piedad* above the entrance arch by Enrique Egas. The only thing left from the time of Cardinal Cisneros is the three *Juan de Borgoña frescos*. These represent the Orán campaign, undertaken by the Cardinal whilst Regent of Spain (1516-1519); since they were made only five years after the event, they are of considerable iconographic interest. The panels for the 15C *reredos* were brought from the Tránsito Synagogue in 1924.

To the right, we next see the *Tombs of the Archdeacons*, recumbent statues sculpted in 1514 by Covarrubias.

Afterwards, we have the **Chapel of the Epiphany**, with an outstanding grille attributed to Juan Francés and a *retable* from the studio of Juan de Borgoña illustrating the Epiphany.

The **Chapel of the Conception** houses an admirable altarpiece containing nine paintings attributed to Francisco de Amberes. On the gospel side is the tomb of the Founder.

Crossing the area of the Puerta Llana, on the left-hand pillar we will see an *Anunciación* by Vicente Carducho.

In the **Chapel of San Martín**, the tombs of the founding priests follow the stylistic lines of Covarrubias. The *grille* is by Juan Francés, as the inscription indicates. The central panel of the *reredos*, with its plateresque masonrywork, depicts San Martín.

Next we have the **Chapel of San Eugenio**, founded as a parish by Ximénez de Rada; it preserves the original 13C architecture. Early in the 16C, it was dedicated to San Eugenio, the first Archbishop of Toledo, and the monumental *grille* by Juan Francés was emplaced. The *retable*, created by *maestros* Pedro and Oliver (based on sketches by Egas and Rodrigo Alemán), is centred around a statue of the saint by Copin de Holanda. In addition to the *plateresque tomb* by Covarrubias, the Mudejar tomb by Fernán Gudiel is particularly noteworthy —one of the few Mudejar ruins in the cathedral other than the triforia and the door to the Chapter Room.

Beyond this chapel is a wall that holds an enormous work, the 1638 painting of *San Cristóbal* by Gabriel Rueda (there was a medieval legend that said anyone who viewed the image of the saint would be assured of living the next twenty-four hours). Behind this wall is a music archive, with this room also providing access to the Emperor's organ.

We can now see the inner face of the splendid frontispiece of the transept, a monumental scenographic work that is an admirable combination of Gothic and plateresque elements and is yet another contribution by Covarrubias. On the lower section is a double door, a mullion and a tympanum whose theme is the Jesse Tree, or the family tree of the Virgin. Above, there is a plateresque-type retable showing the Coronation of the Virgin. Over one rostrum we can see the trumpets of the *Emperor's Organ*, the oldest in the cathedral.

In the apse aisle, we find the ancient **Chapel of San José**, formerly dedicated to *Santa Lucía*. It is an excellent example of 13C architecture, containing a Spanish-Flemish triptych and a number of paintings.

The *Capilla de los Reyes Viejos* or **Chapel of the Old Monarchs** was brought here in 1498, after the original one in the presbytery was dismantled. Of particular interest is the magnificent *grille* by Domingo de Céspedes (dated 1529), and three fine *retables*, of which the central, plateresque one is by Francisco Comontes.

Next we have the *Chapel of Santa Ana*, with a plateresque *grille*, the *retable* with its reliefs, and the praying figure of the founding priest.

The **Chapel of Saint John the Baptist** is also enclosed within a Gothic grille, with decorative stonework. Its altarpiece is neoclassical circa 1790.

The tiny **Chapel of San Gil** contains a small marble *retablo* with a strong plateresque-manneristic flavour and al fresco decorations on the walls and vaults, done in Pompeyan style.

Main Chapel, Cathedral

Next comes the Chapter House (*Sala Capitular*) ▶ *page* 93, then the **Trinity Chapel** a Renaissance grouping with a recumbent statue by Covarrubias and an excellent plateresque altarpiece.

Pause a moment in your wanderings and contemplate the so-called Transparente on the other side of the aisle and to the rear of the altar in the main chapel. Its name comes from the manner in which a lantern installed over the vault throws light on the tabernacle on the main altar. This entire 18C creation, made of marble, jasper and bronze, was the work of a single man, Narciso Tomé, who was its designer, sculptor and painter. Needless to say, this powerful Baroque work imposed on the Gothic structure of the cathedral led to a storm of controversy; nowadays, however, it is universally recognised as one of the high points of the Baroque, comparable to the best of Bernini, Barromini, and others.

In front, there is the Chapel of San Ildefonso, the centre of the cathedral and a pleasant surprise. Its spaciousness is due to the fact that it encompasses the site of three earlier chapels. This octagonal chapel was built in the early 15C, and was to serve as a model for the chapels of the same octagonal style that became popular worldwide in the 15 and 16C. Its original Gothic retable was replaced by the current marble creation of Ventura Rodríguez (18C), which frames a sculpted relief by Manuel Francisco Alvarez. In the centre is located the *tomb of Cardinal Carrillo of Albornoz*, with small Gothic arches and entreating statues, circa 1370. However, its most outstanding feature is the monumental *Renaissance tomb* to the right, the work of Vasco de Zarza. It has a base with frieze, tympanum and several sculptures, whilst its floral decoration and mythological motifs have a certain Florentine flavour. Also attributed to Vasco de la Zarza is the tomb of Iñigo López Carrillo, less ornate and with the recumbent statue atop a sarcophagus with dragons.

The second octagonal chapel in this aisle is that of Santiago, of even greater proportions than the preceding one. Alvaro de Luna, a rather pompous High Constable who was subsequently to be beheaded in Valladolid, purchased the chapel in 1453 in order to convert it into a sumptuous mausoleum as befitted his rank. He even ordered his tomb to be sculpted with a recumbent bronze statue displaying a most curious mechanical twist: during Mass, the statue would rise up and kneel. Work was continued by his wife and daughter. Its outer appearance was that of a fortress, with parapets, battlements and gates; the interior was one of the hallmarks of Gothic-Flemish monumental works, rendered by a team of artists under Hannequin of Brussels. The *altarpiece* is by Pedro Gumiel, with panels by Sancho de Zamora and the sculpture by Juan de Segovia. The ornately-sculpted **tombs** of the Constable and his wife that we now see, which replaced the moveable version, are by Pablo Ortiz.

Alongside this mortuary chapel, we find the Chapel of the New Monarchs or *Capilla de Reyes Nuevos*. Charles V ordered Covarrubias to design this chapel as a last resting place for the kings and queens of the House of Trastámara (they being the New Monarchs), whose tombs were scattered throughout the naves of the cathedral. Covarrubias produced a type of church joined to the cathedral by a vestibule, thus achieving a perfect merger of Gothic and Renaissance art —the Gothic is reflected in the structure and ceiling, with plateresque decoration. The neoclassical altars in the front part are by Ventura Rodríguez, the main altar by Mateo Medina, and the painting is by Maella. (Temporarily closed to the public).

The **Chapel of Santa Leocadia** is a bit dark, since it lies alongside the sacristy. It contains a neoclassical retable with a painting by Ramón Seyro, a student of Maella.

The last chapel in the aisle is the tiny **Chapel of Christ of the Column**, with its titular figure sculpted by Copin de Holanda.

This brings us to the Sacristy ▶ *page 96* and two chapels, the *Tabernacle Chapel* and the *Octagonal Chapel*, whose design was based on plans by Vergara the Younger during the time of Philip II (visits are currently made through the sacristy, part of the museum rooms). The *Sagrario* or **Tabernacle Chapel**, wherein such painters as Carducho and Caxés worked, has been called a *little Escorial transferred to Toledo*. It houses the popular *Virgen del Sagrario*, to whom Calderón dedicated one of his plays.

As we go past the interior side of the *Puerta del Reloj*, we can see a medallion showing the Annunciation (by Nicolás de Vergara), whilst overhead is a 13C *rose window* with the oldest stained glass in the cathedral.

The **Chapel of Saint Peter** constitutes a type of parish within the cathedral, with its simple Gothic interior and Bayev paintings. Next, the **Chapel of Piety** has a woodcarving from the school of Mena. Afterwards come three chapels: *Pila Bautismal* (**Baptismal Font**), with a grille by Céspedes; *La Antigua*, (**The Old**) with its Baroque grille; and *Cristo de las Cucharas* (**Christ of the Spoons**). Following these is the plateresque *Puerta de la Presentación*, which also opens onto the cloister. Alongside is the Chapel of Saint John (commented on later under 'Treasures'). We will end this tour of the chapels by looking at one that stands apart, next to a pillar in the midst of the naves: This is the **Chapel of the Descent** or *Capilla de la Descensión*, a sort of canopy enclosed by a grille, directly over the spot where the Virgin descended to place the chasuble on San Ildefonso, which most likely means that it marks the spot of the sanctuary of the original Visigothic basilica.

Chapter House (*Sala Capitular*)

Here is unquestionably one of the most beautiful and serene interiors handed down by the Spanish Renaissance, one that unites the Spanish-Moorish and Italianate traditions (the so-called Cisneros style). We enter the *chapter anteroom* (the ancient chapel of Santa Isabel) through a spectacularly flamboyant portal with decorations by Copin de Holanda. The coffered ceiling of this vestibule, by Francisco Lara, has beautiful interlacing Moorish arches. The access door to the Chapter Room is of Mudejar plasterwork alternating with plateresque motifs. As we enter the room, we are immediately captivated by the luminosity of its large al fresco *murals*, painted by Juan de Borgoña and with a noticeable Florentine influence. One critic has stated that this striking example of early Renaissance art offers *a fantasy and a collection of perspective planes that are on a par with those rendered in Italy*. Beneath these paintings, forming a type of shelf, is a running series of the prelates of Toledo, from the first (San Eugenio) to contemporary ones. Until Cisneros, they were painted by Juan de Borgoña; later ones are by Tristán, Ricci, Goya, and Vicente López.

Framed by the plateresque frieze, we have the most beautiful Mudejar *ceiling* in Toledo, a work of Francisco de Lara (circa 1510).

The archbishop's chair is a plateresque creation completed in 1514 by Copin de Holanda.

Choir (*Coro*)

To reach the choir, we cross the *vía sacra* (holy way) from the site of the *Sacrificio* (Sacrifice) and go toward *Alabanza* (Praise). It is enclosed by another dazzling *grille*, by Domingo de Céspedes.

The *choir stalls* here are unique in the world, a type of Sistine Chapel of the best of Spanish Renaissance sculpture. The seats on the lower level represent the oldest part, with multicoloured, naturalistic reliefs depicting the battle and conquest of Granada; they are the work of Rodrigo Alemán. Amongst the foliage and border figures, the handrails and the *misericordias* (the small wooden pieces beneath the seat that are used for support whilst standing), a traditional element in many cathedrals can be seen: this is a series of somewhat wild and humorous scenes with apelike, irreverent characters, to which the novelist Blasco Ibáñez attributed strange sociological interpretations. The lower choir stalls, all of which are preserved, were finished in 1495; although the upper level was also finished at the same time, it was decided to re-do the seats in 1533. A competition was announced, with the work consequently awarded to Covarrubias; he was assisted by Diego de Siloé, with the carving undertaken by Felipe de Borgoña and Alfonso de Berruguete.

Alabaster was used on the highest part, with prophets in the niches between columns, all painstakingly wrought. The chairbacks are of walnut, a material that no doubt contributed to what has been described as a violent expressiveness linked to a cherished morbidity.

Felipe de Borgoña took charge of the gospel (left) side, whilst Berruguete worked the epistle (right) side. They were given three years to complete the work, during which time they were assisted by top-notch artists such as the sculptors Isidoro de Villoldo, Francisco Giralte, Manuel Alvarez, and Pedro de Frías, amongst others. Berruguete's creative and outstanding reliefs have made this area a focal point of Spanish art, a work that has been described as *absolutely genius-inspired, animated and enlivened by a pre-Tridentine, almost pagan, vitality that elevates it to the first rank of universal art.*

In 1593, Berruguete was also placed in charge of the archbishop's chair. Here he produced three small classical reliefs —the Final Judgment, the Flood and the Bronze Serpent, a work of sensual beauty and chiaroscuric detail whose style has been compared to that of Benvenuto Cellini.

As the crowning touch to this output, Berruguete produced the alabaster Transfiguration, whose restless and dynamic classicism predated the Baroque sculpture of Bernini by a hundred years.

Also worthy of mention here in the choir is the altar balustrade (Prima) and the canopy (Villalpando). The *White Virgin* on the altar is French 14C marble. The two doric *bronze music stands* are the work of Nicolás de Vergara and his son. The *lecturn* with the bronze eagle was forged by Vicente Salinas in 1664. Rising above the choir rostrums are two wonderful *organs*: the oldest is the one on the epistle side, called the Archbishop's organ, with the workings by Pedro Liborna (1758) and enclosed in a sumptuous churrigueresque casing; the other, on the evangelist side (the Dean's organ) was finished in 1794, during the time of Lorenzana.

Cloister and Tower (*Claustro y Torre*)

Construction of the lower part of the cloister was ordered by Archbishop Tenorio in the 14C, and it is of a simple Gothic design. The original wall frescos were rather severely faded by the weather; Bayev and Maella were therefore given the task of painting new ones, which are what we now see (recently restored, and of course under protection).

In the stretch beginning at the Santa Catalina door (unfortunately closed to the public) there is the *Chapel of San Blas* with its tomb and walls boasting of the best group of 14C paintings in the Siennese style to be found in Castile.

Cisneros had the upper **cloister** built as lodgings for priests; the quarters came to be known as *Las Claverías* (derived from keeper of the keys). The intended residents were not happy with the rooms, and so they were consequently used for housing those who worked in the cathedral, a practice that has continued to this day.

The **Tower**, of Gothic design with Mudejar elements, has a base topped by a black marble frieze and coats-of-arms in white marble. Its prism-shaped main body was finished around 1442. Hannequin of Brussels was the architect who designed the stunningly beautiful structure, with its pinnacles and flying buttresses (one is arrow-shaped with three crowns that resemble a pontifical tiara).

The public is occasionally allowed to climb the tower, entering via c/Hombre de Palo. If one is so lucky, the reward will be a wonderful chance to see the buttressing, the roofs, pinnacles, and gargoyles, as well as to obtain a priceless view of the entire city.

There are nine bells, two per side, plus *la Gorda* (the Fat one), measuring 2.29m high with a diameter of nearly 3m, which is currently cracked. Legend has it that the crack occurred the very first time the bell rang; it shattered every window in the city. It is also a good example of Baroque excess.

Main Chapel (*Capilla Mayor*)

It is not easy to put into words the sensation felt by those who view the *most exquisitely bejewelled site in the world*, in the words of Frenchman Maurice Barrés. We see it now as it was following extensive remodelling in the time of Cisneros, when the Chapel of the Ancient Monarchs was torn down in order to enlarge the presbytery. At the same time, the magnificent *retable*, or altarpiece, was installed.

This *altarpiece* is a gem of the late Spanish Gothic period, and represents the work of a number of artists: the carving is by Copin de Holanda, Sebastián de Almohacid, and Felipe Bigarny; the gilding and colouring are by Francisco de Amberes and Juan de Borgoña; and the decorations and filigree work are by Peti Jean.

The chapel was formerly enclosed on either side by filigreed stone grillework from the 13C, though only the one pertaining to the epistle remains. The grating on the evangelist side has been replaced by the *Renaissance tomb* of Cardinal Mendoza (the so-called third king of Spain). Queen Isabel herself took charge of seeing that the work was carried out, which is attributed to Fancelli and Andrea Bragno.

When the Chapel of the Ancient Monarchs was torn down, crypts of a number of kings and queens were elevated to the free spaces between the pillars: Alfonso VII and Berenguela beside the evangelist, with Sancho IV and María de Molina on the epistle side. The wood-carved images were done by Copin de Holanda, the same artist who carved the Holy Sepulchre located in the crypt underneath the altar.

Among the figures on one of the pillars on the epistle side, we can see the prudent Moorish priest, *alfaquí Abu Walid*, the one who calmed the furore of his subjects after the mosque had been converted into a church. On the opposite pillar is the shepherd who led the army of Alfonso VIII to a miraculous victory at Las Navas.

The *grille*, a work by the Toledan artist Francisco Villalpando, is perhaps the most monumental and exquisite of all Spanish Renaissance grilles; it was finished in 1548.

Sacristy and Octagonal Chapel (*Sacristía y Octagonal*)

The *antechamber* (Vergara and Monegro, with an Herrera-inspired purity) presents us with paintings by Carducho, Caxés, Ricci and Jordán. But we do not receive the full impact until we enter the spacious **Sacristy** itself, its white walls replete with stunning works, whilst overhead is the crowning piece, the Lucas Jordán ceiling.

El Greco's *The Denuding of Christ*, above the marble altar by Ignacio Haan, dominates this museum in miniature. On the wall hangs one of his *Apostols*, as well as a Virgin and a Christ with a cross. Yet, there are many other sterling examples: Goya's *Arrest*, a prime reflection of his black side; Titian's *Paul III*, and Velázquez's *Cardinal*, along with works by Morales, Van Dyck, Tristán, Raphael, Rubens, and others.

To the left side of the Sacristy is the **Octagonal Chapel** or *Octavo*, a luxurious chapel whose dome was painted by Ricci and Carreño, then restored in the 18C by Maella. Under its arches there are shelves filled with dazzling reliquaries. One of the many outstanding items is found under the centre arch, this being a plateresque silver altar by Pedro de Medina and Diego Vázquez.

On the right side of the Sacristy there is another door, leading to the *Vestry* and yet more of the large selection of paintings. There are glass cabinets holding a number of codexes, such as the ornate bible of San Luis or the missal of León X, as well as a unique collection of *fabric* and religious garments, evidence of how the Toledo cathedral has always been served by Spain's leading embroiderers. In addition, the cathedral has an impressive collection of *Flemish tapestries,* though no guarantee can be given as to how many will be on display.

Leaving through the rear of the Vestry, we arrive at the **New Cathedral Museum Rooms**. These five new rooms have recently been opened in the so-called *Casa del Tesorero* (*Treasury House*), a building on the northern side dating from the late 16C.

On display are some of the cathedral's most outstanding works, brought here from the Chapter Room, the chapels, and the Sacristy. Thus we now have Caravaggio's *San Juan,* a Gerard David (formerly in the Chapter Room), some El Grecos, a Bellini, among others. Special mention should be made of the collection of small Bayev and Maella canvases that were used as studies for the cloister frescos.

There are also some sculptures, such as El Greco's *Imposición,* along with gold and silverwork, articles used in religious services, and the garments worn by a number of archbishops, including Mendoza, Cisneros, and Fonseca.

Treasures (*Tesoro*)

We will actually see only a small part of the enormous wealth of cathedral treasures that is to be found in its many areas. In the Chapel of Saint John, for example, one is not always aware of the architectural richness of the *plateresque façade* (Covarrubias), with work by Olarte.

The outstanding attraction of the cathedral's treasury is undoubtedly the famous *processional monstrance* by Enrique de Arfe. Commissioned by Cisneros, it is the most important work in all of Spanish gold and silversmithing. Standing over a metre and a half high, it contains 18kg of gold and 183kg of silver; it has 5,600 different parts, more than 12,000 screws, and 260 statuettes inlaid with countless precious stones.

On either side is a storehouse of reliquaries, chalices, relic-bearers, cups, and other pieces. Looking upward will give us a view of the attractive Mozarabic coffered ceiling.

Churches and Convents

Capuchin Convent

Located in the Pl de Capuchinas, it is quite difficult to visit, since it is usually closed. From the outside, however, one can admire its stately 17C construction and façade adorned with an image of the Conception attributed to Manuel Pereira. The Capuchins, who had settled into the lower part of Toledo in the early 17C, moved to this convent in 1655. It had been built for them by Cardinal Pascual de Aragón, who is buried in the church, as can be seen by a liberal scattering of his coat-of-arms in the building. The church and sacristy also contain impressive works of Baroque art: altars of multicoloured marble, jasper and bronze, as well as paintings and frescos by Ricci and other artists and sculptors, such as Algardi.

Concepción Francisca, Convent of

This stands to the south of the old Palacios de Galiana ▶ *page* 127. (In Toledo, *palacio* is best thought of as meaning mansion). The Catholic Queen Isabel gave this convent to the Conceptionist nuns in 1484 (it had previously belonged to the Franciscans). In 1491, its members joined with the Benedictines of San Pedro de Dueñas. Only the apse of the original church has been preserved, along with its magnificent Gothic frescos. On its left is the so-called *Chapel of San Jerónimo,* which is entered through the forecourt of the convent, or through the interior of the apse. This chapel appears to be topped off

97

by a strange aluminium dome —its interior, however, is a veritable jewel, made entirely of multicoloured glazed ceramic pieces that form geometrical combinations in the Arabic tradition. It dates from 1432. The fabulous *Mudejar arch* on one side was brought here from what was known as the Palace of King Peter. Particularly striking is its wooden Mudejar latticework window, which was once between this chapel and the no-longer-existing church.

At the end of the patio-church, where it meets the present-day convent, is the charming 14C *Mudejar tower*. There are art treasures inside the convent but they are not on view as it is a cloistered convent. These include remains of original *palacios*, utilised in later work; coffered ceilings, frescos, and remains of paintings in the cloister; Mudejar flooring similar to that in San Clemente el Real; and a choir with carved walnut stalls.

El Salvador, Church of

This is one of seven Mozarabic churches. Originally a major mosque continued to function on this site even after the Reconquest. History tells us that during the reign of Alfonso VII, his Queen, Berenguela, was passing through Toledo and had to seek shelter from the storm inside the mosque; during her stay, it occurred to her to convert the place into a church.

The building has been remodelled a number of times, the last being in 1822 following a fire. Yet, it still has its interesting points: the *bell tower*, encrusted with Visigothic stones, and most of all, a recently-discovered *arcade separating the central and right naves*. Here we have a beautiful series of Moorish arches supported by Roman and Visigothic columns and capitals pressed into service, as well as ruins miraculously salvaged from the original Visigothic church and Arab mosque. One must pay special attention to the beautifully-wrought *Visigothic pilaster* to the forefront of the arcade.

At the head of the right nave is another part salvaged from the fire: the *Chapel of Santa Catalina,* which forms a type of building apart. It was founded by Fernando Alvarez de Toledo, the secretary to Ferdinand and Isabel, and is a splendid example of the typical architecture of the day. (The coat-of-arms of the Catholic Monarchs can be seen on the outside wall, next to a lovely window.) There is also an excellent *altarpiece* by Juan Correa de Vivar, and a handsome *grille* by Domingo de Céspedes. Unfortunately, both the chapel and the church are almost always closed. (See worship service schedule.)

Gaitanas, or Convent of the Calced Agustinians

This convent stands in front of San Vicente, near the post office. It belongs to the nuns of the order of *Agustinas Calzadas de la Purísima Concepción*, though they are popularly known as *Las Gaitanas*, since their founder (16C) was Guiomar de Meneses, whose husband was named Lope Gaitán.

The church, open only during worship hours, dates from the 18C and is one of the most original and beautiful examples of the Baroque style in all of Toledo. The colossal altar painting is by Ricci, and there are marvellous altars and images.

Gilitos, Convent of the (Currently houses the Castile-La Mancha Parliament)

▶ *page* 18.

La Magdalena, Church of

Although it was founded shortly after the Reconquest, the church was completely restored in the 18C and once again in more modern times. As a consequence, its only interesting features are its façade, its plain tower, and the classical columns separating its naves. Since it is close to the Alcázar, it suffered considerable damage during the Civil War. Losses included the popular and miraculous *Cristo de las Aguas* (Christ of the Waters), a deep-rooted part of the city's traditions, along with valuable altars and paintings.

Nuestra Señora del Tránsito, Synagogue of ⚬ ⚬

▶ *page 132.*

San Andrés, Church of ⚬
Open only during worship hours.

Behold another of Toledo's hidden charms; to miss it would be unforgivable. Its origins go back to the Reconquest. The original church was destroyed by fire in mid-12C, but was rebuilt around 1200. The chapels on either side of the transept, with their Mozarabic vaults, date from this time. Also from this period is the tomb of Alfonso Pérez (d. 1306), where beautiful Mudejar plasterwork can be seen.

Construction of the transept and main body of the church was begun shortly after 1502 at the behest of Francisco de Rojas, ambassador of Ferdinand and Isabel, who required that the design be based on the contemporary church of San Juan de los Reyes. Juan Egas may have been the architect. Inside are two plateresque tombs belonging to the family of the founder.

The *principal altarpiece* and the ones to each side show the work of Juan de Borgoña (early 16C), probably assisted by Antonio de Comontes. The paintings in the so-called *Chapel of the Lizards*, also known as the *Chapel of the Ambassador*, are by Borgoña as well.

A recent restoration uncovered Visigothic pilasters and capitals in the naves, and a much-needed touch-up was given to the *Mudejar tomb* on the gospel side, as well as to an inscribed Arabic column, a Visigothic capital, and remains of Roman paintings, next to the entrance door.

San Bartolomé, Church of
San Bartolomé de Sansoles (or de San Zoilo) was a Mozarabic martyr from Córdoba who had his chapel here. It was rebuilt at the beginning of the 14C by the Count of Orgaz, though the only part remaining from this reconstruction is the Mudejar apse and arcade. The tower and the rest of the building are modern. At the end of the last century, this old parish church was converted into a convent for nuns, and there are a number of valuable paintings to be found here.

San Cipriano, Church of
Located close to the Mozarabic church of San Sebastián and the Pl de las Mejoras, it was built by Alfonso VI in the 11C. The 17C saw it completely reconstructed, however, with only the original *tower* remaining. Upon entering and crossing a charming atrium or patio, the visitor will be pleasantly rewarded: here are to be found excellent altars and paintings, a trumpet organ, and most of all, the altar and image of the Virgen de la Esperanza (Virgin of Hope), already an object of veneration by 1200. Beneath the niche holding the Virgin is the perfectly-preserved mummy of the man who rebuilt the church, Carlos Venero Leiva. On the walls are a number of delightful and interesting *votive paintings* representing cures, resurrections, and miracles performed by the Virgin.

San Clemente el Real, Convent of ⚬
Open early on Sundays.

As often occurs in eastern Toledo, the visitor can walk right by a simple wall with its beautiful façade, totally unmindful of the artistic treasures concealed inside.

This ancient convent, dating back to 1214 (when Alfonso VIII granted it a number of buildings), was the third to be founded in Toledo following the Reconquest; it therefore has preserved little of its original layout. Outside, half-hidden in the narrow street, rises the *plateresque façade* of the church, which may be considered one of the first works by Alonso de Covarrubias in Toledo.

Toward the end of the 18C, the church was remodelled under Lorenzana; since then it has remained unchanged, and consists of a spacious nave over which stand pointed-arch vaults with plasterwork and paintings illustrating popular 18C motifs. Behind the altar and tabernacle is an enormous *retable*, a splendid late-16C work flanked by statues of angels, all done in multicoloured marble and representative of the age of Baroque restoration. In the centre of the retable, partially hidden by the tabernacle, there is a dated painting of *San Jerónimo*, which some experts attribute to Ribera or Ribalta.

On the wall to the left of the presbytery there is a tomb in a niche; the Latin inscription tells us that it pertains to Fernando, the son of Alfonso VII.

The church has a number of excellent 17C altars, in addition to its attractive frescos. Yet, what most draws our attention is the *communion rail*, at one end. Installed in 1640, it is also made of multicoloured marbles, with a beautiful alabaster relief of The Last Supper in the centre.

The choir can be seen by looking through the grille that separates it from the church. The vaults are Gothic, and here we have another leading example of Toledo's *choir stalls*. The work is believed to be by Borgoña, or one of his better pupils, especially in the case of the priory chair. Next to the splendid *organ*, and dating from modern times, are the *Thirteen Venerated Ones*, thirteen well-preserved, mummified nuns.

Unfortunately, a number of interesting items cannot be seen. These include a woodcarving by Alonso Cano on the retable; two paintings by Tristán, including one that may actually be by El Greco (*Appearance of the Virgin before San Bernardo*); a portrait of Cardinal Bernardo de Sandoval; the *coffered ceiling* in the refectory (Mudejar, 13C); *two cloisters*, probably by Covarrubias; the 12C *parchment collection*; and several *dresses* donated to the convent by Isabel of Valois, the third wife of Philip II. By looking toward the presbytery through the grille shutting off the cloistered part, one may be able to see the *flooring of the Chapter Room*. With the exception of the Roman mosaics, it is one of the oldest and most beautiful in Toledo, if not in all of Spain. The handiwork is Mudejar, with small pieces of glazed, multicoloured ceramic used to form star-shaped rosettes and geometrical designs in the best Arabic tradition. It no doubt belongs to the original convent.

In the same room with this flooring, there is an altar with a large crucifix attributed to Berruguete, whilst the sacristy contains a notable Mudejar coffered ceiling.

San Gines

▶ *page* 23.

San José, Church and Convent of

▶ *page* 21.

San Juan Bautista, Jesuit church of

In simple terms, here we have Toledo's most grandiose Baroque church, one exemplifying the purest of Jesuit styles —and a good example of how in Toledo anything may fit in, as long as it is well done. Its façade is one of the few that can be seen from a certain perspective, and it provides a fascinating roll call of Jesuit history: here are the statues of such saints as San Francisco Javier (Francis Xavier), San Francisco de Borja, San Luis Gonzaga, and San Estanislao de Kostka, whilst standing above all of them is San Ignacio de Loyola. This is indeed the Jesuit Olympus.

The interior follows the same grand design. Until somewhat recently, this church had fallen out of favour, from the standpoint of its architecture, as well as its altars and sculptures. Nowadays, the new sensibility has once again come to appreciate Baroque art. And there is a treasure trove here awaiting reappraisals: the convent's interior and exterior architecture, along with its abundant *retables*, paintings and images (some, however, of a more modern ilk). All in all, we have one of Toledo's outstanding Baroque enclaves —lovers of this period will certainly not be disappointed.

San Juan de la Penitencia, Convent of

Incredibly, this was the only major monument to be completely destroyed during the Civil-war assault on the neighbouring Alcázar. It was one of the crown jewels of Toledo. Founded by Cardinal Cisneros in 1514, the church offered a dazzling array of Gothic, plateresque, and Mudejar styles, as well as housing many priceless chapels, altarpieces, tombs, Moorish rooms and coffered ceilings. All perished in the flames, save a portion of the façade with its late-Gothic decoration and coat-of-arms of its founder, a sad reminder of the style formerly seen in the rest of the building.

The structure we now see is a dormitory for foreign students at the Fundación Ortega y Gasset, which has been built making use of the surviving façade.

San Juan de los Reyes

Visiting hours: 10.00 a.m. to 1.45 p.m. and 3.30 to 6.00 p.m.; in summer open until 7.00 p.m. Private. The church is also open during worship hours.

The victory over the Portuguese in the Battle of Toro was the final blow to the aspirations of Juana la Beltraneja and her followers. In celebration of the victory, the Catholic Monarchs decided to build this monastery, which they also originally conceived of as a royal mausoleum. This explains its lavishness, as well as the large number of coats-of-arms and other heraldic images. Ultimately, however, the King and Queen were put to rest in the Royal Chapel at Granada.

Juan Guas was placed in charge of the project, with work completed in 1476. When Granada was given the nod for the royal tomb, and in view of the reluctance of the *Cabildo Catedral* (Cathedral Council) to allow the premises to be put to similar use, the monastery was handed over to the Franciscans. A second cloister was added in the 16C, though it no longer exists. During the War of Independence, this church was one of those most damaged by Napoleon's troops, who used it as a garrison. Its sculptures were mutilated, and worst of all, its marvellous library was burned, along with the codexes and manuscripts that various monarchs had donated. Later came secularization, and San Juan de los Reyes opened its doors to the parishioners of the nearby broken-down church of San Martín. In 1846, the *Provincial Museum* was installed in its cloister, though it would later be transferred to Santa Cruz. Currently, the monastery once again finds itself in the hands of the Franciscans.

One need not complain about the restorations, whose accuracy can be verified by looking at old engravings and photographs. Its *cloister*, awash in flowery Gothic and mind-boggling detail, has no equal in Toledo. A close look at the carved and painted coats-of-arms on the

Detail of the Cloister, San Juan de los Reyes

coffered ceiling of the upper church will reveal a persistent motif: the many nationalities joined together by Ferdinand and Isabel. Also included is the Cross of Jerusalem, since the king and queen also considered themselves to be the rulers of that city, as well as of the Holy Land. You enter through the *refectory*, going straightaway to the staircase; this gives access to both the upper and lower cloister. The magnificent *dome* over the stairwell is by Covarrubias, and can be closely compared to the one at San Román.

The *chains* hanging on the outside walls are war trophies from the battles fought by the *Reyes Católicos* to free the Christians in Granada.

The splendour of this church, both inside and out, classifies it as the masterpiece of Juan Guas. Above all, the interior of the transept is awe-inspiring in its rich, monumental expression, leaving no doubt as to the original intent of making it the royal tomb. One may find the grandiosity a bit overwhelming, along with a certain insistence on advertising the king and queen and their imperialistic designs by means of all the heraldry, crowns, pages, ornamentation, yokes and arrows, initials of the Catholic Monarchs, and so on. All of the domes are stellar vaults. The original *retablo* was no doubt used as firewood by Napoleon's troops. As a replacement, half way through the last century, a large canvas was brought from the church of San Martín (painted by Simón Vicente, an artist who will not go down in the annals of art history). Consequently, the painting was covered by the main *retablo* from the Hospital de Santa Cruz, the work of Felipe Bigarny and the painter Francisco de Comontes.

The *cloister* was the part that suffered most from the 19C warfare. It is reached through an ogee arch, very characteristic of both the age and the so-called Catholic-Monarch style. The layout of its two storeys is square. Our attention is drawn to the vaulting of the lower storey with the beautiful geometrical decoration of its arches and the exquisite borderwork. The pillars hold numerous images of saints, all from the late 15C. In short, here we have one of Spain's most sumptuous cloisters. Its upper level, ringed by multilinear arches, is covered by a polychromatic Mudejar ceiling (which can be thought of as yet another advertisement). From here we can get a good view of the lavish architectural detail, the whimsical gargoyles, pinnacles, reliefs, and other features.

San Lorenzo, Church of

A Mudejar church built in the 12C, it has undergone numerous modifications. A small square area of the lower part of the tower is ringed by polylobed arches decorated in the *califa* style.

San Lucas, Church of

Open more or less during museum hours.

This church was built in 641 by Evancio, the grandfather of San Ildefonso, during the reign of Chindasvinto. The Moorish domination saw the patio in front of the church used as a Mozarabic cemetery, and is where the parents and grandparents of San Ildefonso are buried, along with other martyrs and prelates.

The church consists of three naves separated by Moorish arches; its structure is Mudejar. In the main chapel there is a Renaissance *retablo* whose central panel represents San Lucas holding the *Virgin of Hope*, to whom the large chapel facing the right nave is dedicated. A popular tradition had it that St. Luke was himself the author of the panel.

There is a legendary story with a miracle attached to the *Virgin of Hope*, a very popular figure in Toledo: an aged Toledan woman, deeply devoted to the Virgin, used to pay for a Hail Mary to be said every Saturday. On her deathbed, she requested that her nephew and heir keep up the tradition, but her dying wish was instantly forgotten. Soon afterwards, the miracle occurred: every Saturday, the residents of the neighbourhood could hear angelic choirs burst forth in song from within the church, whilst rays of light streamed out. Upon entering, the people found a legion of angels intoning the Hail Mary that Diego, the neglectful nephew, had refused to pay for. As a result, he changed his last name from Hernández to De la Salve (Hail Mary) and thenceforth carried out his aunt's wishes. A painting beside the chapel illustrates the moment when Diego discovers the angels intoning the prayer.

There are several paintings we should take a look at, including a Christ tied to a column, by the Granadian Bocanegra, and a crucifix in the style of Tristán. Pay particular attention to a most interesting painting that fits in well with this Mozarabic church: it represents a holy trial by judgment of fire (that occurred following orders of Alfonso VI) to establish which were the right prayerbooks. We see Christians —dressed in Moorish style, hence Mozarabs— tossing the books into the bonfire —the bad books (i.e., Roman) are destroyed, whilst the good ones (Gothic) are left intact by God's fiery justice.

San Marcos

▶ page 25.

San Miguel

▶ page 24.

San Nicolás

▶ *page* 21.

San Pedro Mártir, Convent of

This is another of Toledo's great churches, with a number of fascinating objects and tombs of the illustrious, which make it a sort of pantheon. Located directly beside the church of San Román, it is almost always closed. It formerly belonged to the Dominicans, who came here early in the 15C, remodelling and expanding it at the end of the following century. Then came secularisation, after which the building became a military garrison; subsequently, the Provincial Museum was installed here, having been transferred from San Juan de los Reyes in 1846. The building is presently being used as classrooms.

Only the *tower* remains of the original Mudejar convent. Both church and façade are in the style of Herrera. The main chapel has a large *grille* and a colossal *retable*, both very impressive. There are two *monumental tombs* in the transept, the last resting place of two knights and their wives. The quality of the statues leads us to think of a student of Berruguete, and there is a semblance with work in the now-destroyed church of Carmen Calzado. The left-hand tomb stands out, with its excellent rendering of the knight's noble expression and the fragile beauty of his spouse. This is Pedro López de Ayala, count of Fuensalida, and Elvira de Castañada, the latter being the inspiration for Becquer's legend *The Kiss*.

Another tomb of note pertains to the so-called *La Malograda* (The Ill-fated Lady). It is a Gothic sarcophagus with a recumbent young girl, believed to be María de Orozco, who died at the age of twenty-one —tradition, nevertheless, has her living for three hundred years, one hundred whilst unmarried, one hundred years as a wife, and one hundred as a widow.

One of the chapels holds another, even more interesting, tomb. This is the *tomb of the poet Garcilaso de la Vega* and his father, both carved in alabaster.

Mention should also be made of the so-called *tomb of Mélito:* this is a marvellous plateresque work brought from the demolished Convent of the Calced Agustinians. Inside are three people: Diego Hurtado de Mendoza, Count Mélito, and his wife Ana de la Cerda.

Another treat awaits us at the far end of the church: its *choir.* There are two rows of seats, with the upper level most likely the work of a talented student of Berruguete or Borgoña. Each seat is located in its columned niche, whilst the backs contain reliefs of saints and other figures. Of the many choirs to be found in Toledo, this one may well be second only to the one in the Cathedral.

A short distance away, on c/ San Clemente and a little down from the door to San Román, we find the impressive convent patio with its three-tiered galleries.

San Román, Church of

Visiting hours: 10.00 a.m. to 2.00 p.m. and 4.00 to 7.00 p.m. Closed Sunday afternoons and Mondays. Government-owned.

Could this be Toledo's most interesting and beautiful, as well as strangest church? Be that as it may, it is a veritable treasure that no visitor to the city should miss. As is often the case, its exterior gives us no hint as to what awaits us inside.

This church was already becoming famous by the early 12C. It probably began as a mosque, before that a Visigothic church, and even further back, a Roman building, judging·from the vaults that support the tower staircase.

The current building is *Mudejar*, the most interesting and the most Toledan of all the city's Mudejar churches. Its structure may be the result of remodelling and consecration by Archbishop Ximénez de Rada in 1221.

From the outside, the building is not particularly inspiring, as it stands alongside the church and convent of San Pedro Mártir. Because of its height and the fact that it is on high ground, the slender 13C *tower* can be seen in any panoramic view of the city; tradition has it that as a child Alfonso VIII was proclaimed king by Esteban Illán from this tower, thus putting an end to the intrigues and struggles taking place in the kingdom. In reality, it would have had to be an earlier tower than this one.

Be prepared for a delightful surprise upon entering the church. It consists of three naves separated by wide, thin Moorish arches sustained by *Arabic columns* and *Visigothic, Mozarabic and Byzantine capitals*. The walls are covered by well-preserved paintings. The *main chapel* was remodelled in the 16C, under the direction of Covarrubias, who created a stunning *dome* that is undoubtedly one of his masterpieces and an evident example of how good art can achieve a proper marriage between the old and the new. The presbytery displays an excellent Renaissance *altarpiece* in the Berruguete tradition. The wooden ceilings date from modern times.

The *paintings* are worthy of our closest attention, and we can thank a restoration carried out in the 1940s for their discovery. Most likely dating from the 13C, these works throw light on an unknown chapter in the history of Spanish Romanesque painting, as can be seen in their freedom and naturalness. Nonetheless, Toledo has not failed to place it characteristic stamp on them —thus an Arabic influence can be discerned, and it is not out of place to talk of a completely original Toledo School. (There are more Romanesque paintings in the Cristo de la Luz, whilst others are continually being discovered in monasteries and convents, such as the Convent of Concepción Francisca.)

It is quite clear that Toledan Romanesque painting owes a debt to *califa* influences, which are mainly expressed in Arabic decorative elements such as volutes, inscriptions and background ornamentation. The *califa* panels (*atauriques*), interlaced arabesques and characters, combine with Roman sawtooth designs or meanders. The paintings here at San Román appear to show the handiwork of two artists or studios: one, in charge of the angels, with a Mozarabic semblance; another, the prophets on the arches and certain other figures on the walls, such as paradise, the resurrection of the dead, and God and Eve, that illustrate a greater concern for expression than for correctness of form.

In 1973, the *Museo de los Concilios de Toledo y de la Cultura Visigoda* (Museum of the Toledo Councils and Visigothic Culture) was opened. On display in the glass cases are a number of *Visigothic artefacts*, such as brooches, fibulas, necklaces, rings and other objects that were found in the excavated tomb at El Carpio in the province of Toledo. The walls hold carved stone, capitals, fonts, and pilasters, part of the scant remains left of the civic and religious buildings of the Visigothic capital. In a side chapel can be found reproductions of the *votive crowns* from the Guadarrázar Treasure, a trove found near Guadamur in 1853. Owing to the ignorance of the finders, the articles became dispersed; however, an exchange was carried out with France in 1943, whereby six crowns —including the main one, pertaining to King Recesvinto— were returned to Spain.

The *Concilios* part of the museum name originated with a piece of stone that is on display in one of the cabinets. This is a fragment of the Catholic creed that was found in 1956 during excavations at the Santa Leocadia site (where the famous Councils had been held). The fragment indicates how Arab influences were stamped out and how Catholicism formed the theme for the unification of Spain.

🌶 San Sebastián, Church of

Located on the road of the same name, below the Seminary and in front of the *parador*, it is usually closed, but you can ask for the key from a caretaker at a neighbouring house.

Of Visigothic roots, it may have been built around the year 600, during the reign of King Liuva II. One of Toledo's seven Mozarabic churches, it offers a rewarding experience that should not be missed. Following the Reconquest, it was rebuilt in the Mudejar style, with its structure resembling that of Santiago del Arrabal. In its three naves are found the original *Visigothic columns and capitals* that have been utilised as supports for the Moorish arches. The wooden ceiling is original. The main chapel was built in the early 17C, and its Renaissance *retablo* contains a beautiful image of the titular saint. During a recent restoration, remains of an altarpiece painted by Berruguete were found, as well as pieces of al fresco paintings and gravestones.

San Vicente, Church of

The outer brick building with its authentic and typical Toledan hallmark dates from the early 17C. However, there is another structure within this shell, a Mudejar one, which can be clearly seen through the windows, especially those on the side opposite the tower. Its plateresque façade can be observed from the alley below the church which formerly housed the El Greco retable with the famous painting of the Assumption, currently in the Santa Cruz Museum. For a time this building housed the Fine Arts Museum now moved on to Santa Cruz.

Embedded in the simple masonry of the tower is a pilaster with its late-Roman relief. The church has been closed for many years.

Santa Clara la Real, Convent of

The convent church contains major Mudejar ruins, especially the wood ceiling over the nave and the Gothic chapel founded by the Archdeacon Juan de Meses to serve as a place where he and his parents could be buried. The tombs are 15C French Gothic; paintings from the same period can be seen on the *retable* in the main chapel, along with paintings by Luis Tristán dated 1623.

Santa Eulalia, Convent of

Located on the Cuesta de Garcilaso and near the site of the poet's house, it is one of the seven Mozarabic churches in Toledo. Until recently, its interior was plastered over and consequently classical writers were unaware of the Church's inner secrets.

Its founding dates from the reign of Atanagildo (559); here was another site where the *Concilios de Toledo* were held. The church was kept open for worship during the Moorish occupation; following the Reconquest, El Cid founded a branch of the Vera Cruz brotherhood here.

The current church dates from the 12C, though it may preserve the Visigothic floor plan. Its three naves are separated by graceful Moorish arches resting on *Arabic columns* and *Visigothic capitals*, all that remains of the Mozarabic church. The sanctuary and apse are from a later period, and are topped by Renaissance domes. There are several interesting paintings and woodcarvings.

A curious note: this is the only parish church in Spain whose jurisdiction is based on its members and not its territory, meaning that its Mozarabic parishioners are to be found in Europe and America. Here in Toledo is where the small *Mozarabic community* is being kept alive ▶ page 34.

Santa Fe, Convent of

Belonging to the order of the *Comendadoras de Santiago* (Nuns of Santiago), it owes its name to the ancient chapel (still inside) dedicated to this group, which was founded in the upper part of the mythical Palacios de Galiana following the conquest by Alfonso VI ▶ page 127. *The chapel was rebuilt in 1266 by the knights of the Order of Calatrava. The exterior masonrywork has been preserved, as well as the bell gable, and its polygonal Mudejar apse is decorated with interlaced Moorish arches.*

The chapel of Our Lady of Bethlehem is well worth visiting, with its califa ribbed vault (the style developed during the 10C Caliphate of Córdoba). Inside, the tombs of Prince Fernando and Princess Sancha Alfonso de León are to be found.

Santa Isabel de los Reyes, Convent of

Founded in 1472 by María Suárez de Toledo. Queen Isabel, the Catholic queen, donated the former *palacios* of Casa Rubios and Arroyo Molinos to help the building of the convent, and her daughter

Isabel, later to be Queen of Portugal, was born here. The 15 and 16C saw the building undergo extensive changes.

The church forms part of the former parish church of San Antolín, and it has preserved the 14C *Mudejar apse*. Its interior presents a spacious nave underneath a Mudejar coffered ceiling and a pointed arch vault in the main chapel. Two items of interest in this chapel are the *tomb* of Inés de Ayala (2nd half 15C), sculpted in black and white marble, and the *Renaissance retable* dating from 1572. Look for other recently-restored altarpieces in the church.

The founder, as well as Isabel, the Catholic queen's daughter, lies buried in the *choir*. Turning to the enclosure, the so-called *patio de Laurel* attracts our attention, as do a number of beautifully decorated rooms, which include the queen's bedroom. The patio of the infirmary is Mudejar.

If we look at the exterior façade facing the small plaza, we can see an embedded stone *front* with carved coats-of-arms, part of what is left of the Alcázar of King Pedro ▶ page 127.

Santas Justa y Rufina, Church of

Open during worship hours.

This is the oldest church in Toledo, founded in 555 by the Visigoth Atanagildo. However, nothing is left of the Visigoth church, and very little of the Mudejar one, owing to a fire in the 16C. It was rebuilt, and its structure was further modified in 1800. Its most outstanding feature is the simple, plateresque *exterior façade*, alongside which a Moorish arch has been discovered atop a beautifully-rendered *Visigothic pilaster*. Circling the building will give us a look at another recent discovery, the Mudejar ▶ page 34 apse (its brick arch mostly destroyed) and a delightful popular Baroque painting whose days appear to be numbered.

Santa Leocadia, Basilica of

See 'Cristo de la Vega' ▶ page 110.

Santa Leocadia, Church of

Open during worship hours.

This church should not be confused with the ancient Visigothic basilica (currently the Cristo de la Vega hermitage). It stands on the 4C birthplace of the Toledan martyr saint —a victim of the Diocletian persecutions. In December of each year, visits can be made to the small *crypt* dug out of the rock, in which tradition claims to be the room in which the saint was born. The church was remodelled in the Mudejar style following the Reconquest, and was once again remodelled in the 18C upon orders of Queen María Luisa, the wife of Charles IV. From the Mudejar period we have the elegant tower, decorated with lobed arches. There is a very well restored wall section at the entrance, covered over until recently by an atrium and grating, which served to preserve it.

The sole nave was divided into three parts by Juan Bautista Monegro, who designed the classical doric columns on which the arches rest.

The main altar and the jasper *retable* are also of a classical bent; the painting is by Eugenio Caxés. In an altarpiece carved by Narciso Tomé (epistle side) we find the famous *Virgin of Good Health*, one of Toledo's most venerated miraculous images. There are other interesting *retablos* and paintings as well.

◉ ◉ Santa María la Blanca, Synagogue of

▶ page 131.

Santa Ursula, Convent of

Open during worship hours.

The church was rebuilt in the 14C. Note the interesting Mudejar architectural work above the entrance door. The restored apse is also Mudejar. Inside, the Mudejar structure has been hidden under a Baroque covering. There are a number of magnificent paintings.

However, the main attraction that makes a visit to this humble convent imperative is its splendid *altarpiece of the Visitation,* Berruguete, which was one of the treasures of the Santa Cruz Museum for a long time. Now it is back in its original home, in a chapel with a Gothic ceiling. It consists of three parts: the uppermost shows Calvary; the centre contains a scene of the Visitation; whilst the sides hold two oval paintings, one with San Cristóbal, and another with San Antonio. In the middle of the lower part is a relief of the Virgin of Bethlehem, with Saint John the Baptist and San Sebastián on the two side panels. Notice how the structure of the *reredos* breaks with the concept of Renaissance balance and presents us with Baroque forms and tension, with the latter best seen in the central group of the Visitation, a section virtually free of surrounding structures and with vigorous movement of its figures.

Santiago del Arrabal, Church of

Open only during worship hours.

Here we unquestionaby have one of the most beautiful Mudejar buildings in Toledo, as well as one of the best preserved. It was constructed upon the orders of Alfonso VI (12C) within the newly-

Church of Santiago del Arrabal

conquered area, in the neighbourhood close to the gate through which he had entered the city. Only the original **tower** remains, the oldest part of the complex, which stands apart from the rest of the building. Notice its double Moorish arch windows, framed by the typical Arabic *alfiz* (panel that starts from the impost).

The church is from a later date (mid-13C). It was built under the protection of the deposed Portuguese King Sancho II, and he spent his final years there. Rectangular, with three naves, its proportions are the most elegant of any Mudejar church in Toledo, making it a fine example of the so-called *mudéjar toledano* style, utilizing a mixture of rubblework interlaced with strips of brick.

The woodwork ceiling (15C) is beautifully wrought. One strange and archaic detail is its baptismal chapel, with stairsteps for baptism by immersion. Its *retable* is a magnificent 16C plateresque creation, and there are other beautiful altars and images. Next to the transept is a Mudejar masonry *pulpit.* Tradition tells us that from it San Vicente Ferrer launched his attacks against the doctrine of the unfaithful, leading to the conversion of Moors and Jews by the thousands. Legend also tells us that he set fire to the Jewish quarter (the *Judería*), subsequently instigating a horrible massacre for the greater glory of God. In memory of all this, there is a statue of the saint on the beautiful pulpit-altar.

Santo Cristo de la Luz, Hermitage of
▶ *page* 114.

Santo Cristo de la Vega, Hermitage of
More or less follows tourist hours.

What is today known as the Hermitage of Santo Cristo de la Vega stands outside the walls beneath the Cambrón Gate, on the banks of the Tagus and near to the Roman circus and other ruins.

Originally, this was the ancient *Basilica of Santa Leocadia*, one of Toledo's oldest churches. After Leocadia was martyred in the 4C, the Christians buried her in this spot and erected a hermitage over it. In the 7C, at the urging of Bishop San Eladio, King Sisebuto built a magnificent basilica here. Later it was the site of several of the famous *Concilios de Toledo* (Toledo Councils), probably in the 4, 5, 6 and 7C. In 660, during a meeting attended by King Recesvinto, Bishop San Ildefonso, nobility and clergy, Santa Leocadia appeared before San Ildefonso and left him a piece of her mantle, a deed recorded by the historians of the day. The hermitage hosted a steady stream of kings, queens, and bishops, including the good San Ildefonso himself, San Eugenio, San Julián and Gunderico. Later the building went through a succession of hard times and reconstruction: Mendoza rebuilt it in the 15C; there was another reconstruction in the 18C, and yet another after the War of Independence (early 19C), at which time it became a hermitage dedicated to the *Cristo de la Vega*.

Nowadays, little is left of its former Visigothic splendour, only an archaeological site that has furnished a number of pieces to the Archaeological and Council Museums. Excavation is sporadic, though at times profitable; it has given us an accurate picture of the former Visigothic basilica. The apse appears to be mostly intact, with certain restorations, in its 13C or 14C form, though the paintings have disappeared. In front of the main body of the church is a cemetery for priests dating from 1845.

Despite the tremendous historical and archaeological significance of this basilica, it is much more known through a popular tradition that the poet Zorilla immortalized in one of his works. It involves the legend of the Cristo de la Vega, which originated with the crucifix in the church, wherein one of Christ's hands has pulled free. It dates from the last century, replacing one burned by the French, and represents a possible link with the Descent motif. Many tales surround it —the conversion of a Jew, a soldier who took up the cloth, a maiden who used it as a witness to a suitor's promise, and so forth.

Santo Domingo el Antiguo, Monastery of

👁 👁

Visiting hours: 11.00 a.m. to 1.30 p.m and 4.00 to 6.30 p.m. Closed Sunday mornings. Private.

The name is intended to distinguish it from the other Santo Domingo (el Real). Dedicated to the holy abbot of the monastery of Silos, tradition (supported by some Visigothic ruins) tells us that it was built on the site of a monastery from the days of San Ildefonso, though it was most likely founded by Alfonso VI. First occupied by Benedictine nuns, it later adopted the Cistercian reforms in 1140. Its archives hold documents that link the convent to high-ranking personalities, including popes, kings and queens. When María de Silva (Philip II's first wife) was to be buried here in 1576, the church was rebuilt and enlarged, sketches by Herrera being utilized, replacing work by Vergara the Younger.

The *retables* were the work of a newcomer to the city —El Greco— and they represent his first efforts here. There are three of them, the main one and those on either side, the dual labour of the famous artist and Juan Bautista Monegro, the sculptor. Thus we would have a privileged look at a seminal work by the painter from Crete... if it weren't for the fact that practically all the originals were sold by the nuns, leaving mostly copies. Yet *three originals by El Greco* do remain *in situ*: the two *Saint Johns* on the main altarpiece and *Resurrection* on the epistle side. The copy of the retable on the evangelist side is by Jerónimo Seisdedos.

In front of the entry door is the *chapel* known as the *Capilla de Doña María de Silva*, with its striking retable and Gothic *Cristo de la Victoria*. Peeking through the grille will give us a look at the *Chapter Room* and its 16C Toledan tilework.

From inside the grille that separates the present choir from the rest of the church, a glass window opens onto the *crypt* where El Greco has been buried. The Register of the church of Santo Tomé in which his death has been inscribed is now on display in the El Greco house. The site of the crypt has only recently been discovered, giving us the chance to see the urn containing the artist's remains.

The present-day choir, a modern structure atop a base made from wood taken from the Mudejar roofs of the convent, contains several interesting paintings and altars, especially a Gothic *virgen sedente* a 16C *Santa Ana*, and a 17C *Ecce Homo*, along with a stunning Renaissance *communion rail* in the form of a retable.

If we go through a door on the left, we will enter the *choir* itself, recently open to the public, and a truly fascinating museum. The rectangular area sits under a coffered ceiling with lacunars; the flooring is of brick and Renaissance stone.

The presbytery also has its surprising treasures: a large *plateresque altarpiece* with frontispiece of Toledan tile; communion rail below the altar; and various plateresque *tombs* of polychrome plaster on either side.

There are also several valuable images, particularly a *Madonna* attributed to Alonso Cano, and a *Head of Saint John the Baptist* by Pedro de Mena. The walnut choir stalls are of a Renaissance simplicity.

Notice the *organ* and paintings. A glass case displays the contracts signed by El Greco for painting the *reredos* in the church.

Walking toward the rear will bring us to the *antechoir*, with a flat coffered ceiling overhead. Here is found a very beautiful alabaster Gothic *recumbent statue* of the Lord of Ajofrín in a Renaissance niche. The glass cases hold many fascinating documents from the archives, and the public display is continually updated. There are also several wood carvings, reliquaries, and rich gold and silverwork.

A great many *Mudejar remains* are to be found in the cloistered area, such as 14C paintings of the infirmary, coffered ceilings, plasterwork, and the Gothic balustrade pertaining to the *patio de los laureles*.

Santo Domingo el Real, Convent of

Open during worship hours, holidays and vespers.

Here we are in what may well be the most characteristic plaza of Toledo's hidden, peaceful side —a veritable route of tranquillity close to the *covered walkways*. Stone tablets on the walls of the plaza are reminders of the literary tradition of this tucked-away spot.

The Convent of Santo Domingo el Real, with its *Toledan portal* supported by graceful doric columns, offers a touch of originality to this location. The monastery was founded by Inés García de Meneses in 1364; it was later enlarged by Teresa Gómez de Toledo, who had a daughter by the King of Castile, Peter I. She withdrew with her child to this place, and eventually became its prioress. In the 16C, the building and church were once again remodelled. Other famous residents include the Queen of Portugal, Leonor de Aragón, and a granddaughter of King James II of Aragón. The princes Sancho and Diego, illegitimate sons of King Peter of Castile, are buried here. All things considered, the application of the name *Real* (Royal) to the monastery is quite justified.

The church is laid out in a quite original fashion. Its large nave is covered by an elliptical vault painted in *trompe l'oeil* and with pendentives on which the four evangelists are found. Two chapels open up at one end of the rectangle, including the *main chapel*. At the other end is the *nuns' choir* belonging to the cloistered part. There are excellent 17C *reredos*, particularly in the smaller chapel and in front of the entry screen. Approach the communion rail (made of Talaveran tile), and you will be able to see the spacious choir, its *choir stalls* and beautiful coffered ceiling. The church has been recently restored.

Particularly noteworthy in the cloistered monastery is its *medieval patio* and two-tiered gallery with Gothic arches and doors covered with Mudejar plasterwork. This is the so-called 16C *patio de la Mona*; there is also a *pulpit* with Mudejar plasterwork from the refectory.

Santos Justo y Pastor, Church of

Located in yet another of Toledo's tucked-away and tranquil plazas is a church whose modern appearance is misleading, because it was founded shortly after the Reconquest. Later, in the 14C, it was remodelled under the sponsorship of the Count of Orgaz, and underwent further changes in the late 18C. The main body of the church dates from this period, with the remaining structure of the Mudejar church having been covered up, though we can get an idea of it from the small arches in the apse. The tower is capped by a strange *churrigueresque spire*.

Inside the church, on the epistle side, there are a number of interesting chapels. In one of them, which features a beautiful Gothic arch, we find the *tomb* of Juan Guas, the grand architect of the Catholic Monarchs. The 14C *Chapel of Corpus Christi* contains some excellent Mudejar plasterwork decorating the tombs along the walls,

Altarpiece, Church of Santo Domingo

whilst overhead is a coffered ceiling with its polychromatic interlaced arches. The painting on the main altarpiece is by Gregorio Ferro (1807). To the left and near the door is a small retable with the popular *Merciful Christ*, the source of a curious legend: during the 15C, a feud existed between two families, the Ayalas and the Silvas. One night a member of one of the families was captured; he began to pray, whereupon the wall tumbled down and the man found that he was inside the church, thereby safe from harm. The cracks in the wall are said to have been caused by the knives of his infuriated captors.

Santo Tomé, Church of

Burial of the Count of Orgaz. Visiting hours: 10.00 a.m. to 1.45 p.m. and 3.30 to 6.00 p.m.; in summer open until 7.00 p.m. Private. Church is open during worship hours.

Located in one of the main areas of the city, its fame and interest can be attributed to two things: the church itself, with its beautiful Mudejar *tower*, and secondly, the fact that it houses one of the world's indisputable masterworks of art, El Greco's *Burial of the Count of Orgaz.*

There are references to the existence of this church in the 12C, though it was rebuilt in the early 14C by the Count of Orgaz, Gonzalo Ruiz de Toledo, the Notary of Castile. The *tower*, one of the best examples of Mudejar architecture in Toledo and one of the city's most characteristic landmarks, dates from this period. Look for stones and Visigothic niches amongst its glazed ceramic incrustations.

Its modern interior has a number of interesting items, especially the platerasque *retable of San Jerónimo*, by Hernando de Avila (16C). In addition, there is another Baroque altarpiece with the Virgin of Guadalupe, a 16C marble baptismal font, and a striking *Smiling Virgin*, a polychromatic marble from the 13C. Its extraordinary sweetness is reminiscent of the *Virgen Blanca* at the Cathedral here, and here too, the child is lovingly caressing the Virgin. Also of importance is the painting by Vicente López that hangs in the presbytery. The *Burial* has its own chapel at one end of the church, with a separate entrance to avoid disturbing worshippers.

🔵 🔵　In the words of the critic Camón Aznar, the *Burial of the Count of Orgaz* represents *not only the pinnacle of El Greco's work, but also that of universal art as a whole*. A strong statement, yet one that has been seconded time and time again.

The painting dates from 1586, during a period when El Greco was at the peak of his maturity. It was painted specifically for this chapel, and it has never left it —perhaps in part due to its measurements: 7.7 x 4.7m. In reality, the painting represents a miracle, a miracle expressed so naturally in the action lived out by the participants that one is hardly aware of it: Count Orgaz, who had taken part in the founding of a convent dedicated to San Agustín, had left provisions in his will for the dedication of a church to San Esteban. At the moment of his burial, both saints appeared in the flesh and laid the Count to rest in his grave, a miracle that occurred in 1312.

The structural force and organic unity of this painting are extraordinary. For a long time, it was looked at from a dual-level standpoint: historians focused on the lower part, whilst critics directed their attention to the upper, heavenly region. With the mountain of criticism that currently exists, the tendency now is to recognize the overall unity and naturalness that unite terrestial and celestial beings as the Count's soul passes into glory.

A brief summary of factual material: all the men in the painting were living at the time, including the architect Covarrubias, Andrés Núñez and the Count of Benavente. The one that is looking directly at us from the left is El Greco; he and the child —his son, Jorge Manuel— appear to be the only ones who have drawn out of their shell in order to engage the onlooker. The handkerchief protruding from the boy's pocket has a date, 1578, the year of his birth.

Mosques

🔵 Cristo de la Luz, Mosque of

This small building is found close to the Bab-Mardón and Sol Gates, and is one of those most dearly linked to the cycle of Toledan legends. One of them, from which its name comes, tells of a Visigothic church that was once on this spot and how a Jew came to spread poison on the foot of the venerated figure of Christ; however, each time a Christian started to kiss the foot, it would pull away. Infuriated, the Jews attacked the statue with a pick and tossed it into a dungheap. Soon after, the blood that had flowed from the wound left a miraculous shining trail of light leading to the dungheap and to the discovery of the desecrators. The site was later named the *patio del Cristo*. There is another legend dealing with the entry of the Moors into the city. The Christians hid the image inside a hollow wall, along with a burning candle. Centuries later, when Alfonso VI liberated the city, he was crossing in front of the mosque on horseback when his horse suddenly dropped to its knees. No one could make it stand up until the image was discovered, with the candle still burning. There is a white stone marking the spot where the horse knelt down. The image of the Christ is now in the Hospital de Santa Cruz Museum.

Legends aside, the building was constructed in 980 by Muza Ibn Alí as ordered by a Toledan Walí, perhaps to be used as a burial chamber. In the 12C, it was converted into a Christian church, with the transept and apse being added at that time.

The exterior is profusely and richly decorated. There is a *brick inscription* on the façade, with the date and architect's name. The mosque itself, a square building, is divided into nine sections by four columns with *Visigothic and Moslem capitals* that support Moorish arches. Each of these nine parts is covered by a ribbed vault in the *califa* tradition. Each vault is different (note that the ribs do not meet in the centre), which makes the building a showcase for the architect who designed it.

The Christian apse, also made of brick, has its interior covered over with rather damaged *Romanesque paintings*, though they are of considerable interest: these are among the few *Romanesque paintings* still preserved in Toledo; together with the ones at San Román and a few others, they have led to the idea of a Toledan school of Romanesque painting, quite different from the other Castilian schools and strongly influenced by the surrounding Islamic elements.

Christ of Light Mosque

Tornerías, Mosque of

It takes its name (meaning lathework) from the street where it is located —the street that leads to the *Reloj* Gate of the Cathedral. There is controversy over whether it actually was a mosque, since it is on a second-storey, and not at ground level as the Koran requires. Nor is its age free of controversy, though most probably it was built during the latter part of the 10C or the early part of the 11C. In either case, it is closely modelled on the previous design of the Cristo de la Luz. By the same token, its small size has led some to believe that it may have been a sort of private chapel. Square in shape, its four columns and their simple capitals serve to divide it into three naves, each with three sections. The result is nine spaces, the same as for the Cristo de la Luz. It was acquired by the General Office of Fine Arts in 1968, with reconstruction beginning at that time.

Museums

● Casa de El Greco (El Greco House)
Visiting hours: 10.00 a.m. to 2.00 p.m. and 4.00 to 6.00 p.m.; in summer open until 7.00 p.m. Closed Sunday afternoons and Mondays. Government-owned.

The entire area around the Sinagoga del Tránsito, where the house is located, was at one time part of the *Palacios de Samuel ha-Leví*, King Peter's treasurer and the builder of the synagogue. A century later, the *palacios* passed into the hands of Juan Pacheco, Marquis of Villena. There is a legend that says they were also the home of the necromancer Enrique de Aragón (incorrectly misnamed the Marquis of Villena), a man who once practised his witchcraft and necromancy in the very basement where the treasures of Samuel ha-Leví were supposedly hidden.

At a later date, the mansions once more became the scene of a famous episode, this one with a more knightly flavour. A celebrated romance poem by the Duque de Rivas, *Un castellano leal*, tells of how the Count of Benavente set fire to his *palacio* after the Emperor had forced him to provide lodging for a traitor, the Constable of Bourbon.

Toward the end of the last century, as the Generation of 98 promoted the 'El Greco' revival, the Villena houses were identified, lying in ruins as they were. The houses, ruins, and underground structures were purchased, and a group of Toledan artisans were given the work of restoring the premises. Thus the present-day El Greco House came into being. It should not be considered a reproduction, since there has never been any trace of the actual building; instead, it is simply a living monument in memory of the great painter, and a remembrance of the times in which he lived. Along with the house, another building has been constructed by utilizing a nearby Renaissance mansion, the site of the projected Museum of Toledo.

Although the house is of relatively recent construction, it nonetheless is a very faithful copy of an elegant house of El Greco's day (1541-1614). The furniture and decorations were very carefully chosen by the Marquis de la Vega-Inclán and his enthusiastic collaborators, who combed antique shops and towns throughout the province. It was inaugurated in 1910.

● ● *El Greco's paintings* naturally stand out among the treasure-trove of works in the house and museum. Here we have the series *Christ and the Apostles*, paintings from the defunct Hospital of Santiago. According to Manuel Cossío, critic and author of a major study of the

painter, it represents *the utmost limit of the restlessness, and abnormality attained by his painting in his search for greater spiritual exaltation.* Of prime interest amongst this group is the strikingly beautiful *Saviour.* There is also the *View of Toledo,* which provides us with a faithful photographic rendering and an accurate layout of the city at the time. In addition, there are various portraits and an enormous painting of San Bernardino, which El Greco painted in 1603 for the Colegio de San Bernardino (also destroyed). The altarpiece holding the canvas was also designed by the painter; at one time, they were separate, but they were later joined and the present **chapel** was built to house them. (The Mudejar coffered ceiling is from Valladolid.)

However, the El Greco paintings are not the only thing of value to be found here. There are several 15C panels, as well as paintings by Tristán, Ribalta, Jerónimo Jacinto de Espinosa, Herrera el Viejo, Carreño de Miranda, Murillo, Valdés Leal, Juan Bautista del Moro, Alonso Martínez Espinar, and others.

Casa de las Cadenas, Museo de Arte Contemporáneo (House of Chains, Museum of Contemporary Art)

This typical *Toledan house* is also the home of another legend. It once belonged to the Zárate family, and was later sold to a Jewish *converso* (a convert to Christianity) named Ismael, who set up a blacksmith shop in the basement. Night and day, his neighbours could hear him hammering on his anvil. Although he turned out doorknockers, horseshoes, farm equipment and the like, he was particularly prolific at making chains. According to his neighbours, these fetters were loaded on muleback in the dead of night, and were transported to Andalusia, to Granada, where the Moors were using them to shackle their Christian captives. Upon the liberation of the Christians, these same fetters were brought back to Toledo and hung from the walls of San Juan de los Reyes, where they remain to this day. As proof of their manufacture at the hands of Ismael, it was said that their expert forging could only have come from the Jewish hatred of Christians, mixed with the waters of the Tagus...

Thus goes the tradition, and the likely source of the name, *Casa de las Cadenas*; no doubt there was a drawing of chains in some place, indicating that asylum could be sought here —in addition to the notoriety of its owner. This is one of Toledo's most incredible houses, and we are fortunate that the installation of the **Museum of Contemporary Art** has led to its preservation.

The architecture of this 15C house is admirable. The capitals in the patio are finely wrought, the wooden galleries are well-proportioned, and a number of murals, plaster artwork, coffered ceilings, and shutters have been preserved, as well as the *arrabases*, or Arabic-style decorative trims around the arches and windows.

The museum was inaugurated in March 1975. Since space is a bit cramped, and modern-day production rather copious, it was decided to offer an exhibition of contemporary Spanish *figurative art*. One exception is Room I, where we can see a number of impressionistic landscapes of Toledo by Aureliano de Beruete and Arredondo.

A selection of artists to be found in the remaining rooms includes Agustín Redondela, Barjola, Menchu Gal, Andrés Novillo, Benjamín Palencia, Pancho Cossío, Vaquero Turcios, Echauz, Oscar Estruga, Alcorlo, Beulas, Peinado, and Agustín de Celis.

The rooms dedicated to *Alberto Sánchez* deserve our special attention. This painter, born here in 1895, was a self-taught man who earned his living by working as a baker, blacksmith, shoemaker and apprentice to a sculptor. His work, shown at the 1925 Exposition of Iberian Artists, was an instant success. This led to a pension from the Toledo provincial government, effectively the beginning of his professional life. He emigrated to Russia in 1938, and for the remainder of his life he was an art professor in Moscow, dying there in 1962. Alberto Sánchez was a banned artist during the Franco years, a man who lived in obscurity. Only recently has he begun to be revived and recognised, along with many other Spanish artists and intellectuals dispersed by the Civil War.

Hospital de Santa Cruz (Museum of Fine Arts, Provincial Museum of Archaeology and Museum of Applied Arts)
Visiting hours: 10.00 a.m. to 6.00 p.m. Sundays: 10.00 a.m. to 2.00 p.m. Closed Mondays. Government-owned.

If we descend from Zocodover through the *Arco de la Sangre*, on our left we will find the Hospital of Santa Cruz. Tradition tells us that this spot was where the mythical *Palacios de Galiana* were located (the ones in the city, since there were others in la Vega). Here lived the celebrated Moorish princess whom Charlemagne would take back with him to his kingdom. Here is the site of another deep-rooted Toledan legend, that of Santa Casilda, Moorish princess and daughter of Alamún. One day she was surprised by her father as she was taking buns to the Christian captives, whereupon the buns turned into roses.

After Toledo was retaken by Alfonso VI, the Santa Fe chapel was founded in the upper part of the city. A Benedictine community was founded in the central part, the *Monastery of San Pedro de las Dueñas*. In the 14C, under the regency of María de Molina, the lower part was ceded to a Franciscan community. The Franciscans later moved to their new church of San Juan de los Reyes, and the Benedictines came to occupy the vacant convent, which is the present *Convento de la Concepción Francisca*. The *palacios* in the central part were therefore vacated, and the Cardinal of Spain, Pedro González de Mendoza, subsequently created a home for foundlings in them, the present Hospital of Santa Cruz.

The building was constructed between 1509 and 1514, based on designs by Enrique Egas. Both the upper and lower storeys consist of two spacious naves that cross in the centre, forming a Greek cross, the idea being to place the altar at this point so that it could be seen from all four arms. The intersection sits underneath a stellar vault, whilst there are Mudejar coffered ceilings over the naves. In addition to the layout, Egas was also responsible for the Gothic vault in the chapel, the coffered ceilings and the *califa* vault, as well as the parietal, isabelline decoration of the transept. The second stage of work saw the introduction of the new Renaissance style that was beginning to take hold in Spain; the building was one of the first to reflect this new form. The architect in charge of this stage was Covarrubias, possibly assisted by other illustrious artists. The construction included the façade, the vestibule doors, the main patio and the splendid staircase between the two floors.

Hospital of Santa Cruz

The *southern façade,* or the main one through which the building is entered, is a lavish, harmonious and beautiful example of early Spanish Renaissance, where we can still see a mixture of Gothic and the new plateresque decoration. Looking at the relief on the tympanum, we can see the Empress Santa Helena showing the Holy Cross to a kneeling Cardinal Mendoza. Equally interesting is the interior of the façade, inside the vestibule.

The *main staircase* also surprises us with its ornateness: an overall embossed surface is seen in the well, whilst all the hangings on the arches and balustrade are done in delicately-rendered grotesques. Particular attention should also be paid to the *porch* on the upper gallery (leading to the exhibition of popular art), with its finely-worked plateresque decoration. Only one *patio* can be visited, the most grandiose of the three. The second contains columns with Visigothic capitals, and the third dates from a later period and is simpler.

The hospital continued to operate until 1846, when it was turned over to the military (being promptly sectioned up and otherwise disfigured). A restoration was initiated in 1902, and in 1919 the collection from the Provincial Archaeological Museum was installed in the building. The structure was divided up even further, along with the addition of more collections from churches and convents, leading to its current status as a three-pronged museum, as will be explained.

The *Museo de Artes Aplicadas y Populares* or **Museum of Applied and Popular Arts** is a bit chaotic, as regards arrangement as well as content (data may also be on the hazy side). Nonetheless, we can admire old Talaveran pottery, an exhibition of popular pottery, textiles and embroideries galore, wrought iron, and more.

The *Museo de Santa Cruz,* or Fine Arts Museum, occupies the four arms of the basic Greek-cross layout, each with two storeys. The museum has acquired an extremely large collection, not all of which is on display. This includes a magnificent collection of paintings, a representative amount of sculpture, a tremendous array of textiles and liturgical vestments, and an equally large collection of gold and silver pieces. Rounding out this treasure are such items as furniture, documents and seals.

Outstanding amongst the paintings are *twenty works by El Greco,* including his *San Francisco, San José with the Child,* and in particular, the *Assumption.* The latter, still to be found in its original *altarpiece* from the church of San Vicente, may well be the most representative work of the artist's late period (it was exuberantly praised by Rilke).

Other highly-interesting paintings are the *Crucified Christ,* by Goya; a *Holy Family* by Ribera, illustrative of his later, dark *tenebrista* style; the *Descent from the Cross* by Lucas Jordán; several works by Tristán and Orrentes, and a good cross-section of Castilian masters from the 15 and 16C (Comontes and others).

The sculpture collection is also noteworthy, such as the *Ecce Homo;* the *Madonna,* attributed to Mena; the bust of Juanelo by Juan Bautista Monegro, the beloved *Cristo de la Luz,* and a number of retables.

The huge flags decorating the chapel are the standards borne by Don Juan of Austria at the Battle of Lepanto.

The glass cases hold a wide variety of documents, seals, coins, arms, textiles and religious objects.

Also noteworthy is the Flemish tapestry collection from the 16 and 17C, with particular emphasis on the so-called *Astrolabe Tapestry* (15C). As a final touch to the exemplary collection at this museum, there are a number of fine rugs and furniture pieces.

Library, Hospital of Tavera

The *Museo Provincial de Arqueología* or **Provincial Museum of Archaeology** is located in the buildings surrounding the main patio. The museum has been subjected to a series of structural upheavals: most of its Mudejar section was carted off to the *Taller del Moro* (Moor's Workshop) in 1963, whilst in 1973 the greater part of its Visigothic collection was transferred to the new *Museo de los Concilios*.

Thus, its most attractive collection most likely involves the prehistorical and Roman exhibitions. The *prehistorical section* has just been installed in the building basement, which has been splendidly prepared for this purpose (for example, polychromatic coffered ceilings have been obtained from other sites in Toledo). The focal point of this exhibition has long been the private collection of the enlightened Cardinal Lorenzana, and it includes fossils, mammoth remains, pottery, stone and bronze weapons, and more. Of particular note is the pottery and Iberian relief figures, all of which come from the province. On view in the *Roman section* is a series of mosaics found in Toledo's la Vega, highlighted by the reconstruction of a burial site from the period and numerous carved stones. The Arabic and Mudejar sections contain pottery, carved wood, and inscriptions, among other interesting pieces.

Hospital de Tavera

Visiting hours: 10.30 a.m. to 1.30 p.m. and 3.30 to 6.00 p.m. Private.

Founded by Cardinal Juan Pardo de Tavera, it is also known as the Hospital of Saint John the Baptist, to whom it was dedicated, as well as the *Hospital de Afuera* (Outside Hospital), since it stands outside the city walls. Cardinal Tavera ordered it to be built in 1539. Its architect was Bartolomé de Bustamante, who later became a Jesuit and passed the work on to the Vergaras (the Elder and the Younger). Tavera died not long after work began; the result was delays that postponed the completion of the church until 1624, with the hospital having never been finished. Even today, one can see that the upper part of the main façade and rear half of the building are incomplete. The *portico* of the main façade was installed in the 18C. The hospital was under the patronage of the ducal house of Medinaceli, whilst today the patroness is the Duchess of Lerma, who fitted out the building and opened the museum in 1962.

Most of all, you must visit the formidable *patio* —or rather, the patios, since there is one on either side of the building, separating the main façade of the church. The entry to the church is a beautiful *portico* by Berruguete, to whom we also owe the crowning jewel of the hospital: the magnificent white marble *tomb* of Cardinal Tavera. (A work, however, that the artist did not finish; he died suddenly in this very hospital.)

The *Museum* is actually a number of *palacio* rooms which have been made into an exhibition space, and which at times are used by private parties.

Visits can be made to the Duchess's dining room, the Hospital library, certain second-storey rooms, the bedroom belonging to the Duke and Duchess, and other areas.

Because paintings and other objects may get shifted around from time to time, we will only comment in a general sense on the more significant items that can usually be found somewhere in the museum.

● There are a number of *El Grecos*, including such major works as the *Holy Family*, which many believe to be the artist's family. There is also a magnificent version of *Saint Peter's Tears*, a congenial portrait of Tavera, the founder; and a San Francisco. We are drawn to another work by El Greco, the small statue of *The Saviour*, whose beauty and brazenness is almost pagan, not a common trait of the mystical painter.

Another centrepiece of the museum —and most certainly a strange one— is Ribera's *Bearded Woman*. It represents a curiosity of the day, a woman from Naples who was masculine to the point of growing a beard, a fact that Ribera exaggerated somewhat by using a male model. Also by Ribera is the portrait of a philosopher... whose head has overheated to the point where it is necessary to pour water on it.

Though it is a copy, Titian's *Charles V in Mühlberg* is no less impressive than the original in the Prado Museum. Zurbarán is represented by a fine portrait of the Duke of Medinaceli, and there are two magnificent portraits by Moro. Rounding out the paintings are works of varying quality —by Synder, Tintoretto, Lucas Jordán...

The ambience of the museum is substantially enhanced by furniture and other valuable objects, such as mirrors, cabinets, tables, *bargueños*, braziers, etc. The visit should also include the splendid and recently-restored *Farmacia del Hospital*, or hospital pharmacy (16C).

Museos Catedralicios (Cathedral Museums)

▶ *page 88*.

Museo de Armas de la Real Fábrica de Armas (Arms Museum of the Royal Arms Works)

▶ *page 128*.

Museo de Santo Domingo el Antiguo (Santo Domingo el Antiguo Museum)

▶ *page* 111.

Museo Romero Ortiz (Romero Ortiz Museum)

▶ *page* 85.

Museo Sefardí (Sephardic Museum)

▶ *page* 130.

Museo Victorio Macho (Victorio Macho Museum)

This museum occupies the former house and workshop of the sculptor from Palencia. It is located looking out over the *Roca Tarpeya* with a majestic view of the cliffs above the Tagus and the San Martín Bridge.

Inaugurated in 1967, it holds materials bequeathed by the artist: sketches, drawings, models, and a number of sculptures by this 20C sculptor. The museum is presently closed for renovation.

Museo Visigótico y de los Concilios (Visigothic and Council Museum)

▶ *page* 106.

Taller del Moro (Moor's Workshop and Mudejar Museum)

Visiting hours: 10.00 a.m. to 2.00 p.m and 4.00 to 7.00 p.m. Closed Sunday afternoons and Mondays. Government-owned.

The *Taller del Moro* is unquestionably one of Toledo's most interesting and significant secular Mudejar monuments. It pertains to the oldest part of the *palacios* of Ayala and Fuensalida —one cannot find a more Mudejar structure. Outside, we are greeted by little more than blank walls; inside, we are in the presence of a finely-wrought piece of art. The name *taller* may have come from its ancient use as lodging for the stonemasons who worked on the cathedral during the 16C, although it has also been a sort of catch-all —convent, match factory, even a garage. Be that as it may, we most definitely have a stately Mudejar mansion that is an incredibly faithful reproduction of a Moorish-Andalusian *palacio*: a large room with a small bedroom (or *alhamía*) at either end; lavish *coffered ceilings;* walls and their *plasterwork* profusely decorated with geometrical designs, plants, and inscriptions in both Arabic and Spanish. It was the custom of eminent Christian families of the 14 and 15C to outfit their mansions in this lavish style, for which they hired Mudejar or Moorish masons.

The building we see today has been extremely well restored (especially if we compare it to old photographs that show the deteriorated plasterwork). Adding to its delights, a part of the Arabic and Mudejar section of the Santa Cruz Archaeological Museum has been brought here. There are examples of *tilework* from the 15 and 16C, glazed ceramic well curbs, Arabic and Mudejar vats, beams and wood carvings, flagstones, stones with Spanish and Arabic inscriptions, and so on.

Palaces, Mansions and Civic Architecture

Ayuntamiento (City Hall)

The current building, extremely harmonious and well-balanced, was built in the 17C from plans by Jorge Manuel Theotocópulus, the son of El Greco. It occupies the site of the original *Casa de la Ciudad* (City House) that had been there since the 15C. Before then, the city council met in the house of the magistrates or in the cathedral cloisters.

From the entrance hall at the northeastern façade, you arrive at the *Summer Chapter Room*. This spacious room is decorated with 17C tile representing events from the Battle of Flanders. Whilst in the hall, observe the stone staircase from whose walls hang two large portraits of Charles II and his wife, Mariana, the work of Carreño de Miranda. There is also a stone tablet on which some verses attributed to Jorge Manrique are engraved.

Upstairs is the *sala capitular alta*, or *Upper Chapter Room*, decorated with Baroque mouldings and frescos. Above the entrance is a marble tablet with the record of the conceptionist oath sworn by Toledo in 1617, when the city vowed as one to defend the theory that the Virgin Mary was conceived without original sin. The walls hold portraits of distinguished Toledans who have been honoured with pensions and other grants by the city council.

Baño de la Caba (La Caba's Bathing Spot)
▶ *page 15.*

Bridges
▶ *page 14.*

Casa del Diamantista y Embarcadero (Diamond-cutter's House and Dock)
▶ *page 14.*

Casa de El Greco (El Greco House)
▶ *page 116.*

Casa de Garcilaso (Garcilaso House)
▶ *page 23.*

Casa de los Armiño (Los Armiños House)
▶ *page 22.*

Casa de los Templarios, o del Duende (Templars House, or House of the Spirit)
▶ *page 24.*

Casa de Munárriz (Munárriz House)
▶ *page 24.*

Casa de Padilla (Padilla House)
▶ *page 23.*

Castillo de San Servando (Castle of San Servando)

There may have been a Moorish fortress here previously. We know that Alfonso VI, upon regaining Toledo, restored or rebuilt a castle as a defence for the city, and brought in a Cluniac community to occupy it. The Moors returned several times in an attempt to retake the city, which prompted the monks to leave the castle. Its defence was then handed over to the mayor, Alvar-Yánez Minalla, and subsequently to the order of the Templars. When this order was suppressed in the 13C, the castle was left vacant and slowly fell into ruins. It was later restored twice, though all attempts at making it functional have proved unsuccessful, resulting in an abandonment only interrupted by its use as a temporary livestock pen.

Most of what we see now is an extensive restoration in the Mudejar style that was carried out by Archbishop Tenorio in the 14C. Next to the entry door, dug out of the rock, are several *rupestrian graves*, almost certainly dating from the days of the monks.

Circo romano (Roman Circus)
▶ *page 13.*

Colegio de Doncellas Nobles (School of the Noble Maidens)
▶ *page 22.*

Colegio de Santa Catalina (School of Santa Catalina)
▶ *page 130.*

Cueva de Hercules (Cave of Hercules)
▶ *page 23.*

El Nuncio, formerly a lunatic Asylum

The name comes from Francisco Ortiz, the papal nuncio of Pope Sixtus IV. In 1483, he established a lunatic asylum in his own house, on the street currently called Nuncio Viejo. In the 18C, the enlightened and illustrious Cardinal Lorenzana wished to endow the establishment with a worthy building; the task was given to Ignacio Haam, who designed and built the structure we see here.

The stone and brick building is, obviously, Neoclassical. Its large, two-part façade, crowned by a sizeable coat-of-arms pertaining to Lorenzana, reminds us of the University.

Within the rectangular layout of the building are four interior and quite simple patios. If we climb the wide stone staircase from the vestibule, we will arrive at the elliptical chapel, located in the exact centre; a division into two equal parts is therefore created, one for women and the other for men.

The building is currently being used by the regional government of Castile-La Mancha to house its Territorial Policy and Economic Affairs departments.

Gates
▶ page 15.
Hospital del Rey (King's Hospital)
▶ page 23.
Hospital de Santa Ana (Santa Ana Hospital)
▶ page 22.

Interior, El Greco House

Palacio Arzobispal (Archbishop's Palace)

Originally on this site there was a group of houses, in front of the mosque, that King Alfonso VIII gave to Archbishop Rodrigo Ximénez de Rada. Successive Cardinals remodelled and enlarged the premises, mainly Cardinals Sandoval y Rojas and Lorenzana. Most of what we see was done by the former, though there is still a façade that pre-dates the time of Tavera, whose coat-of-arms is seen supported by a host of angels (an emblem that has been called cold, austere, sombre, out-of-proportion, and more). Cardinal Lorenzana was responsible for the remodelled eastern façade, where the arch that stands between the *palacio* and the cathedral is found; he was also responsible for changes on the northern and western sides. The interior is of less interest, save for an occasional gallery, the coffered ceilings, and certain paintings. Nonetheless, two rooms do merit our attention: The *capilla arzobispal*, and most of all, the so-called *Council Room*.

The name of the latter comes from its having been the site of meetings of the provincial and diocesan councils during the 16C. Here, too, Cardinal Lorenzana set up a sort of *Natural History Museum*. This collection subsequently led to the creation of the Archaeological Museum we see today, with the addition of other antiquities and artifacts the diligent cardinal salvaged from digs. The *Salón de Concilios* later served to house part of the *Provincial Library* yet another contribution of the good Cardinal —who had at his disposal the library of the recently-expelled Jesuits (shown the door in 1767). A restoration carried out by Cardinal Segura in 1930, however, was not kind to the room. In one section of the tower there is an interesting plaster frieze, along with coats-of-arms of Castile and of Archbishop Palomeque (1299-1310).

Palacio de Benacazón (Benacazón Palace)

Palacio de Fuensalida (Fuensalida Palace)

This mansion comes down from the former *palacio de los Ayala*, the family who had Santo Tomé for its private chapel. It was built circa 1440 by the first Count of Fuensalida, Pedro López de Ayala, whose coat-of-arms can be seen on the façade. At one time, this was the residence of the Empress Isabel of Portugal, wife of Charles V and mother of Philip II. Her death here (in childbirth) led to a celebrated conversion: the sight of the funeral cortege caused the Duke of Gandía to begin reflecting on the misery and vanity of this world; as a result, he became a Jesuit, and was later canonized as San Francisco de Borja.

Pay particular attention to the outside *façade*, which follows the design of *palacio* architecture that was popular throughout the 15C. Inside, a number of interesting Mudejar, Gothic and plateresque elements can be seen, especially the former (friezes and plasterwork).

The *patio*, also adhering to this style, is two-storeyed, with brick pillars and magnificent lintels. Over the staircase is a plateresque coffered ceiling, whilst there are Ayala coats-of-arms scattered throughout the building.

This mansion is currently the presidency headquarters of the Castile-La Mancha regional government, and is not open for visits.

Palacios de Galiana (Galiana Palaces)

This name covers two different locations: the mythical *Palacio de*

Galiana, originally found on the site of the present-day hospital of Santa Cruz ▶ page 118, and another building outside the walls, currently known *as the Palacio de Fuera* (Outside Palace), in the *Huerta del Rey*.

Linked to the former is a cycle of legends and romantic literature dealing with the beautiful *Princess Galiana*, daughter of the Moorish King Galafre, whose hand was won by Charlemagne as a result of a knightly battle with the Moorish King Bradamante. Another legend unfolding in these buildings tells of *Santa Casilda*, daughter of Almamún, who emigrated to Burgos and later attained sainthood.

The *Palacio de Fuera*, also lauded in poetry, stands on the banks of the Tagus with its clepsydras, or water clocks. Here Alfonso VI hid as a political refugee in the court of Alamamún, before he became King of Castile. The area where he went out to stroll is now known as the *Huerta del Rey*.

The building we see may date from the 14C, and could have been rebuilt by Archbishop Gómez Manrique (1362-1377), whose coats-of-arms are on display. Another more-recent proprietor of the building was the Empress Eugenia de Montijo. After having been urged to undertake a restoration, she was —as had the earlier Princess Galiana— also kidnapped, in this case, whisked away to become the bride of France's Napoleon III. Her plan to create a fairyland palace was never carried out. In 1960, a more sensible restoration was carried out; today we can see the true elegance of the rectangular brick building, with its tower on either side and its Moorish-arch entryway. Inside we will find paintings and 14C Mudejar decorations, as well as a garden that lends its charm to the atmosphere of this celebrated structure.

Although it is privately owned, it may be visited by asking the guard for the key.

Palacio del Rey Don Pedro I (Palace of King Peter I)

The original *palacio* no longer exists; the building given this name is a stately house whose architecture is more closely linked to the mid-15C, rather than the 14C, when King Peter lived.

However, it is true that once there was a *palacio* here, one that stood where we see the monastery of Santa Isabel and the *seminario menor*. Only a few scattered remains are left, including the strikingly beautiful *façade*, through which the cloistered convent of Santa Isabel can be entered from the small plaza. Here we see coats-of-arms bearing a castle, wolves and saltires (X's), pertaining to the Ayala family, the maternal surname of King Ferdinand. And in reality, this misnamed Alcázar del Rey Don Pedro once belonged to the Catholic Monarch and the Ayala family. Inside the convent of Santa Isabel are some outstanding remains of Mudejar architecture ▶ page 34, though they cannot be visited (again, we have a cloistered convent). We can, however, go into the *seminario menor*, which will bring us to a large *Renaissance patio* on whose walls remains of *Mudejar plasterwork* are found, no doubt a part of the original, fragmented mansion.

Palacio de Trastámara (Trastámara Palace)

In the 15C, this spot was occupied by the so-called *Corral de Don Diego*, or Diego's Playhouse, named after Diego García de Toledo. A theatre at the time, it is now a neighbourhood courtyard (thus spanning the two meanings of the word *corral* in Spanish). At its entrance stands a *Mudejar façade* with floral decorations on its lintel. This is a survivor of the magnificent *palacio* of Henry of Trastámara, the bastard brother of Peter the Cruel. (In 1369 Peter was killed in battle, and Henry assumed the throne of Castile.)

There is a room at the rear of the patio with an octagonal wood ceiling and plasterwork bearing various coats-of-arms and inscriptions. Here we have evidence that Henry's *palacio* was of Mudejar style similar to the residences of the eminent families of 14 and 15C Toledo —the *Salón de Mesa* or the *Taller del Moro* stands as additional proof.

Posada/Cárcel de la Hermandad (Inn/Jail of the Brotherhood)

In 12C Toledo, an armed organization was formed under the name of the Holy Brotherhood as a protection against bandits. The group received generous privileges from Ferdinand III, and it was reorganized by the Catholic Monarchs. Charles V later renewed all of its privileges. The magnificent building here served as a prison for the Brotherhood, which remained in existence until it was disbanded by Isabel II in 1835; it then became a privately-owned *posada* (inn), as it is now called.

Here is an instance of a painstakingly-restored structure from the age of the Catholic Monarchs. Its handsome *façade* reflects the Toledan architecture of the day, with its two side columns and projecting lintels. Beneath a pointed arch in its second section, we can see the coat-of-arms of the Catholic Monarchs, along with yokes and arrows, and an imperial coat-of-arms. Surrounding it are statues of *Hermandad* crossbowmen, along with polychromatic remains.

Inside are *calabozos* (cells, hence calaboose) in the basement, damp, dark and unprotected places that open onto a gloomy and narrow patio. (We are reminded of Poe's *The Pit and the Pendulum*, his gruesome tale that takes place in a Toledo *calabozo* during the Inquisition.) There are other cells arranged around a chapel and in a less-foreboding patio. Upstairs we will find an uninviting room in shambles, the *Sala de Juntas* (Meeting Room) or *Sala de Justicia*. In spite of its splendid coffered ceiling and the remains of 16C murals (more *Hermandad* crossbowmen), it is hard to avoid a sense of oppression and desolation emanating from this fearful area.

Royal Arms Factory

The famous Toledan swordsmiths of yore gradually became scattered to the four winds. Toward the late 18C, Charles III gathered together those he could find and founded the *Real Fábrica de Armas*, with the building (Sabatini) being inaugurated in July, 1783.

Current production at this plant mainly deals with modern firearms; hand weapons are of less importance. At the same time, the swords made here are virtually the only ones still manufactured according to the age-old process ▶ *page 142.*

The *Fábrica de Armas* is a military installation; therefore it cannot be visited. However, you can visit the Hand Weapon Museum, the *Museo de Armas Blancas*. Opened in 1960, it contains an amazing collection of weapons that date back to prehistoric times: axes from the neolithic period, as well as from the Iron and Bronze Ages (be advised that they are copies of those in the National Archaeological Museum); medieval swords, including one belonging to King Pelayo (8C), to whom went the honour of winning the first reconquest victory over the Moors; two swords belonging to El Cid; and swords of other famous Spaniards and Moors, along with sabres, daggers, knives, halberds, lances, etc.

Also on display are a number of devices used to test the temper of the swords, such as the machete test, the flex test and the steel pillow.

Here, too, you can purchase or place special orders for any model of sword or *damasquinado* (damascene), with the confidence that the traditional handicraft method will be maintained.

Salón/Casa de Mesa (Mesa House)

Its name, Mesa, comes from one of its many owners. And, indeed, it has had quite a few: it may have been the ancestral home of the Toledo family, descendants of the Greek Count Peter who came to the aid of Alfonso VI during the siege of the city; it then most likely passed to Estéban Illán; afterwards, Cardinal Silíceo utilised it as a temporary home for his School for Noble Maidens; then came private owners, later the Carmelites, and so on. It is currently owned by the Spanish government, who has restored it. Those who wish to visit must ask a guard for the key.

We first cross a delightful little patio, arriving at an elegant *Mudejar room* with its splendid *coffered ceiling* and *plasterwork* around the doors and windows. The bottom level has an excellent frieze made from 16C Talaveran tile.

This room, the only part of a Mudejar mansion remaining (remindful of the Taller del Moro and many other Toledan mansions), was the headquarters of the *Economic Society of the Friends of the Country* during the last century. Currently, it is the headquarters of the *Real Academia de Bellas Artes y Ciencias Históricas* (Royal Academy of Fine Arts and Historical Sciences) of Toledo, where its members meet every two weeks. Next to the main room is the small Academy *library*. Amongst its offerings are a number of history books that contain secrets regarding the constantly-unravelling history of this city. The Academy, founded by Rafael Martínez de Arellano, has 25 members.

Taller del Moro, Museo Mudéjar (Moor's Workshop and Mudejar Museum)

▶ *page* 123.

Teatro de Rojas (Rojas Theatre)

The *Plaza Mayor* in front of this building was used to stage both serious plays and farces during the 16C, with the former *Mesón de la Fruta* (Inn of the Fruit) that stood here also being put to use. The inn was torn down in the 17C and a true *Corral de Comedias* was built, based on plans drawn up by El Greco's son; this *corral* continued to function in fits and starts until the middle of the last century. In 1878, the building we now see was inaugurated. An impressive structure for its day, it was named after the Toledan dramatist Rojas Zorrilla (1607-1648), one of the outstanding figures of the Spanish Golden Age and its so-called *teatro de honor*. The theatre has been carefully restored.

Typical patios

▶ *page* 38.

Typical Toledan houses

▶ *page* 38.

University

Toledo has a long-standing tradition as an educational centre. During the Visigothic period, there were a number of monasteries that enjoyed a reputation as seats of learning and provided Spain with some of its most notable intellectuals. These included the *Agaliense Monastery*, the monasteries of San Cosme and Damián, among others. Throughout the Moorish occupation and well into the Middle Ages there were flourishing Moslem schools and Jewish *yesibot* where philosophy, theology, medicine and other scientific subjects were taught. Alfonso X the Wise took advantage of this intellectual climate and ordered that teachers and translators be brought to his court from Seville. During the last third of the 14C, Diego Gómez, the magistrate of Toledo, set up a school in his own house for the teaching of theology and the arts, placing the Augustines in charge of instruction. In 1494, the prebendary Pedro de Rivadeneira also entrusted the Augustines with a centre of learning in the *Convento de las Nieves*.

Beginning in the mid-15C, the Dominican convent of San Pedro

Mártir imparted classes in theology, the arts, and canon law, and conferred academic degrees.

In 1485, the priest Francisco Alvarez de Toledo founded the *Colegio de Santa Catalina* near the parish church of San Andrés. The school grew rapidly, both in terms of its reputation and the range of subjects taught; consequently, in 1520 King León X granted it the title and privileges of University, which represents the birth of the modern university in Toledo.

For two and a half centuries the *colegio* and the University kept their ties; in the mid-18C, however, they were separated by a decree of the Supreme Council of Castile. At first, the university was given classrooms that had belonged to the recently-expelled Jesuits, though their unsatisfactory condition led to a subsequent move to the convent of San Pedro Mártir (1789). Later, Cardinal Lorenzana decided that the University needed its own premises; thus, construction of the current building began in 1795. Nevertheless, the University was fated to exist only for a short time longer, being abolished in 1845. During the next hundred years or so, the building served as a secondary school; finally, in 1968, the *Colegio Universitario de Toledo* was founded.

Here we have a typical Neoclassical construction in the style of Villanueva; nonetheless, it is not out of place within its surroundings, owing to its well-balanced proportions. The two storeys in the front section are cancelled out by the uneven ground in the rear. There is a double staircase at the entrance, and a gigantic coat-of-arms (Lorenzana's) over the cornice high up on the portico. The sculptures at each end of the façade are by Salvatierra. The spacious patio, with its ionic columns, is ringed by classrooms, with an auditorium at the rear.

Synagogues

Museo Sefardí (Sephardic Museum)

Opened in 1971, it consists of three small rooms. Most of the objects on display here are from fairly recent times, along with maps and explanations serving as an orientation to the Jewish presence in Toledo and the rest of Spain.

Of particular note amongst the more interesting items is a *marble baptismal font* from the 1 or 2C. Notice its Hebrew and Latin inscriptions and bas-reliefs depicting a *menorah*, or seven-branched candelabrum, a *shofar*, or ram's horn, as well as peacocks and the Tree of Life.

There are also large *gravestones* with Hebraic inscriptions that come from various sites. The glass cases contain books, manuscripts and a number of items used in worship: *Shofars*; *moreh*, or pointers for following the reading of the scrolls; a *tallith*, or woollen prayer shawl; *tefillin*, or phylacteries with their boxes; *rimmonio*, or liturgical bells; and *magillot*, or scrolls of Esther. Other objects are related to Jewish holidays, such as *Purim*, *Hanukkah*, *Succoth*, circumcisions, weddings and the like.

● ● Santa María la Blanca, Synagogue of

Visiting hours: 10.00 a.m. to 2.00 p.m. and 3.30 to 6.00 p.m.; in summer, open until 7.00 p.m. Private.

This was the main synagogue (*Sinagoga Mayor*) in Toledo, located in the heart of the Jewish quarter (*judería*). According to tradition, it was built in the late 12C by Ibrain, a favourite of Alfonso VIII (whose love affair with the Jewish girl Rachel became the subject of another cycle

of legends). The Jews enjoyed such prosperity that evil and envious tongues began to wag, alleging that the synagogue was founded atop dirt that had been brought from Jerusalem. The situation worsened, until at the beginning of the 15C the building was burned to the ground —the reason being, according to tradition, the fiery sermons of St. Vincent Ferrer, which also provoked a massacre in the *judería*. It was later rebuilt and consecrated to Christian worship, being dedicated to Santa María la Blanca. In 1550, Cardinal Silíceo turned it into a shelter for repentant women, adding three chapels to the sanctuary at the time. Over the years, it was put to a variety of uses —hermitage, military garrison, and lumber warehouse.

The building has now been carefully restored. The outside is of no special interest, except for the peacefulness of the garden through which we enter. Inside, however, we are plunged into an almost unreal play of backlighting and the stunningly white and diaphanous aura it produces. The five naves are separated by *Moorish arches* atop octagonal pillars with stylised *capitals,* all different, formed by large pinecones with intertwining ribbons. The pinecone motif is repeated in the *atauriques* and plasterwork; here also is the lily, a symbol of purity and decency, and a star of David. The plasterwork bears no inscriptions, for this custom came later.

In the sanctuary, where the holy scriptures used to be read, we see the three chapels added in the 16C. The main chapel houses an

131

excellent plateresque retable carved by Bautista Vázquez and Vergara the Elder, bearing the coat-of-arms of Cardinal Silíceo. The coffered ceilings are made of larch.

🕽 🕽 Sinagoga del Tránsito o de Samuel Leví (Tránsito, or Samuel Leví, Synagogue)

Visiting hours: 10.00 a.m. to 2.00 p.m. and 4.00 to 6.00 p.m.; in summer open until 7.00 p.m. Closed Sunday afternoons.
Government-owned.

This synagogue marks the finest moment in Toledan Jewry. It is the sole remaining element of importance from the sumptuous mansion that Peter I's Jewish treasurer, Samuel ha-Leví, commissioned the architect Meir ab-Deli to build in 1366; most likely it was the *chapel.* (The entire mansion included the space where the El Greco House now stands.) After the expulsion of the Jews from Spain in 1497, the synagogue was handed over to the Order of Calatrava, who turned it into the church of San Benito; it subsequently became the hermitage of *Nuestra Señora del Tránsito.*

Samuel ha-Leví undoubtedly wished to duplicate Solomon's gesture, but since for the Jews the only true temple was at Jerusalem, he built a synagogue. The best craftsmen to be found worked here, with an example of their skills seen in the *coffered ceilings* made of expensive cedar.

The exterior is in the Mudejar style, and is a poor indication of the richness and beauty of the inside. The single story of the building measures 24 x 10m. The eastern wall, or sanctuary, is the most lavishly decorated: in the central part is a triple lobed arch, which would have held the case with the holy texts. Displayed on the *panels* on either side are the coats-of-arms of Castile, each with its inscription in Hebrew. Along the side walls is a *frieze* with plasterwork on which psalms have been inscribed in Hebrew, together with warm words of praise for Samuel Leví, the craftsman, Rabbi Meyr Abdeli, as well as for the King and Christian protector himself. There are a great many pinecones, fig leaves, palm leaves, lilies, stars of David, Castilian coats-of-arms, and the letter T, which is the initial of the word for strength. In the arcade above the frieze, with its polylobed arches atop multicoloured marble columns, there are elegantly-wrought latticed windows, all different. The coffered ceiling (12m high), is of cedar and is incrusted with delicate mother-of-pearl.

On the southern wall can be seen the *gallery* reserved for women. The altar beneath it is a reminder of the Christians who were here. The area once held tombs of the knights of Calatrava, but they have been removed so as to restore the synagogue to its original appearance. A roped-off part of the sanctuary contains an excellent example of the *original flooring.* The magnificent *plateresque door* of the Christian sacristy is also from this period.

At the far end of the nave, a small door leads to where the ancient *archives* of the military orders of Alcántara and Calatrava were kept; it is now the *Sephardic Museum.*

POLICE AND SECURITY

The **police emergency number is 091**. The police are at your service: don't hesitate to ask for their help if you need it.

Public order in Spain is the responsibility of three different police groups, and they are all available to help the visitor. The ***Policía***

Municipal (municipal police) is principally responsible for traffic problems within the cities. This city police corps usually wears blue uniforms and white.caps. The *Policía Nacional* (national police) wear brown. They protect public buildings and patrol urban areas. Their *comisarías*, or police substations, are seen in all major cities and provincial towns with populations of more than 20,000. The *Guardia Civil* (civil guard) polices rural areas, the coasts and customs, and is in charge of traffic surveillance and highway assistance. Their uniform is green with a visored cap of the same colour —or they will be wearing the traditional and celebrated tri-cornered, black patent-leather hat.

Never lose sight of your personal belongings; you could lose them. Don't leave anything of value lying about in your car, and lock the vehicle carefully when you leave it. Be especially careful with purses and handbags in cities and other built-up areas. Take care with car stereos as well: most Spaniards either cover them or have removable car radio cassettes that they take out of the car when they leave it unattended. Be equally careful with your luggage; in the event of any problem contact your consulate or the police. It's wise to have the number and date of issue of your passport noted down separately; this information is useful in speeding up the resolution of several problems.

It's legal in Spain to possess up to 8g of **hashish**, or what the Spanish commonly call *chocolate* or *costo*. But having more than that can get you into serious trouble.

Hitch-hiking is not illegal in Spain, but it is quite rare except among some young people. It you do try hitch-hiking be sure to position yourself so that you do not interfere with traffic and so that anyone stopping can do so without danger to you or other traffic. Avoid the highways and, in general, hitch-hiking at night. A woman is strongly advised to hitch-hike only with a friend of the opposite sex.

RELIGIOUS SERVICES

The only religious services available in Toledo are Catholic. People of this faith will have no problem, since the city abounds in churches and convents. In addition, a **Mozarabic-rite Mass** is held in the Cathedral, in the *capilla mozárabe*, every Sunday morning.

RESTAURANTS

Toledo is brimming with restaurants, given the size of the city. The reason, naturally, is the tourist trade. Most of the restaurants that cater to this line will have their tourist menu. Variety however, is not easy to come by, be it in regard to price or quality. In addition to the restaurants, many cafeterias, as well as some bars and taverns, will offer *platos combinados*, literally combination plates, a fairly complete meal served on a single dish. A Toledo feature is the *venta,* a rather stereotyped throwback to the age of Don Quixote with its roadside inns and perhaps an outdoor patio or garden, which is generally more frequented by Spanish visitors than by foreigners. Don't judge them entirely by their average appearance, however, because some serve food that is far better than average.

Given the abundance of restaurants, there is no way to avoid it —we must be selective. Our choice is mostly limited to those establishments that are outstanding because they serve high quality food. At the same time, we have included some with perhaps less quality but which have something else to offer, such as a panoramic view, a long-standing tradition, and the like.

Chirón

☆ ☆ ☆ **Paseo de Recadero, 1 (in front of Puerta Cambrón)** ☎ **22 01 50** ✳ ≪ ♨ **AE, DC, EC, MC, V $$$.**
Wonderful view of the *Vega baja* and the Tagus; terrace dining in the summer. Comfortable surroundings with the stereotyped Toledo decor. Manchegan cuisine that shuns innovation with its traditional dishes: *tortilla a la magra*, stewed partridge, roasts, and so on.

El Abside

☆ ☆ ☆ **c/ Marqués de Mendigorria, 1** ☎ **21 26 50** ✳ **AE, DC, EC, MC, V $$$$.**
This restaurant is found in the *María Cristina* hotel complex, which in turn occupies what is left of the ancient 15C *Hospital de San Lázaro* (subsequently a military garrison and then an orphanage, the latter created at the urging of the 19C Queen after whom the hotel is named). The city has thus been able to rescue a major building whose quite dilapidated remains were simply a Mudejar apse, the walls and the main façade. The exterior restoration is exemplary, perhaps less so in the case of the interior, since it attempts to be openly modern and even *avant garde*. The inspiration is traditional, though results are not always satisfactory. The colours are light and bright, there is a feeling of spaciousness, with refinement and attention to the smallest details. Service can be a bit careless. The menu embraces the *nouvelle cuisine* wholeheartedly (and for the most part successfully), with all the consequences. From the selection of the basic traditional ingredients, imaginatively prepared and combined, until they make their final appearance on the platter, the touch is exquisite and colourful. Among the outstanding dishes are salmon pie with spinach, avocado and nut mousse, warm anglerfish salad, poached salmon in champagne sauce, cod *al ajo confitado*, venison with pears, *cabracho* pie, and venison stew with mushrooms. There is also an *Arabic-Sephardic menu* (almond soup, orange duck, sherbets), as well as low-calorie menu and children's plates.

Hostal del Cardenal

☆ ☆ ☆ **Paseo de Recadero, 24** ☎ **22 08 62. Open from 1.00 to 4.00 p.m. and from 8.30 to 11.30 p.m.** ✳ ≪ ♨ **AE, DC $$$$.**
Located by the Alfonso VI Gate in a 17C palace that belonged to Cardinal Lorenzana, this has been Toledo's most elegant restaurant for many years (it was opened in 1966 by the owners of Madrid's *Botín*). An evocative and distinguished ambience, with impeccable service. The food, although having had some ups and downs, has regained its customary excellence. Exquisitely decorated, with patio dining in the summer. Castilian and Toledan dishes: Castilian garlic soup, partridge *a la toledana*, sea bream *al ajoarriero*, lamb stew, roast suckling pig, and more. There are also general Spanish dishes (*paella*, Basque food, and so on.)

Venta de Aires

☆ ☆ ☆ **c/ Circo Romano, 12** ☎ **22 05 45. Open from 1.00 to 4.00 p.m. and from 9.00 to 11.00 p.m. Closed Mondays** ✳ ♨ **AE, DC, EC, MC, V $$$.**
Another of Toledo's classics. Founded last century by Dionisio Aires, the restaurant has been passed down through four generations.

Customers have included Lorca, Buñuel, and Dalí, (who created a comic Brotherhood here), and Marañón. Excellent food prepared over wood fire. Dishes include many of the traditional ones, such as cream of crab, *tortilla a la magra*, and partridge stew, though with some new creations (partridge paté). Marvellous soufflé. Good wine cellar.

Asador Adolfo

☆ ☆ c/ Granada, 6 (on the corner of c/ Hombre de Palo, in a sort of covered walkway: may require a bit of searching to find it) ☎ 22 73 21. Open from 1.00 to 4.00 p.m. and from 7.00 p.m. to midnight ✽ AE, DC, EC, ME, V $$$.

Located in this 14C building since 1979 (right in the heart of Toledo, beside *Casa Aurelio*), its ambience and decorations are refined, though perhaps not artistic. Castilian cuisine, menu indicative of a certain restlessness leading to some innovations based on the season and the *nueva cocina*, such as leek pie (*pastel de puerros*), partridge with green beans, *tiznao de merluza*, venison with mushrooms, sea bass in mushroom sauce and almonds, roasts prepared in wood oven, in addition to salmon *al cava* and seafood puff. Desserts include house pastries, sherbets, crêpes, and marzipan. Perhaps another example of its experimental attitude is that each year the restaurant presents a *Puerta Bisagra Poetry Prize*.

Casa Aurelio

☆ ☆ c/ Sinagoga, 6 ☎ 22 20 97; Pl del Ayuntamiento, 3 ☎ 22 77 96; c/ Santo Tomé, 21 (the latter only open during the lunch hours). Open from 1.00 to 4.00 p.m. and from 8.00 to 11.00 p.m. Closed Wednesdays ✽ AE, DC, EC, MC V $$$.

Aurelio Montero is yet another of Toledo's classic chefs. Following in the footsteps of his father, who opened a restaurant in c/ Sinagoga more than thirty years ago, he now runs four: the original one; one in front of the original in c/ Sinagoga (new); another in the Pl del Ayuntamiento; and the Hostería de Aurelio in c/ Santo Tomé. Authentic Castilian cuisine though not terribly innovative. Moderately-high prices. Reservations suggested at weekends. Good house wine. Recommended dishes include cream of crab, sea bream *a la espada*, partridge *a la toledana*, and sirloin *a la espada*

Hierbabuena

☆ ☆ c/ Cristo de la Luz, 9 $$$.

Occupying a house and patio with remains of Mudejar plasterwork, though decorated with a certain *belle-époque* brio, the atmosphere is quite romantic and hospitable, especially in the evenings (reservations suggested at weekends). The food shares the romanticism, with such dishes as plum turkey, mushroom, shrimp and garlic-sauce omelettes, and sherbets. Service and ambience are distinguished, yet also personal.

La Botica

☆ ☆ Pl de Zocodover, s/n ✽ AE, DC, EO, MC, V $$$.

A newcomer to the portals of Zocodover (cafeteria and terrace downstairs; restaurant upstairs), it strives to add a touch of elegance to the city's core. Decoration is refined, managing to avoid the cliché of typical decor. By the same token, the menu seeks to add elegance and dignity to the traditional dishes, orienting them to the taste of a special clientele with a certain cosmopolitan air. Innovation and experimentation, however, are not taboo. Recommended: eggplant gratineé with shrimp, seafood salad with watercress, stuffed sole, anglerfish with lobster, lamb *Tahona*, sirloin *al cabrales*, braised veal with mushrooms, *suspiros del Greco*, Moorish pudding in vanilla sauce, and fruit sherbets.

La Tarasca

☆☆ c/ Hombre de Palo, 6 ☎ 22 43 42 ✹ AE, DC, EC, MC, V $$$.
Located on the busiest street in Toledo. The locale and the certain air of modernity that blows betwixt its cafeteria and restaurant may prove a bit restricting owing to its lack of space, with the resultant noise and lack of intimacy. The food is traditionally based, though with modern trends, with offerings that are somewhat impersonal: crab bisque, hake *a la Tarasca*, omelette of baby eel with mushrooms, *escalope San Jacobo*, suckling pig *a la Teja*, tournedós, fruit pudding, and crêpes Suzette. Prices are high and out of proportion to the service and food.

Sinaí

☆☆ c/ Reyes Católicos, 7 ☎ 22 58 23 ✹ AE, DC, EC, MC, V $$$.
In the midst of the Jewish quarter (*judería*) facing the two synagogues. This restaurant has come to fill an obvious gap in the city's needs, though its offering of oriental dishes is unfortunately very limited. However, there is chicken paté, *shaslik kebaba* (shish-kebab) or tangerine steak, on the Jewish side, whilst of particular merit is the Moroccan *alcuzcuz* for those who have an enormous Arabic hunger to assuage. A kosher Rioja wine is also available. Service and decor are very discreet.

Tourist restaurants of special interest:

El Aljibe
☆☆ Pl Padre Mariana, 9 (in front of the Jesuit church).
Located in ancient caves or dungeons; ideal for summer. Tourist menu.

El Patio
☆☆ c/ Plata, 2 (in front of the post office).
Another typical Toledan patio, with an Andalusian touch.

El Porche
☆☆ Paseo del Tránsito, s/n (next to the Tránsito Synagogue and the Casa El Greco).
A neat and peaceful establishment in the midst of the tourist route.

Emperador
☆☆ Ctra del Valle, 1.
Good view of the city. Excellent rabbit with garlic (*conejo al ajillo*).

La Cubana
☆☆ Paseo de la Rosa, 2 (next to the Puente de Alcántara).
Typical decor, well-established, and known for a long time for its partridge.

Los Arcos
☆☆ c/ de las Cordonerías, s/n (next to the apse of Santas Justa y Rufina, behind c/ Comercio).
In the heart of the city. A trim and proper place of the tourist variety, but with aspirations.

Los Cuatro Tiempos
☆☆ c/ Sixto Ramón Parro, 5 and 7 (next to the cathedral sanctuary).
Toledan decor with dining rooms in ancient basements or caves. Centrally-located and comfortable.

Monterrey
☆☆ Ctra Piedra Buena, 42.
A short distance from the centre, but with excellent views. The dining room is beautiful and spacious (there is a hotel), with good price-quality balance.

Plácido
☆☆ c/ Santo Tomé, 6.
Located in a typical Toledan patio, with a certain charm.
Price-quality ratio, however, is not good.

SHOPPING

Arts and crafts have long been a flourishing tradition in Toledo, and the burgeoning masses have stimulated and expanded them. However, this same mass phenomenon has, in many areas, led to a decline in the quality of the handicraft trade. Stereotyped and even shoddy goods have made their appearance, a far cry from the original and much-admired creations.

For this reason, the shopper must always exercise great caution and inspect potential purchases carefully. One example is the Toledo sword, seen everywhere and at quite affordable prices. Yet, if one wishes to have the real thing, manufactured to tried-and-true standards, then it is necessary to seek out the proper place and pay a logical price, which may be ten, fifteen or twenty times that of a cheap replica. The same can be said of gold *damasquinado* (damascene) work. Low-quality objects may turn black within a few weeks.

The most widespread and noticeable handicraft traditions involve the production of swords (including other arms and armour, and reproductions of antique versions of the same); damascene work and embossed leather; embroidery and lace; ceramics (both pottery for everyday use and decorative tile, a deep-rooted tradition in the city); marzipan and other gourmet treats; *toledano* (Toledo-style) and *castellano* (Castile-style) furniture; antiques and reproductions. A few traditional handicraft industries, such as silk and rugweaving, have completely died out during this century.

Ceramics

The **Toledo style of pottery** has created a world of its own. As one draws closer to the city, the number of pottery shops increases at a dizzying rate. This craft is one that has not become totally automated, save for a few techniques; in other words, it is a handicraft that for the most part is authentic. However, the rising tide of tourists has led to hasty potterymaking, crudely-drawn designs and blatant copies of other types being employed. Pottery can often be totally unrelated to traditional designs. The name of the game is a fast output.

The obligatory simplification of concepts that accompanies the tourist trade has allowed the ceramics produced in two towns in the province of Toledo —Talavera de la Reina and Puente del Arzobispo— to achieve a mythical status. The traveller rarely goes elsewhere in the province in search of popular pottery. That said, it is true that the two towns have a tradition of ceramics equal to that of Toledo steel.

Potterymaking in Talavera goes back at least to the 16C. In the 18C, the historian Ponz noted that the town contained *seven or eight workshops that called themselves potterymakers.* Contrary to current belief, archaeological remains are being found that suggest potterymaking in Puente dates back just as far, and that its output was even greater. However, the War of Independence (early 19C) proved to be disastrous for potters, as well as for many other industries.

Toward the mid-19C, Juan Niveiro created the *El Carmen* pottery works, for which he had to bring in potters from the town of Manises, in the province of Valencia. The establishment was taken over by his son, Emilio, who had as a co-worker the great Sevillian artist, Enrique Guijo, a man who was dedicated to potterymaking as an art. Guijo, however, found Niveiro's support insufficient, and so he joined forces with another potter, Ruiz de Luna, in 1908. This signalled the beginning of a true potterymaking rebirth in Talavera, to the point where Niveiro's workers at El Carmen, along with others, shook off their lethargy and began to imitate the creations of Guijo and Ruiz de Luna.

With the Talaveran renaissance, local pottery began to be exhibited at major art exhibitions, in Spain as well as abroad. In 1925, the **Museum of Antique Ceramics** was inaugurated in Talavera, with its focus on pieces collected by Juan Ruiz de Luna, Platón Páramo, and other partners.

Following the Spanish Civil War (1936-39), Talaveran ceramics once again fell into decline. However, in 1963 a new renaissance began, one that coincided exactly with the tourist boom that hit Spain in the 1960s.

Demand is now such that a great deal of potterymaking is directed solely toward the tourist trade, and frequently departs from the idea of traditional handicrafts. Thus we have a massive output of clever pieces intended to please the tourist —ashtrays, telephones, ceramic irons and flowerpots, among others. And when traditional items are made, they result in the most haphazard mixture of styles and designs, highly-simplified and crude patterns being utilized.

Toledo Style Pottery

Yet, there are other types of popular ceramics that do not come from Talavera. Overall, Toledo is one of Spain's richest potterymaking provinces. Yet, in many of its towns only a single potter is to be found, often with no apprentices; this means that time will soon see the disappearance of specific styles, which will remain only as museum pieces.

Fortunately, a few years ago there was a strong outburst of interest in this authentically popular style of pottery. In spite of its virtually total isolation and the lack of interest among potential buyers, it has managed to survive. Proof of this isolated condition is the fact that only a few pottery shops in Toledo offer a selection that goes beyond pieces from Talavera or Puente, and the hybrids expressly created for the tourist trade.

The province of Toledo still contains a large number of pottery shops that continue working along traditional lines. Some of the most representative towns and establishments are: **Cuerva**, perhaps the most characteristic, or at least the most recognisable, with its glazed pieces decorated with white clay on a honeylike background (jugs, *ollas majas*, or fancy pots, *cuerveras*, etc.); **Consuegra**, glazed fireproof pottery (there are a number of pottery makers in this town); **Ocaña** and **Puebla de Montalbán**, unglazed and stunningly white ceramics (pitchers, jugs, pots, etc.); **Valdeverdeja**, red glazed and unglazed pottery that has maintained its traditional designs (*escarfadores*, ovenproof dishware, soup bowls, etc.). Major pottery works producing traditional items can also be found in **Madridejos, Villafranca de los Caballeros** and **Los Mavalucillos**.

These traditional pieces can also be obtained in the city of Toledo, though the usual selection from Talavera and Puente is generally what is sought.

Nonetheless, the city does have a number of potters who are mainly involved in turning out plates and decorative tile, and who at times search for new directions, or else incorporate present-day forms. *Aguado*, c/ Toledo de Ohio, 5. Pieces from Cuerva and other towns. *Pablo Sanguino*, c/ Matías Moreno, 2 ☎ 22 30 92. Bric-a-brac, modern, and Picassoesque ceramics.

Damascene and Embossed Work

Damascene is not only used for sword decoration; it is also applied to plates, small boxes, bracelets and a wide range of souvenirs. As the name implies, this handicraft originated in Damascus. It was later brought to Toledo by the Moors, where it soon became a deeply-entrenched art.

The process is as follows: the article to be decorated is first prepared by being grooved (*rayado*) or indented (*picado*); in other words, the surface is roughened so that the gold will adhere. A burin may be used, as well as acid. The next step is the inlaying of the gold wire. This is the actual damascening. Here the artisan creates the patterns and decorations. The craftsman may be as imaginative as he wishes but normally patterns are standarized. Once the gold wire has been inlaid, it is then affixed to the metal by light hammer and burin taps. Next comes the blueing or *pavonado*. In order to prevent rust in the steel that holds the inlaid gold, the piece is given a flame bath with caustic soda and potassium nitrate. The steel portion turns black, while the gold (or, at times, silver) is unaffected. Lastly, the final touches are applied, which consist of livening up the gold area, putting it in relief using the hammer and burin, and completing the gold pattern.

The difference between a well-wrought, handmade damascene piece and a tourist version is that a cheaply-made item will employ poor-quality gold, and it may well rust and become quite unsightly in a short while. Such pieces are not handmade, but are instead mass-produced by machines. It is not always easy to recognize properly-made damascene; needless to say, price is not a criterion. How do the experts make a distinction? Machine-made pieces usually have a minimum of pattern detail in the gold, and leave large areas bare. An even better method of evaluation is to look closely at the work: handcrafting can be accurately noted by the artisan's hammer marks. To be safer yet, it is best to buy a piece and have it made while you wait. This can be done at the swordworks where damascene is also produced, or by going to one of the numerous establishments in the city where craftsmen can actually be observed at work. The buyer should also be aware of another aspect of quality: a handmade piece is not a sure thing; there is also the consideration of the detail and beauty of the design, as well as the skill demonstrated by the artisan. Thus, in the final analysis, the basic rule is to inspect carefully before buying.

Another handicraft similar to damascene, which is frequently employed in sword decoration, is **etching** (*grabado*). Designs are painted on the steel surface with varnish; the piece is then placed in a nitric acid solution, and the acid eats into the non-varnished area, thus producing the etching. The etched part may then be painted with lacquer of various colours.

There is also **embossing** (*repujado* or *cincelado*), which consists of placing the metal leaf over a pattern and hammering on a burin to obtain the desired relief pattern. Embossing and openwork are the two most expensive techniques.

Leather can also be embossed, and is used for sword sheaths and furniture. However, a less expensive method of working in leather is by gouging, or cutting away a pattern that has been previously traced.

Furniture and Antiques

Toledo is a major supplier of **furniture** to the Spanish market. Pieces are always given the general label *mueble castellano* (Castilian furniture); however, prospective buyers should turn a careful eye toward verifying the actual quality, since most of this so-called Toledo or Castilian furniture is nothing more than mass-produced copies. At the same time there are wonderful reproductions of genuinely traditional tables, chairs, *bargueños* (a decorative cabinet with many small drawers), and other items, which are manufactured in the best craftsmanship tradition.

Virtually all furniture stores are located on the Toledo-Madrid highway, within an area of some 10km just outside the city. The following furniture and antique stores are recommended:

Balaguer, Pasadizo del Ayuntamiento and c/ Puerta Llana, s/n. Antiques, old books, parchments and tiles.

Linares, c/ de los Reyes Católicos, s/n, in front of San Juan de los Reyes. Antiques.

Olrey shopping complex in Olías, 10km from Toledo on the Madrid highway. Antique furniture and reproductions.

Other recommended purchases are **marzipan**, sweets, and gourmet items ▶ page 30. Recommended semiartisans and shops where marzipan and gourmet items can be bought are:

Barroso, c/ Real del Arrabal, 11.

Casa Telesforo, Pl de Zocodover, 17.

Santo Tomé, c/ Santo Tomé, 5 and Pl de Zocodover, 11.

For those visiting Toledo on a Tuesday, this is the day of the outdoor fleamarket, a long-standing tradition where regional artists and people from the countryside come to buy and sell.

Toledo Steel

There are three countries famous for their swords: Germany, Italy and Spain. In the case of Spain, Toledo swords enjoyed worldwide renown back in the days when the Spanish Empire included a signifcant part of the world. Spanish literature, as well as that of Europe in general, is full of references and allusions to **Toledo steel**. As time passed and military tactics changed, the manufacturing of steel weapons for hand-to-hand combat declined. In the 18C, Charles III gathered together the last remaining swordsmiths scattered throughout Toledo and put them to work in the **Royal Arms Factory** ▶ page 128.

Nowadays, the demand for large quantities of inexpensive souvenirs to satisfy tourists has led to automation among the ranks of the craftsmen, with the result that swords and other steel weapons are now mass-produced, rather than handmade. Only two or three places maintain the former handicraft tradition. The Royal Arms Factory —unquestionably the best— keeps up the ancient, painstaking methods. Other manufacturers have, logically, implemented semi-automation. Even so, arms forging is still a craft that is in danger of dying out.

The process of making an authentic Toledo sword is unbelievably complex. The blade is all important. First, a straight piece of iron leaf, called the *alma*, or soul, is chosen, along with two curved steel leaves. The *alma* is placed between the two steel leaves, and the assembly is forge-heated until it is redhot. The smith then begins hammering the metal in order to obtain a weld, initially working with what is to be the point. As the hammering continues, the leaves fuse together over their entire length, until the iron *alma* remains enclosed inside the two pieces of steel. Then comes the drawing. This is a process whereby the desired length is obtained by repeated heatings and continuous hammering while the piece is held in a chuck, or mould. Other sword parts are the *mesa* and the *vaceo*, the former being the flat, or face, and the latter the long groove that normally runs down the centre. The Royal Arms Factory is the only place that carries out this entire process. Other manufacturers simply take a piece of steel and draw it, without filling it with the iron *alma*.

Then comes the *temple*, or tempering. Once again it is necessary to heat the blade redhot, immediately plunging it into a container of water. Care must be taken that the blade enters edgewise, from the point to the tang (where the grip is attached), shaken gently all the while so that it will cool properly. Tradition requires the water to come from the Tagus. When tempering is finished and the blade is removed from the water, it has a milky or dull white finish, as if it were tin-coated; at this point, the blade is completely brittle —a single blow would shatter it.

The next operation is annealing, a softening process for partially reducing the hardness of the blade; it allows for a subsequent and more uniform tempering that will add flexibility. Annealing consists of reheating the metal to a violet colour, then cooling it under carefully-controlled conditions until the desired temper is obtained.

Thus the blade is given its two essential characteristics: hardness and, of no less importance, flexibility. If it were not for the latter, a blow struck against armour or another hard surface would shatter the metal, leaving the swordsman unarmed.

Once the blade is completed, work shifts to the hilt. This is often done in filigree and it is frequently an art work. Hilts may be embossed, engraved, rendered in openwork, damascened, and so forth. In the 16C, it was customary to attach a handguard which incorporated all these decorative techniques. A display in the Royal Arms Factory Museum shows the evolution of the various types of swords, as regards their hilts as well as blades, and ranging from the days of the Celtiberians up to the 16C.

A standard forged sword, without nickelplating or decoration, may cost from 3,000 to 5,000 pesetas. If, however, it is nickelplated and damascened, its price could rise to around 10,000 pesetas. Beyond this point, everything depends on the model and how it is decorated, with prices of 50,000 to 100,000 pesetas not uncommon.

Yet...if one's fantasy allows, a mass-produced Toledo sword can be purchased for 2,000 pesetas at any of the numerous souvenir shops that dot the city. But beware if the price is higher; a fully-guaranteed sword bought at one of the forges mentioned earlier could well be a better buy than one of the bargains to be found on the street.

Some of the places where traditionally-made swords are sold are the following: *Real Fábrica de Armas*; *Casa Martos* (Ctra Madrid, about 5km from town); *Fábrica Bermejo* (next to Santiago del Arrabal); and *Fábrica Garrido*, one of the largest and oldest. The latter occupies the former España hotel (Rilke stayed here), next to the Bullring, and also does work in damascene, leather embossing, woodcarving, and other artisan techniques.

Various Other Regional Arts and Crafts

Toledo once had a thriving silk industry, no doubt a legacy from the Moorish period, which is now totally nonexistent. However, as late as the end of the past century there was the renowned Molero Factory, which was famous for its rugs. Nowadays, all that is left of the textile industry is embroidery, lace and the Lagartera needlework, the latter named after a village near Oropesa. The fame and success of this needlework has served to keep the art alive in the village itself and others nearby.

There are a number of shops in Toledo where this type of needlework can be purchased: the *Tienda Oficial de Artesanía Española* (Official Spanish Handicraft Shop), c/ Samuel Leví, s/n, located in front of the El Greco House, offers handmade pieces with guaranteed authenticity. In addition, the shop exhibits relics of paintings and plasterwork from the former Leví Palace (subsequently owned by the Marquis of Villena), which once stood on the same site.

Other recommended shops are the following:

Manuel Oliva Martín, c/ Chapinería, 4. The shop has a typical Toledo patio.

Mauricio Jiménez, c/ de la Plata, 9. The shop has a typical patio.

SPANISH WAY OF LIFE: INFORMATION FOR FOREIGNERS

Spain is in many ways the most easygoing country in the western hemisphere. Its extraordinary **youthfulness** reflects, in part, the fact that Spain is demographically young. In addition many are surprised by the extent to which the country's key professional, business and political posts are held by people who are barely 45 years old. As an unhassled, young society, Spain is **hospitable** toward strangers. Pride in the recent recognition of his country as both newly democratic and European —and the determination to keep it that way— has given the Spaniard a special respect for the differences and peculiarities of foreigners.

The first thing to remember is that Spain is a patchwork of **very different lands and peoples**. The second is to forget the clichés and commonplaces of the past: a profound and rapid process of change has modernized this country, even while traditional life remains more alive in Spain than probably in any other European country. The Spaniard is cultured, hardworking and efficient, but he nonetheless retains his personality, his *joie de vivre* or *alegría*.

Freedom Spanish-style extends to shopping hours and to ways and rhythms of living. This unhurried life, together with the ingrained youthfulness of its contemporary society, makes Spain a particularly easy place to visit. The foreigner can choose from among a host of lifestyles the one that suits him best.

Bars, Wine Bars, Taverns and Cafeterias

Alcoholic beverages can be bought in virtually any grocery store; furthermore, they can be legally consumed almost anywhere, the street included. Wine bars, taverns, bars and cafeterias offer their drink according to their peculiar grading system. The **wine bar** or *bodega* usually sells wine from small barrels, more often than not purchased from local vineyards; draught beer served as a *caña*, a fifth of a litre serving that takes its name from the cane-shaped glasses it usually comes in; and low-grade brandies and anisettes. **Taverns** or *tabernas* serve cheap bottled wine and beers and bubbly refreshments. In both *bodegas* and *tabernas* drinks are often accompanied by small servings of tinned goods such as mussels or smaller shellfish as well as bread. **Bars**, which usually offer sandwiches (*bocadillos*), cigarettes and, nearly always, coffee and tea, specialize in that wonderful Spanish creation, the *tapa* —a small plate containing one of an enormous variety of appetizers. Among the usual fare are stews, sausages (*embutidos*), cheeses, conserves and fried foods: tuna, almonds, salads and dried fruits, cheese, salami or ham, clams in red sauce, grilled shrimp, cold omelette with potatoes (*tortilla*), small fish *boquerones* that come fried or in vinegar, skewered marinated meat, octopus and snails. In some places, the fare includes *garbanzos guisados*, or stewed chick peas, tripe and offal and *paella* —the seafood, saffron flavoured rice dish for which Spain is justly famous. *Raciones* are simply somewhat larger orders of 12 tapas. A very Spanish way of eating lightly and informally is simply to order *raciones*; better yet, if you're in a group, the best thing to do is order a variety of these appetizers and share them around.

The *tapa* is a sensible gastronomic institution in Spain, derived from the lightness of the morning meal: usually a simple *café con leche* (coffee with hot milk) with toast, or the traditional *churros*, fried dough normally accompanied by thick drinking chocolate. The *tapa* also supports the Spanish habit of drinking before the day's first major meal, which is eaten in the afternoon. A tradition of socializing has grown up around the *tapa*, and the name *tapeo* has been given to a series of drinks which are each consumed with their proper *tapa*. This custom has made its way as far as New York City.

The **cafeteria** is subtly different from the bar. It is more modern in conception, adding a range of services, milk products, sweets and other foods to its offerings, and service is rapid at both bar and tables.

The Spanish **eating and drinking schedule** is full of surprises. Bars and cafeterias usually serve breakfast until 11.00 or noon, when they begin offering *tapas* and aperitifs (wine and wine spritzes made with a sweet soda pop or soda water, beer, vermouth, *vino fino* and other varieties of sherry); this continues until the lunch hour, which in Spain is generally between 2.00 and 4.00 p.m. After lunch, the diner usually has a coffee, normally *solo* (without milk), and a cup of brandy or anisette, often accompanied by a cigar. Round about 4.30 is the traditional *siesta*, but this is pretty much a relic of the past except during vacations and weekends. Towards 6.30 or 7.00 p.m. many Spaniards have a snack, or *merienda*. This is usually *café con leche* or a chocolate drink, and those most often seen taking it are women finishing up their afternoon chores and meeting their friends. After about 8 o'clock, the bars and cafeterias begin to fill up again with a mixed crowd, who will continue drinking and eating until 10.00 or 10.30, when the dinner hour —finally— arrives. The evening meal can last until midnight or later, although most restaurants close at that time. Specialized eateries such as hamburger bars, pizza parlours and other late-closing restaurants often remain open after midnight, particularly in the big cities.

Beverages

Aside from cheap and excellent wines (see 'Wines'), Spain also produces soft drinks and a great deal of **beer**, both draught and bottled. Some of the better-known bottled brands include *Aguila, San Miguel, Mahou* and *Cruzcampo*. Among the **fizzy non-alcoholic beverages** are *Coca-Cola, Trinaranjus, Kas* and *Pepsi-Cola*. An enormously popular brand of *gaseosa* —a sweetened bubbly water— is *La Casera*, so much so that its name has become interchangeable with *gaseosa* as a generic term. *La Casera* is often mixed with wine.

Spanish **coffee** is very good, and is normally served as an Espresso-type beverage rather than the lighter, American-style drink. It comes *solo* (without milk), *con leche* (with milk) or *cortado* (only a small amount of milk is added). *Irish coffee* is very popular, especially among the middle and upper classes; another variant, *carajillo*, or black coffee served with brandy, is more popular with the less affluent. **Tea** and other quality infusions are usually prepared with tea bags, although some places still retain the traditional tea-pot.

The Spanish drink best known to the world is almost without doubt *sangría*, made with red wine, lemon, brandy, slices of orange and peach, and some sugar and cinnamon. A purely alcoholic drink, strictly for the seasoned drinker, is the *sol y sombra*, which combines anisette and brandy. On the other hand, **fresh, non-alcoholic drinks** are varied, from the *horchatas*, which are milky-like cold drinks, made of earth almonds, to the *granizados*, sherbet drinks that come in flavours of lemon, orange, and coffee. Also available are the *aguas de cebada* or *de arroz*, literally barley and rice water.

Bullfighting

Summer afternoon is the time of the **bullfight**, or *corrida de toros*, that festival of light and death in which animal is measured against man for bravery, astuteness and skill. The fight usually begins at 7 o'clock sharp, lasting between 90 and 120 minutes and consisting of a *lidia* of six bulls.

Much like a play, each of the six bullfights is divided into three *tercios*, or acts: first come the *picadors* who, mounted on a horse, jab the bull with a long lance; second are the *banderilleros*, men who scamper in front of the bull and plant brightly coloured barbed darts (*banderillas*) on the nape of his neck; and finally the *matador*, the master bullfighter who passes the animal with his cape before delivering the death stroke with his sword. *Novilladas* are fights featuring apprentice matadors and young animals (between two and three years old). *Rejoneadores* are bullfighters who pass and kill the bull while mounted on a horse.

The bullfighting season runs from the end of March through October it is somewhat longer in the south. The principal rings are the *plazas* of Madrid and Seville. Matadors like *Joselito, Belmonte, Manolete* and *El Cordobés* make up the legend of Spanish bullfighting. Today, *Manzanares* and *Espartaco* are among the better known fighters. Every season, however, new bullfighters make their names.

Customs and Courtesy

Pressures of formality and convention are scarcely felt in Spain outside the workplace. Most people dress in sports wear, much of it manufactured by Spain's well-developed fashion industry. In any case, the spirit of living together that characterizes the country means that conventional dress takes its place alongside the more bizarre clothes worn by those people the Spaniards call *new-look postmodern* or *punkie*. The variety of clothes is even wider in the cities and the popular summer resorts. The establishments that require formal dress are few, most of them casinos and very expensive restaurants. These latter often stock a whole wardrobe of their own ties to lend to the improperly attired customer.

Spanish men normally greet one another with a handshake; women, and very often teenagers of both sexes, normally kiss each other once on each cheek. The formal form of conversational address is *Usted* but among young and middle-age people, even those who do not know each other, the more familiar *tú* is more usual. Very often what may be taken for arrogance is simply a reserved way of showing respect. The Spaniard is proud of his nationality. He is sharply critical of his own country; but at the same time he does not like to hear others criticize it so freely.

It is general practice in Spain to heap courtesies on women, opening doors and the like; the rule applies also to senior citizens and invited guests. Queuing, on the other hand, is not a Spanish virtue and is not widely practised.

Electricity

Electricity in Spain is normally alternating current at 220v, although many hotels have a special 110-120v plug so that travellers may use electric razors without danger to the appliance. The plugs are generally of the universal two-pronged, round-shaped variety.

Gambling

For those who are interested in **games of chance**, there are many to sample in Spain. These include the *Lotería Nacional*, or national lottery, the popular *Loto*, or *Lotería Primitiva* which has weekly draws and the *Cupón de los ciegos*, a lottery run by the organization for the blind, ONCE, which has daily draws. There are also football pools and horse racing punts both known as *quinielas*. In the vast majority of bars and many other establishments as well, you will find electronic gambling machines. Lastly, casinos abound in major tourist sites.

Mailing Addresses

To address mail in Spain, or to Spain, you should write out the envelope like this (the *c/* stands for *calle*):

> D. Manuel Pelaez
> c/ Velasco, 3
> 28043 Madrid

Pharmacies

Pharmacies in most cities have a rotating system whereby one is always open round the clock; a listing may be found in local newspapers. In this same list, the opening and closing times of others are given. Pharmacies in Spain sell many drugs over the counter that require prescriptions elsewhere. An example is antibiotics. Contraceptives are available without much difficulty.

Public Washrooms

The apparent scarcity of public washrooms shouldn't cause panic to the stranger: there's an informal network of public services in bars, cafeterias and other eating and drinking establishments. Most owners won't be bothered by non-customers walking in off the street.

Some of the rest rooms in bars, restaurants and railway stations are not models of cleanliness. For that reason, the visitor may prefer to stick to better eating and drinking establishments, hotels, museums and so on. If there is an attendant, a small tip is customary.

The Spaniards' Schedule

The conversational image of Spain is that of a country that stays up late —true in terms of meals, shows and bedtimes, but far less so in other areas of life. Factories start work at 8.00 and offices open at 9.00, just as in any industrialized country. Nevertheless, lunch is not until 2.00 and dinner until 10.00 p.m.: evening sessions of cinemas and theatres generally start at 10.30 p.m., and it is unusual to go to bed —on a working day— before midnight.

Spain's **banking schedule** is quite strict, normally running from 9.00 a.m. until 2.00 p.m. or 9.00 until 1.00 on Saturdays. The **schedule for other establishments**, especially shops and boutiques, varies more widely, according to both locality and season. Generally, establishments of all kinds are open from 10.00 until 1.30 or 2.00, and again from 4.00 or 5.00 until 8.00 p.m. The department stores or *grandes almacenes*, literally warehouses, don't usually close during lunch hour and many are open all day Saturday and even Sunday. Of course, there are also many places of all types that remain open longer hours.

The normal thing in the evening is to walk the streets, taking the air, socializing, perhaps indulging in a little flirtation. Spain, after all, is known for its **tradition of night life**.

Taxis

A taxi is usually identified by a horizontal or diagonal stripe on the body and a sign marking it as a taxi on the roof or behind the windshield. As a general rule, the rates charged are set by local authorities. In the cities, at least, the rate schedule is posted where the traveller can easily read it. There are many taxi ranks, marked by signs in blue that carry the letter T or the word taxi. There are also a good many radio-dispatched taxi companies that you can reach by telephone. And of course you can pick one up in the street. Unoccupied taxis carry a card in their windshield marked *libre* in the day; at night, they are marked by a green roof light.

Telephone

Spain has a good telephone communications system that has a fully automated national and international network. International telephone calls may be made easily and without the help of an operator to most countries (see the instructions and list of prefixes below). Apart from the many **telephone booths** along the streets, the majority of restaurants, bars and cafeterias have **public telephones** that work with coins. You insert the coins, listen for the dial tone and then dial. You can make local, national and international calls on these phones. It's advisable to use these rather than hotel phones in general —hotels often charge more than 25% extra. If you are planning a longer international call you should either provide yourself with a good supply of coins or find a phone marked **international**. Better yet, go to the local **public office** of the utility CTNE, better known as *Telefónica* (*Compañía Telefónica Nacional de España*), where you can pay with bills after making your call. Rates are substantially lower at night and on holidays.

When you dial a number, the sound of the ringing phone will be long intermittent tones. A busy signal is more rapid.

All Spanish **provincial prefixes** begin with **9**, followed by the number in the province. These prefixes must always be used when calling from another Spanish province. Within a province they are dropped. When calling Spain from another country the provincial 9 prefix is also dropped.

To make **automatic calls from Spain to another country** —calls without the assistance of the operator— you need to dial **07**, followed by the country code for where you are calling (see the list of international prefixes below), the area (dropping the zero if there is one) and finally, the number of the party you wish to reach. If you don't know the area code, or need the help of an operator for another reason, dial **008** (Europe) and **005** (the rest of the world) if you're calling from Madrid; dial **9198** (Europe) or **9191** (the rest of the world) if you are in any other province of Spain. Remember that Spanish time usually runs an hour ahead of Greenwich Mean Time (GMT).

International Prefixes

Algeria: 213
Andorra: territorial code 9738
   (don't dial 07)

Argentina: 54
Australia: 61
Austria: 43

Bahrein: 973
Belgium: 32
Bolivia: 591
Brazil: 55
Cameroon: 237
Canada: 1
Chile: 56
Colombia: 57
Costa Rica: 506
Cyprus: 357
Czechoslovakia: 42
Denmark: 45
Dominican Republic: 508
Ecuador: 593
Egypt: 20
El Salvador: 503
Federal Republic of Germany: 49
Finland: 358
Formosa: 886
France: 33
Gabon: 241
German Democratic Republic: 37
Greece: 30
Guatemala: 502
Haiti: 509
Honduras: 504
Hong Kong: 852
Hungary: 36
India: 91
Indonesia: 62
Iran: 98
Ireland: 353
Israel: 972
Italy: 39
Ivory Coast: 225
Japan: 81
Jordan: 962
Kenya: 254
Kuwait: 965

Liechtenstein: (first dial Swiss prefix 41) 75
Luxemburg: 352
Mexico: 52
Monaco: (first dial French prefix 33) 93
Morocco: 212
Netherlands: 31
New Zealand: 64
Nicaragua: 505
Nigeria: 234
Norway: 47
Panama: 507
Paraguay: 595
Peru: 51
Philippines: 63
Poland: 48
Portugal: 351
Puerto Rico (USA): 80
Rumania: 40
San Marino: (first dial Italian prefix 39) 541
Saudi Arabia: 966
Senegal: 221
Singapore: 65
South Africa: 27
South Korea: 82
Sweden: 46
Switzerland: 41
Thailand: 66
Tunisia: 216
Turkey: 90
United Arab Emirates: 971
United Kingdom: 44
United States of America: 1
Uruguay: 598
Vatican City: (first dial Italian prefix 39) 6
Venezuela: 58
Yugoslavia: 38

Tipping

Tips generally don't need to be more than 5% to 10%, depending on the size of the bill: the larger the bill, the smaller the percentage. Bills for many services already include a service charge of 5%. Some establishments do not permit individual tipping, and instead use a common tin, or *bote*, for all tips. For those cases where a service charge isn't included in your bill, here is a general guide to some key services: a hotel porter might normally get a tip of between 100 and 150 pesetas; a taxi driver usually gets about 5% over what shows on the meter; parking lot attendants, 15 to 25 pesetas above the cost of the ticket; 25 to 100 pesetas to a cloakroom attendant. Of course the size of the tip depends on the type of place and how expensive it is. And it is always up to the customer to decide how well he has been served and what he wants to leave.

Tobacco

Most bars and restaurants sell **cigarettes** for a few more pesetas than the local government licensed tobacconists, or *estancos*. The *estancos* sell two varieties of cigarettes: *rubio*, the or American tobacco, and *negro*, the stronger black tobacco. The most popular brand of Virginia cigarettes is *Fortuna*; the most popular *negro* cigarette, far cheaper than the blonde tobaccos, is *Ducados*. The best-selling pipe tobacco is *Gravina*. Cigarettes are also made locally under licence from American companies like *Winston, Camel* and *Marlboro*. You can usually also find English cigarettes and European cigars, along with those from the Canaries and Cuba. The *estancos* also sell postage stamps.

SPORTS

One of Toledo's great traditions is bicycling. On any Sunday you can see hordes of people of all ages engaged in this vigorous activity. It is a sport that comes naturally to Toledans, owing to the lay of the land as well as to one of their native sons, the cyclist Bahamontes, who became a living legend after he won the *Tour de France*. There are a number of bicycling *peñas*, or sports clubs, some of which are named after this hero.

○ Fishing

Fishing is also a popular sport in these parts. Offerings include speckled trout, rainbow trout, Pacific salmon, crab, pike, black bass, barbel, carp, tench and boga.

The law considers all ICONA reserves and private lakes not classified as public property to be **waters subject to special regulation**. To fish in such places, a proper fishing licence as well as permission to enter the reserve must be obtained from ICONA, or from the owner of the lake. Such permits must always be in writing. In the case of ICONA, there is an official form that can be obtained at the *Jefatura Provincial* overseeing the reserve; otherwise, they must be got at the site before fishing. Do not overlook getting this permit, for you might get into trouble.

Toledo's main reserves are the following: **Las Becerras**, on the Pusa y Chorro River; **El Chorro**, on the Chorro River; **Guarajaz**, in the Guarajaz reservoir; **Torcón Reservoir; Municipal reservoir of Portiña; Cazalegas Reservoir**, and the **Castrejón Reservoir**, to name a few.

The best course of action is to request detailed information concerning seasons and schedules, licences and reserves, among others, from the *ICONA Jefatura Provincial* in Toledo, Pl de San Vicente, 6 ☎ 22 21 66 and 22 21 62.

● ○ ○ Hunting

This is a favourite sport amongst many Toledans, and the one that attracts most foreign visitors to the province.

It has been said, and truthfully so, that if Spain is the great game reserve of Europe, then Castile-La Mancha is the heartland of this reserve. Going further, the *Montes de Toledo*, or Toledo highlands, represent one of the most-distinguished hunting areas, especially for larger game.

Large game that can be found here along with hunting methods used includes the following:

Spanish deer (*ciervo español* or *cervus elaphus*). Stalking and Spanish-style hunting; 6-9mm rifle or bullet-loaded shotgun.

Roe deer (*capreolus capreolus*). Stalking, decoy during rutting season, and *battue*. Small-calibre high-velocity 6mm rifle.

Fallow doe (*dama dama*). Stalking and *battue*. Medium-calibre rifle, 6-8mm.

Wild boar (*jabalí* or *sus scrofa castilianus*). Spanish-style hunting, *battue* and stalking. Rifle of calibre not less than 7mm.

Spanish wolf (*lobo español* or *canis lupus*). Rifle of calibre 9.3 x 74R or similar.

Moufflon (*muflón europeo* or *ovis musimon pallas*). Introduced into Spain in 1954, it is hunted by stalking. 7mm rifle or larger.

The following is a list of **small game** to be found in the province:

Red partridge (*perdiz roja* or *alectoris rufa*). Beating, stalking shotgun with #6 or K7 shot.

Wood pigeon (*paloma torcaz* or *columba palumbus*). Decoy bird, fields, blinds, drinking troughs, etc.

Turtledove (*tórtola* or *strepto pelie turtur*). Very prevalent in Toledo; hunted from blinds.

Rabbit (*conejo*). If one wishes to have a live specimen, a ferret and hood can be used. 12-gauge shotgun with #6 shot.

Hare (*liebre*). Ferreting or stalking as other small game. A typically-Spanish method is *battue* with greyhounds. 12-gauge shotgun with #6 shot or larger.

Quail (*codorniz*). Stalking, with game dog. 20-gauge shotgun or larger, fine shot #8 to #10.

Thrush (*zorzal*). Species are varied and plentiful, thus an ideal game for beginners.

Bustard (*avutarda*). Stalking during mating season; beating.

Current law in Spain has established two types of **hunting areas**: those for general use (*aprovechamiento común*) and those subject to special hunting regulations (*sometidos a régimen cinegético especial*).

The **general use areas** are those where you can hunt with no limitations other than general ones imposed by law. They are known as free areas, with the game not particularly abundant and where anyone may hunt.

The **areas subject to special hunting regulations** include National Parks, Game Shelters, National Hunting Reserves, National Game Reserves, Regulated Hunting Areas, Local Reserves, and Private Reserves.

The province of Toledo has no reserves or national preserves, though there are local preserves and a number of private ones. Information related to preserves and hunting licences in Toledo may be obtained by calling:

Jefatura Provincial de ICONA en Toledo (Provincial office of ICONA, the government office in charge of natural resources), Pl de San Vicente, 6 ☎ 22 78 99, 22 21 66 and 22 21 62.

Junta Nacional de Homologación de Trofeos de Caza (Hunting Regulation Board), c/ Goya, 25, in Madrid. Representative in Toledo: Mr. Meco, Pl San Vicente, 6 ☎ 22 21 62.

If you are going to request a licence or information from abroad, you should write to the Spanish Tourism Administration in advance.

Dirección de Empresas y Actividades Turísticas, c/ Almagro, 36, 28004 Madrid, Spain.

USEFUL ADDRESSES

Auto Repair Shops

BMW, Ctra Madrid-Toledo, km63.3 ☎ 35 79 99.
Citröen, c/ Duque de Ahumada, s/n ☎ 22 08 46.
Ford, Ctra Madrid-Toledo, km64.4 ☎ 35 80 56.
General Motors, Ctra Madrid-Toledo, km63 ☎ 35 77 66.
Mercedes, Ctra de Ocaña, km8 ☎ 23 01 35.
Peugeot-Talbot, Ctra Madrid-Toledo, km66.6 ☎ 22 78 50.
Renault, c/ Cervantes, 5 ☎ 22 13 24.
Seat-Audi-Volkswagen, Polígono industrial, parcela 146 ☎ 23 07 00.

Emergencies

Civil Protection ☎ 22 60 50 extension 45.
Emergency oxygen ☎ 22 87 04.
Fire Department ☎ 22 60 80.
First-aid Clinic ☎ 22 81 57.
Hospital ☎ 22 16 98.
Municipal Police ☎ 22 34 07.
National Social Security Health Clinic ☎ 22 15 16.
Police Headquarters, Pl de Zocodover, 1 ☎ 22 14 06.
Red Cross Ambulance (Toledo) ☎ 22 29 00.
Social Security Ambulance ☎ 22 37 73.
Talavera Ambulance ☎ 80 03 60 and 80 20 73.
Talavera Fire Department ☎ 80 30 80.
Talavera First-aid Clinic ☎ 80 02 93.

Governmental Agencies

Ayuntamiento de Toledo, City Hall, Pl del Ayuntamiento, 1 ☎ 22 28 00.
Consejería de Agricultura, Agricultural Council, c/ Dr. Lerma, 13 ☎ 21 12 40.
Consejería de Cultura, Cultural Council, c/ Trinidad, s/n ☎ 22 34 50.
Consejería de Industria, Industrial Council, Cuesta del Alcázar, s/n ☎ 21 09 00.
Consejería de Política Territorial y de Economía, Council of Territorial Policy and Economic Affairs, El Nuncio, c/ Real, s/n ☎ 21 24 00.
Consejería de Presidencia y Gobernación, Council of the Presidency and Government ☎ 21 30 53.
Consejería de Sanidad, Health Council, c/ Dr. Lerma, 13 ☎ 21 20 12.
Cortes de Castilla-La Mancha, Castile-La Mancha Parliament, Old Convent of Gilitos, c/ de Gilitos Desca, s/n.
Diputación Provincial, Provincial Delegation, Pl de la Merced, 4 ☎ 22 52 00.
Gobierno Civil, Civil Government, Pl de Zocodover, s/n ☎ 22 60 50.
Palacio Arzobispal, Palace of the Archbishop, c/ del Arco de Palacio, 1.
Presidencia de la Junta de Castilla-La Mancha, Presidency of the Castile-La Mancha Autonomous Government, Palace of Fuensalida ☎ 22 45 00.

Information and Tourist Offices

Delegación Provincial de Turismo, Pl de Zocodover, 11 ☎ 22 14 00.
Puerta de Bisagra, Paseo de Madrid, s/n ☎ 22 08 43.

Parking Lots Inside the City

Corral de D. Diego, (public) Pl Corral de D. Diego, s/n.
Corralillo, (public) behind the Alcázar.
El Miradero, (private) c/ Gerardo Lobo.
Garage Alcázar, (private) c/ Gral. Moscardó, 8.
Garage Santo Tomé, (private) c/ Santa Ursula, 3.
Garage Toledo, (private) c/ Instituto, 5.
Padilla, (public) Pl Padilla, s/n.
Plaza San Marcos, (public) c/ del Salvador, s/n.

Press and Radio

Antena 3 Toledo, c/ Comercio, 46 ☎ 21 24 21.
Newspapers ▶ page 82.
Radio Cadena Española, c/ Núñez de Arce, 12 ☎ 21 17 17.
Radio Toledo, Pl de la Merced, 1 ☎ 22 53 00.

Transportation and Communications

Autobuses Continental Auto, S.A., new bus station, Ctra Circunvalación,
s/n.
Autobuses Galiano, S.A., new bus station, Ctra Circunvalación, s/n.
Centro de Información de Tráfico, traffic information centre ☎ (91)
742 12 13.
RENFE, Spanish national railway, c/ Sillería, 7 ☎ 22 23 96.
Taxis (all points) ☎ 22 19 68.
Taxis Cuesta del Alcázar ☎ 22 23 96.
Taxis Cuesta de la Vega ☎ 22 16 96.
Telephones and telegraphs ▶ page 82.
Train Station, Paseo de la Rosa, s/n ☎ 22 12 72.

Travel Agencies

Vincit, c/ de la Sinagoga (in the alley), s/n. IBERIA tickets and
excursions from Toledo to foreign countries.
Wagons Lits Cook, c/ Hombre de Palo, 16. RENFE tickets at official
prices; also bus tickets.

WINES

Spanish wines are a mosaic of different tastes and types, but they are
singular both for their **high quality** —under the control of the Institute
of Officially Regulated Wine Regions, *Instituto Regulador de
Denominación de Origen*, whose mark appears on the label opposite
the name of the wine— and for their **genuinely low prices**, which
compare very favourably with European and American wines.
   The most famous Spanish wine, with the longest tradition and the
highest prestige, is **sherry** (in Spanish *Jerez*, after the southern city of
that name). Sherry is a tasteful wine, strong, as one might expect of the
hot climate of the south of Spain. It is drunk, generally, before meals,
with hors d'oeuvres, during a *tapeo*, that is a round of appetizers or
with desserts. From the more temperate north come a variety of wines:
Rioja, which competes in quality and taste with French table wines;

Catalan table wines of many types, including **cavas**, bubbly wines that are similar to French champagnes; and white wines, young-tasting and made from grapes grown in humid Galicia, in the northwest, that are commonly drunk with Galician dishes and shellfish. The robust table wine produced in central Spain are quite varied, from those carrying the **Ribera del Duero** label, very good wine with strong body, to the many varieties of **Valdepeñas**, produced in vast quantities and very popular in Spain as a table wine.

Catalonia

Catalonia is the area with the widest variety of wines, from sparkling wines like the **cavas** to still wines. **Alella** mainly produces whites that are pale, young and fruity, with a distinctive bouquet and flavour; they are good with shellfish, white-fleshed fish and mild cheeses. *Marqués de Alella (82)* is a good example. The most characteristic wines from **Ampurdán** are rosés that are cherry-coloured, fruity-tasting and aromatic. They go well with fish, light meat, pastas and other foods. A very good, young white is *Blanc Pescador (83)*. The reds are robust and full-bodied, best suited for expert drinkers.

Penedés may be the Catalonian wine best known to the rest of the world, with the sparkling **cava** wines the most important in the province. Still, Torres, for one, has worked to produce several lesser-known whites of very high quality. The **cava** wines are one of many sparkling wines, a very well regarded beverage distilled and aged in the same bottle —that is to say in the same way as champagne is made. The cavas are relatively cheap and quite good, and so they have made a major impact on the international markets. The *brut* and *seco* varieties are good for any occasion, while the *dulces* (sweets) and *semisecos* (semi-dry) are well-suited to desserts. Sant Sadurní d'Anoia is home to Codorniú, Freixenet —the best two wineries—, Castellblanch, Conde Caralt, Juve and Camps, Segura Viudas, Marqués de Monistrol and others.

Miguel Torres, in Villafranca del Penedés, is one of the most famous of Spanish wineries. Its non-sparkling wines are excellent and include, among the whites, *Gran Viña Sol (83)* and *Viña Sol (83)*, and among the reds, *Gran Coronas Etiqueta Negra (77)* —described by a Paris jury as better than the mythical *Chateau Latour*. Rene Barbier produces excellent whites such as *Kraliner (83)*.

Central Spain

From La Mancha come the ubiquitous **Valdepeñas** wines, at the moment the most popular and best-selling type of wine in Spain. *Clarets* are the variety seen most often; they are light-coloured and light-bodied, not very alcoholic, and can be drunk on all occasions and with all kinds of food. They are frequently served in bars and taverns. Like the reds, the whites are also light. Among the latter are *Viña Albali (78)* and *Los Molinos*, interesting wines of good colour and body.

A quite wide range of wines is produced in Castile and León, from the strong reds of **Toro** or **Cebreros** to the delicate whites of **Rueda** —like the excellent *Cuatro Rayas (83)* of La Seca— and the clarets of **Cigales**. **Ribera del Duero** is the nomenclature of some of the greatest and most famous Spanish reds, the Vega-Sicilia wines, and of the excellent *Valbuena (80)*.

Galicia

Albariño wines —whites of great delicacy, a yellow-straw colour, acidic and young, producing a tickling sensation in the mouth— are made with grapes from high vines. They have a relatively low alcoholic content and go well with shellfish and fish. **Ribeiro** offers several whites, good with fish and shellfish, and reds that are well-suited to such local specialities as octopus and hake.

Rioja and Related Wines

The **Riojas** have a tradition of high quality —only Bordeaux and Burgundy come out ahead, and that may be in name only. Although the Rioja tradition in the area may go back to pre-Roman times, today's principal wineries date to the 19C. They include Bodegas Bilbaínas, Martínez Lacuesta, Muga, CVNE, Paternina, López de Heredia, Berberana, Marqués de Cáceres, AGE, Lan, Franco-Española and Marqués de Murrieta. All these wineries are good, and they produce wines up to Rioja Alta, literally High Rioja. Most Riojas are red

—although both white and fruity Riojas have been made for several years now—, light-bodied, with a light aroma and a noticeable taste of oak, deriving from the barrels in which they are made. **Excellent** years were 1964, 1970, 1978, 1981 and 1983. **Very bad** years were 1972 1977 and 1980.

Among others, some of the excellent red wines produced after 1970 are *Marqués Villamagna (70), Viña Cumbrero (78), Prado Enea (76), Viña Albina (73), Imperial Gran Reserva (73), Viña Vial (78), Viña Ardanza (76), Marqués de Murrieta Reserva (70)* and *Viña Tondonia (sixth year)*. Among the rosés we can include *Cerro Añon (73)*, and among the whites, *Monopole (81)* and *Marqués de Cáceres*.

The young white wines go well with grilled fish and shellfish, while older whites are better suited to fish with sauces. Rosés are usually taken with egg dishes, pastas, rice and so on. Young reds go well with dark-fleshed fish and light meats. The better, older reds, according to their age, make an excellent accompaniment to a variety of foods including non-red meats, fish with sauces, game and similar dishes.

Navarre produces heavy-bodied red wines of great character, aromatic and sweet rosés, and clarets.

Sherry and Andalusia

Sherry is known to date back to before the Middle Ages. Sherrymakers of today can trace their lineage back, in many cases, to the 18C. Some examples are Terry, Duff Gordon, Garvey, González Byass (19C), Agustín Blázquez, Osborne, Domecq, Sandeman, and Williams/Humbert (19C). Under the all-embracing name of *Jerez*, however, there is a rainbow of sherries. The most important are the *finos*, sherries that are dry and light, straw-coloured, pale, and marked by a distinctive aroma, both pungent and delicate. They are graded between 15.5° and 17°. *Tío Pepe, La Ina, Carta Blanca, San Patricio, Perla, Quinta* and *Tío Mateo* are some of the most famous names. The *manzanilla* wines from Sanlúcar de Barrameda are similar to the *finos*, but there is a subtle difference, perhaps owing to the fact that they come from an area closer to the sea. *La Guita* is one of the popular *manzanilla* labels, but there are many more. The *amontillado* wines are amber-coloured, smooth, with much body, a hazel tint and graded between 16° and 18°. Some well-known labels are *Coquinero, Don Zoilo* and *Etiqueta Blanca*. The *olorosos*, the sweet-smelling, or odorous, ones, are dark, very aromatic, dry and heavy-bodied and graded between 18° and 20°. *Río Viejo* and *Dry Sack* are among the better-known olorosos. **Palo cortado** wines lie midway between the *olorosos* and the *amontillados*. Finally, there are the **sweet wines**: *Moscatel, Pedro Ximénez* and *Cream*.

The *fino* sherries are drunk chilled and, like the *amontillados*, are ideal served with hors d'oeuvres; both are excellent with fried or grilled fish or serrano ham. The *olorosos* and *palo cortados* go well with dry fruits, serrano ham and sausages. The sweet wines are usually drunk as dessert accompaniments.

Famous Córdoba wines include **Montilla-Moriles**, which is similar to sherry, and wineries like Alvear, Crismona, Navarro; some popular labels are *C.B., Moriles* and *Montilla*, all finos, and *Oloroso Viejo*. **Málaga** is known for its sweet wines, notably the *moscatels* and *Pedro Ximénez*, made to go with sweets and pastries. **Condado de Huelva** makes a sweet wine as well, but it is little known outside the area of Huelva and Seville.

Maps

STREET INDEX

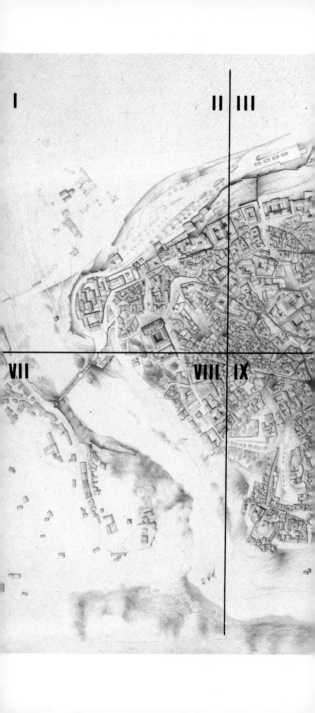

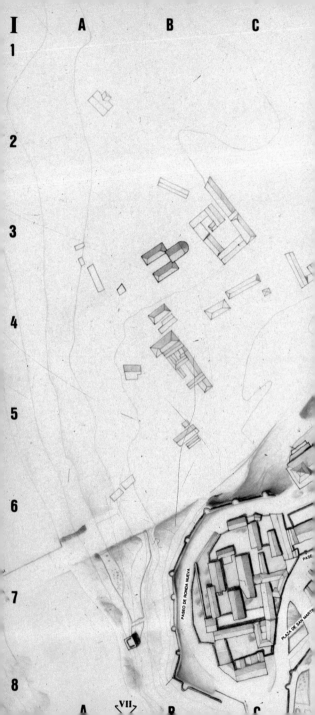

I   A   B   C

1

2

3

4

5

6

7

8

PASEO DE RONDA NUEVA

PLAZA DE SAN MARTIN

PASE

A   VII   B   C

PASEO DEL RECAREDO

III

REA

REAL

PLAZA DE LOS CARMELITAS

CUESTA DE SANTA LEOCADIA

VALLEHERMOSO

PLAZA DE LA VIRGEN DE GRACIA

COLEGIO DE LAS DONCELLAS

VIRGEN DE GRACIA

PLAZA DE SAN JUAN DE LOS REYES

CERRO VIRGEN DE GRACIA

CUESTA DE LO

VIII

PASEO DEL RECAREDO

CUESTA DE LA GRANJA

CUESTA DE LA GRANJA

CUESTA DE LA GRANJA

LA MERCED

REAL

LOS ALJIBES

TRAVESIA DE SAN ILDEFONSO

CUESTA DE SANTA LEOCADIA

PLAZA DE PADILLA

CUESTA DE GARCILASO DE LA VEGA

PLAZA DEL

COLEGIO DE LAS DONCELLAS

COLEGIO DE LAS DONCELLAS

PLAZA DE SANTA EULALIA

PLAZA DE LA CRUZ

SAN CLEMENTE

COBERTIZO DE SAN PEDRO MARTIR

LAS BULAS

V A B C

1

BAJADA DE ANTEQUERUELA

PLAZA DE ALFARES

PLAZA DE AZACANES

2

AZACANES

CUESTA DE GERARDO LOBO

CUESTA DE GERARDO LOBO

3

PASEO DEL MIRADERO

4

CUESTA DEL ÁGUILA

PLAZA DE SAN AGUSTÍN

IV

5

LA SILLERÍA

LA SILLERÍA

NUEVA

PASEO DE LA CAVA

PLAZA DE ZOCODOVER

CUESTA DE LAS ARMAS

6

PLAZA DE LA ROPERÍA

TOLEDO OHIO

PASEO DEL COMERCIO

TRAVESÍA DE SANTA JUSTA

PLAZA DE LAS CONDONERÍAS

PASEO DEL COMERCIO

BARRIO REY

TRAVESERA DE ERRIO

PLAZA HORNO DE LA MAGDALENA

CALLEJÓN DE LUCIO

CUESTA DE LAS ARMAS

PLAZA DE ARMAS

7

TORNERÍAS

TRASTAMARA

SAN JUAN LABRADOR

CUESTA DEL HORNO DE LOS BIZC...

CUESTA DEL ALCÁZAR

MARTÍN GAMERO

8

PLAZA MAYOR

A XI B C

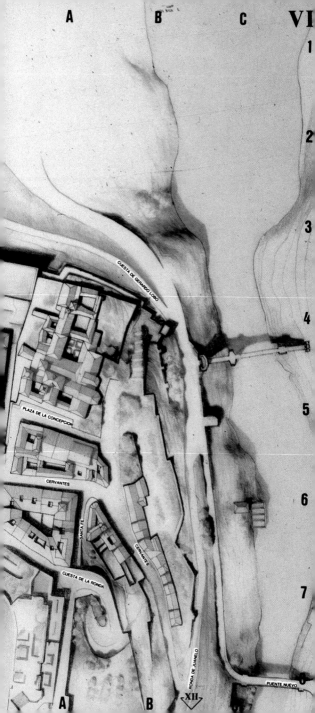

A B C VI
1
2
3
CUESTA DE GERARDO LOBO
4
PLAZA DE LA CONCEPCION
5
CERVANTES
SANTA FE
CERVANTES
6
CUESTA DE LA RONDA
7
RONDA DE JUANELO
PUENTE NUEVO
A B XII

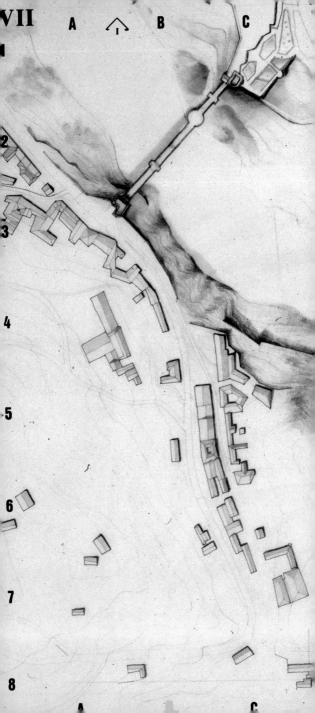

VII   A   B   C

2

3

4

5

6

7

8

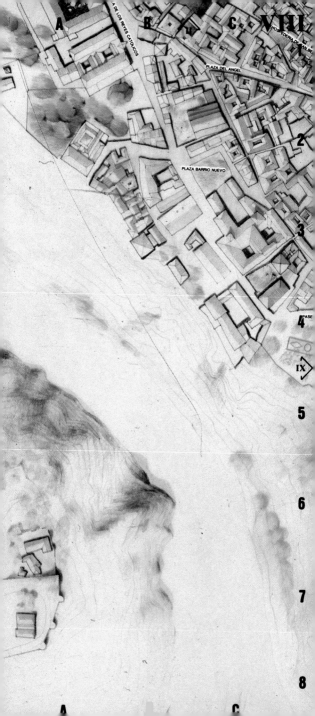

A   B   C   **VIII**

A DE LOS REYES CATÓLICOS

PLAZA DEL ANGEL

2

PLAZA BARRIO NUEVO

3

PASE

4

IX

5

6

7

8

A   C

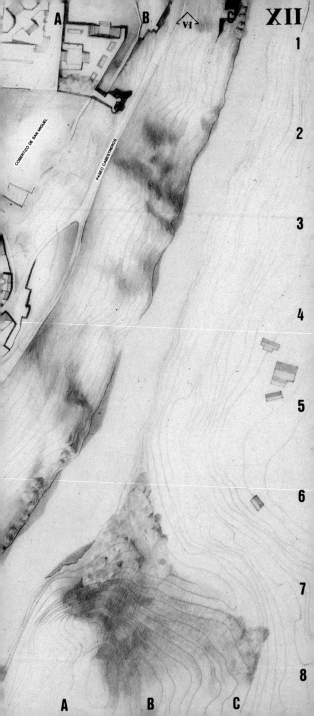

XII

A   B   VI   C

COBERTIZO DE SAN MIGUEL

P.º DEL CABESTREROS

1

2

3

4

5

6

7

8

A   B   C